MUGABE

AND THE

WHITE AFRICAN

This book is dedicated to a brave African – who happened to be white. Mike Campbell died for what we believe in – leaving his legacy for us all.

This book is also dedicated to all who have done so much to help the victims of Mugabe's land programme, whose stories are very similar to this one. Our prayer is that we will one day rebuild our country on the right foundations.

MUGABE

AND THE

WHITE

AFRICAN

BEN FREETH

LION

A Lion Book
an imprint of
Lion Hudson plc
Wilkinson House, Jordan Hill Road,
Oxford OX2 8DR, England
www.lionhudson.com
ISBN 978 0 7459 5546 9 (print)
ISBN 978 0 7459 5985 6 (epub)
ISBN 978 0 7459 5984 9 (Kindle)
ISBN 978 0 7459 5986 3 (pdf)

Distributed by:
UK: Marston Book Services, PO Box 269, Abingdon, Oxon, OX14 4YN
USA: Trafalgar Square Publishing, 814 N. Franklin Street, Chicago, IL 60610
USA Christian Market: Kregel Publications, PO Box 2607, Grand Rapids, MI 49501

First edition 2011
10 9 8 7 6 5 4 3 2 1 0
First electronic format 2011

Acknowledgments
Scripture quotations taken from the Holy Bible, New International Version,
copyright © 1973, 1978, 1984 International Bible Society. Used by permission of
Hodder & Stoughton, a member of the Hodder Headline Group. All rights reserved.
"NIV" is a trademark of International Bible Society. UK trademark number
1448790.
p. 71: Scripture quotation taken from the Holy Bible, Today's New International
Version. Copyright © 2004 by International Bible Society. Used by permission of
Hodder & Stoughton Publishers. A member of the Hachette Livre UK Group. All
rights reserved. "TNIV" is a registered trademark of International Bible Society.
pp. 78–79: Extract from The Authorized (King James) Version. Rights in the
Authorized Version are vested in the Crown. Reproduced by permission of the
Crown's patentee, Cambridge University Press.
Cover image © 2011 Jude May, Lion Hudson plc
Inside images © Ben Freeth unless specified otherwise

This book has been printed on paper and board independently certified
as having been produced from sustainable forests.

A catalogue record for this book is available
from the British Library

Typeset in 10/13 Latin 725 BT

Printed and bound in America

CONTENTS

FOREWORD

A story that has had a profound influence on my life is that of David and Goliath. It seemed so extraordinary that this small chap could defeat such an enormous giant, just by using his brain. For many of us in South Africa, it served as an inspiration in our efforts to bring down the colossus of apartheid. At times it was a seemingly impossible task as the apartheid government was very powerful, but today it no longer exists. Injustice and oppression will not have the last word.

Mugabe and the White African is in essence a David and Goliath story. Appalled by the state-orchestrated crimes against humanity on a massive scale countrywide, with horrific violence perpetrated against white commercial farmers, their farm workers, and the rural population, a farming family takes on President Mugabe's government in a landmark court case heard by the SADC Tribunal in Windhoek, Namibia. They know the risks, but they believe it is what God requires of them.

Set on Mount Carmel farm in the Chegutu district of Zimbabwe, this deeply moving book is the chronicle of a Christian family's struggle to survive, to protect the land it purchased legally from the government, and to protect the lives and livelihoods of all those working on the farm. The support of their farm workers is crucial and the loyalty of these vulnerable men and women in the face of grave danger is remarkable. Mike Campbell was the owner of the farm and Ben Freeth, his son-in-law, worked alongside him. Ben's wife Laura ran a small linen project to empower the wives of their farm workers. All were viewed as model employers.

Mugabe and the White African explains how the shocking acts of violence and wanton destruction committed in the name of land reform have demolished property rights and all but ruined commercial agriculture in this once highly successful African country. In benefiting the chosen few in high office, the land invasions have forced Zimbabweans into poverty and dependence, discarding the ideals for which the independence struggle was fought.

Numerous books on this turbulent period catalogue the horrors, injustice, and oppression that have defined the last decade. A fascinating feature of Ben Freeth's book is that he also explores the conflict between good and evil under the Mugabe regime. At the heart of Christianity is a struggle and Freeth grapples with the root of the evil in his country and the malevolent spirits that have allowed the leaders to cause people such suffering.

The incomprehensible greed, appalling lack of compassion, and unspeakable cruelty demonstrated by the Zimbabwean elite contradicts the classical African concept of *ubuntu* – the essence of being human. *Ubuntu* speaks particularly to the fact that you can't exist as a human in isolation since we are all interconnected. The spirit of *ubuntu* is diminished when others are humiliated or diminished – and when others are tortured or oppressed. It is encouraging that throughout the book there are examples of extraordinary courage, humanity, and neighbourliness that embody the philosophy of *ubuntu*.

There have been too many abuses since the launch of the Universal Declaration of Human Rights over sixty years ago. I would like African leaders to be the kind of leaders that many of us hoped they would be. The suffering of our brothers and sisters in Zimbabwe is a blight on our region and beloved continent. All of us Africans must hang our heads in shame for having allowed such a desperate situation to continue and for doing so little to try to stop it.

Citizens need to be galvanized to shame governments and create an ethos in which it would be more difficult to act with impunity. If everyone who wants to see an end to poverty, hunger, and suffering speaks out, then the noise will be deafening. Politicians will have to listen. We are one family, the human family, God's family. Zimbabwe's plight is all of our plight. To ignore its suffering is to condone it.

Reconciliation, when change comes, will be a long haul, and will depend on all of us making a contribution. Reconciliation must be a national project, as we learned through South Africa's peaceful transition to democracy. Our Truth and Reconciliation Commission (TRC) presided over the process of healing a traumatized and wounded people and is regarded as the most ambitious of its kind – a benchmark against which truth commissions in other countries are measured. We acknowledge that there were shortcomings in the process – as there are in any process, especially in one so challenging.

As the TRC evolved, the inadequacy of the criminal justice system in exposing the full truth of, and establishing clear accountability for, what happened in our country became apparent. Unsuccessful prosecutions of perpetrators of gruesome crimes led to bitterness and frustration in the community. Furthermore, we realized that all communities must be involved in the reconciliation process, otherwise the burden of guilt could not be assuaged. From a practical point of view, the healing of those who came to the TRC also hinged on their receiving more substantial reparations and the stalling of this process caused further pain.

When we look around us at some of the conflict areas of the world, it becomes increasingly clear that there is not much of a future for them without forgiveness and reconciliation. God has blessed us richly so that we might be a blessing to others. If South Africans could reconcile, despite the terrible legacy of apartheid, then this can certainly happen anywhere, including Zimbabwe.

I commend the many learnings contained in this book and the courage of all those who lived on Mount Carmel farm or who continue to live there because they have nowhere else to go. They have all suffered mentally, physically, and emotionally, and many will never recover fully. A number have lost their lives because they stood up for what they believed to be right. May their supreme sacrifice lead to a better country and to a better world.

Archbishop Emeritus Desmond Tutu

April 2011

FOREWORD

Mugabe and the White African is a courageous endeavour by Ben Freeth to present the true nature of President Mugabe's controversial "land reform" programme, the breakdown of the *rule of law* and the need for justice for the people of Zimbabwe. He explains that control of the rural areas is strategically vital for the retention of power by ZANU–PF since this is where an estimated 70 per cent of the Zimbabwean population lives, and they have borne the brunt of the onslaught.

The book begins with Ben's first encounter with President Mugabe in the late 1990s and provides brief historical context prior to the farm invasions that were unleashed in 2000. He describes appalling acts of violence perpetrated against farmers and farm workers and the wanton destruction of highly successful commercial farming enterprises, which were the backbone of Zimbabwe's agri-based economy. I have had the privilege to visit this previously thriving country on nine occasions and am shocked by the ruinous policies of President Mugabe and the fact that so many people have been displaced, brutalized, and killed.

Racism has returned to haunt Zimbabwe in a different form and, by his actions, Mugabe demonstrates that he is the worst kind of racist dictator. He has enacted an awful Orwellian vision, with the former freedom ideals being transformed into the worst kind of totalitarian oppression. Like Idi Amin before him in Uganda, Mugabe's perceived enemies are tortured and jailed, the press is censored, and people are starving. In the past Mugabe has successfully used food as a mechanism for control and at least 1.7 million Zimbabweans currently need food aid.

As someone who went on countless marches to campaign for the ending of Ian Smith's Unilateral Declaration of Independence (UDI), I am deeply ashamed of the decade of suffering endured by Zimbabweans. We all know the truth of the situation and we cannot continue to look the other way. Zimbabwe is a scourge on the conscience of the entire world.

As this book goes to print, the situation in the country is of escalating concern. A brutal ZANU–PF crackdown is once again being unleashed to terrorize the population and force victory in the next election. Fuelling the climate of fear are unlawful arrests, beatings, torture, murder, and the manipulation of the rule of law. Tragically all the apparatus of a totalitarian regime is again being brought to bear on a people betrayed by those African leaders who refuse to condemn President Mugabe. Zimbabweans have been robbed of their dignity, their rights, their identity, and their hope. Manipulated by Mugabe and his party to achieve their own objectives, the tenuous transitional government has failed.

The international community must coalesce in putting pressure on Mugabe and ZANU–PF. The African Union has been promising that they will provide an African solution through the intervention of South Africa and the Southern African Development Community (SADC), but they haven't done this. What needs to happen now is for a world voice to say: "Enough is enough. This cannot be tolerated." The United Nations must make Zimbabwe a priority and ensure that peacekeepers protect the people of Zimbabwe so that they are free to vote for whom they want under an internationally supervised election. If it does not, the blood that is spilled will also be on their hands.

It is time for Mugabe to answer for his crimes against humanity, against his countrymen and women, and for justice to be done. The winds of change that once brought hope to Zimbabwe and its neighbours have become a hurricane of destruction resulting in a health crisis, destitution, starvation, and the systematic abuse of power by the state. As the country cries out for justice, we need to become more proactive. Mugabe and his henchmen must now take their rightful place in the Hague and answer for their actions. They must be removed from power so that democracy and the rule of law can be restored.

As an Anglican, I am deeply concerned about the welfare of Anglican bishops, clergy, and laity in the Dioceses of Harare and Manicaland. Week by week, they are experiencing horrific violence and intimidation. Their courage, like the courage of Ben Freeth and his family, is a remarkable witness to the grace of God in Christ. As a Christian community, we must all stand together with our brothers and sisters living under the tyranny of Mugabe and pray they will find deliverance. If everyone who wants to see an end to poverty, hunger, and human rights abuses has the courage to speak out, the noise will be deafening. Politicians will have to listen. We, the people of Britain and the United Nations, need to hear the voices of our own consciences and heed the cries of the suffering people of Zimbabwe.

Most Revd Dr John Sentamu, Archbishop of York

April 2011

CHAPTER 1

I first met him in the 1990s, in a dusty bit of *veld* a little to the north of the farm.

The dry heat was palpable as I turned off the tar road onto a rutted dirt track leading to a run-down butchery, hoping to buy a cold bottle of Coke. Having found one, I bumped along sipping it, asking the people I passed where the rally was to be held.

I soon found the place. An old army tent had been erected for the lesser dignitaries. A little to the right of it was a platform with Dralon-covered chairs and with some more canvas over it. The ordinary people stood or sat in a large rough semicircle beneath the burning sky.

Apart from people from the nearby villages, numbers had been swelled with bussed-in school children in their white shirts and various coloured shorts and skirts. They were chattering away, their smiles flashing in the sunlight against their black skins.

I had been told by my boss, the president of the Commercial Farmers' Union (CFU), to go to the event. It came with the job, attending political rallies. I knew what to expect by now: dusty, hot, thirsty days, mostly of waiting for enough people to turn up for it to be worthwhile for the politicians to address them. When the minister, or whoever the speaker was, finally arrived – invariably many hours late – it was always with a fresh flourish of authority, slogan chanting, and fist raising.

He arrived as if from nowhere. Suddenly he was right there, in the centre of a large group of security people and important dignitaries. There was a fantastic energy about him. He was walking so quickly. His face was animated and he was talking and gesticulating and moving on all at the same time. He acted like a man in his mid-fifties, not his mid-seventies. He was almost like a man possessed.

I remembered trying to fight a fire on the farm once when I was caught in the path of a dust devil. The fire had already burned through where I was standing and the ground was black and full of soot where the grass had been. As the dust devil hit, the whole world went black and I was suddenly engulfed in a blinding, swirling, dark confusion of choking debris, which settled as suddenly as it had arrived.

As Robert Mugabe moved unpredictably in different directions, the people around him moved too, just like the trees and leaves and other objects caught up in the path of a dust devil, leaning over, flying up, twirling around, and falling back down again. He was the centre. Whatever he did affected everything and everyone.

I had never seen him close up before. I was struck by how small he was and yet what tremendous energy emanated from that tiny frame. The little Hitler moustache and the elegantly tailored suit added to the aura of authority that surrounded him, to the confusion of all those around.

In the heat haze and the dust I could imagine bullets cracking as he spoke from the podium, his voice snapping and whispering, rising and falling, breaking from English to Shona and then back again. His fist always seemed to be upraised, as though anger had completely mastered him and even the *veld* was his enemy. I wondered whether the trees and golden swaying grasses all around recognized in what he was saying the haunting echo of his promise, years ago, at a different rally in the 1970s, when he proclaimed that bullets and the power of the gun barrel were the way forward for Zimbabwe. "We came to power through the barrel of a gun and that's how we intend to keep it."

We were a small group of whites there in the army tent. Suddenly, in the middle of it all, I was asked to make a speech about the help that the CFU was giving to black farmers. I don't know why we were asked, or, least of all, why I was asked. I was the youngest and the least senior of the white men present. I'd never made a speech in front of thousands of people before, and never in front of a president.

I was thrust forwards to the podium, not really knowing what I was going to say. I had to think quickly.

"Your Excellency," I began. "I'm sure that in the evening you and your wife, Comrade Grace, like to sit down and listen to the piano being played by a master musician. I'm sure you love the beauty of the notes as they harmonize together into a delightful tune."

I went on speaking slowly and clearly into the microphone so that all the people could hear – and so that I had time to think.

"Your Excellency, on the piano there are black keys and there are white ones too. The pianist can't play the harmony if he just uses the black keys and he can't play the harmony if he just uses the white ones. The harmony happens when both the black and the white keys are played skilfully together. In Zimbabwe," I said, "we have black people and white people and we each have our role to play. We can make harmony together; or we can choose not to. The choice is ours. But disharmony will not be good for our nation, just as disharmony on the piano is not good for our ears."

There was a huge round of spontaneous applause from the thousands of people present. They were all black apart from the handful of white farmers who were with me.

I stopped speaking, stepped away from the microphone and walked instinctively toward Mugabe. He was sitting above me on the dais, about 1.5 metres from the ground. I approached him from his left and held my hand up to him. He looked ahead, away from me, toward the crowds who were clapping and cheering and ululating. But he was looking straight past them, toward the past. Toward the bullets. There was a pent-up storm of anger in his face, like a menacing black cloud hovering above me. I could feel hatred tearing him apart from the inside. His hand came down mechanically and I took it. The instant I touched it I knew it was unlike any hand I'd ever touched before. It was cold, despite the heat of the day, and it had a clammy softness to it. It also felt lifeless, as though the body that it came from was dead. I looked at his face and into his eyes but he couldn't look at me. It was as though I had shaken hands with a reptile and not a warm-blooded human being.

I will carry the feeling of that touch to my grave. I can't forget it. I had a premonition of overwhelming evil.

CHAPTER 2

As a child, I loved camping out in the African bush. One night, heading out on a safari with Laura Campbell (who'd grown up on Mount Carmel farm in the Chegutu district of Mashonaland West Province) and my best friend James Egremont-Lee, I slept out under the stars by an albida (acacia) tree on the banks of the Zambezi, the most beautiful river in the world. The next morning we had to search for James's boot, which he'd used to peg out his mosquito net next to his head. The spoor showed that a hyena had come in and devoured the boot without trace. Perhaps that was the beginning – a sign of what was to come...

I spent part of my childhood in Harare, during the *Gukurahundi* massacres, which began just three years after Zimbabwe gained independence in 1980. *Gukurahundi* means "the early rain which washes away the chaff before the spring rains", and during this period thousands of people – mainly innocent black civilians – were murdered, although I was unaware of it at the time. It passed me by like a faraway storm at night and was gone before I awoke.

The seeds of fear that had led up to the "bush war" of the mid -1960s and 70s were sown as the winds blew in from the north. Between March and September of 1962, ZAPU (Zimbabwe African People's Union) carried out thirty-three petrol bombings against black Africans. In some cases petrol was poured over people and they were burned to death. Eight African schools were burned, ten churches were destroyed, and numerous farm animals were burned alive in order to spread fear throughout the land.

ZANU (Zimbabwe African National Union) was formed on 8 August 1963. In July 1964, Ndabaningi Sithole was elected as the president of ZANU and Robert Mugabe became Secretary General. On American Independence Day in 1964, Sithole's gang, known significantly as the Crocodile Gang, killed Petrus Oberholtzer, a civilian farmer, at a makeshift roadblock.

On 28 April 1966, twenty-one men armed with AK-47s and grenades, and calling themselves the Armageddon Group, entered Zimbabwe (then Rhodesia) from Zambia. A group of seven of them was killed by police in a firefight. The campaign had begun. It was war.

A second group of seven men moved south. They got to Nevada farm, fifteen kilometres from Mount Carmel, where I was later to live. They knocked on the door of the house and shot the farmer, Johannes Viljoen, through the door, before gunning down his wife, who came to his aid. Bullets lodged in the wall above and below the cot, narrowly missing the baby who was sleeping there. The other child, little Tommy – who was three – was unscathed. Both children had to face life growing up as orphans. The first white farm murders had taken place.

The war proper started when Solomon Mujuru, who took the *chimurenga* (revolutionary war) name of Rex Nhongo, led an attack on Altena farm in the Centenary district on 21 December 1972. The owners survived but their seven-year-old daughter was injured. They went to stay with a neighbour on Whistlefield farm and were unlucky enough to be attacked there two nights later by another of Rex Nhongo's groups. Another of their daughters was injured. From there the attacks escalated.

It was against this backdrop that my future in-laws, Mike and Angela Campbell, bought Mount Carmel farm in 1974. Mount Carmel is right in the middle of Zimbabwe, with the Biri River running through the centre of the farm.

Mike and Angela both came from true white African stock. Mike's mother's family had been farming continuously on African soil since 1713. His father's family, the Campbells, came out to South Africa from Scotland as transport outfitters and set up in the semi-desert region of the Karoo. Mike grew up on his family's farm in the Western Transvaal during the Great Depression of the 1930s. It was a hard place to grow up in, and an equally hard time.

A picture of one of Mike's ancestors, called "Oom Jan Hell", used to hang in the house at Mount Carmel. The inscription read, "He was afraid of no man." We used to laugh about it because he looked so stern and the epitaph seemed to fit Mike himself so well. Mike was the most tenacious person I have ever known. When he wanted to achieve something, he was like a dog with a bone and he wouldn't give up until the task was done. He was a gifted horseman, hunter, and wildlife man, and had a lion-hearted courage. To those that didn't know him well, he could seem quite hard at times, but you only had to see him with a little child or with one of his beloved animals to know that underneath he had a very soft heart.

Angela's family came to South Africa's Natal province (now known as KwaZulu-Natal) at more or less the same time as the Campbells, in the 1860s. Her father's family started a farm mission called Impolweni, which they developed and then gave over to the people. Angela is a very caring person with a radiant smile, a big heart, and a deep peace within her that comes from her Christian faith. From the bottom of my own heart I can sincerely say I couldn't ask for a more wonderful mother-in-law.

There are some days in a man's life when his dreams come true. It had been a childhood dream of Mike's to bring game back into areas where it had once roamed. His mother's family in the Free State conserved game, so the seeds of a passion for its protection were sown in Mike's heart from an early age.

Close to Mount Carmel was a farm called Rainbow's End. Its owners, the Brackenridges, became great friends of Mike and Angela Campbell. Often the two families would head out into the bush with their children and some guitars and build a fire to camp out in the beauty of the wilds, where dreams became reality.

Ben Brackenridge was also a keen conservationist, and he and Mike started bringing game animals back into the district.

Those were pioneering days. Back in the 1970s the relocation of game wasn't simple and it wasn't a common thing to do. Mike and Ben each brought fifty impala in from Mana Pools National Park on the banks of the Zambezi River, where there was an over-population, and settled them on Mount Carmel and Rainbow's End. They then started bringing in the other animals. Ben brought up some giraffe from the *lowveld*. Within a few years of their first successful capture and relocation, Mike and Angela had brought in wildebeest, eland, kudu, sable, warthog, giraffe, waterbuck, and zebra, in small populations, to protect and breed up. They even brought up some nyala from nearly 2,000 kilometres away in Natal. Mike became a founder and the first chairman of the Wildlife Producers' Association, promoting the reintroduction of wildlife back into many areas around the country.

But below this idyllic surface, like a crocodile lurking below the water, conflict was close at hand. From 1973, when Mike and Angela began farming in Zimbabwe, to 1979, 320 white farmers were murdered. This accounted for more than half the total number of white civilian deaths over that whole period. In the "hot" areas near Mozambique and Zambia, up to 20 per cent of white schoolchildren had lost at least one parent.

Mugabe declared in October 1976: "In Zimbabwe, none of the white exploiters will be allowed to keep a single acre of their land!" By 1978 there was, on average, one farm murder of a white civilian every three days. Every farm was a target.

Every child who grew up on a farm in the 1970s remembers the unbridled terror of those days. Laura Campbell, who was just a little girl at the time, remembers crawling down the passage to the toilet at night, petrified that a *terr* might see her and shoot her through the window. Sandbags surrounded the house and everywhere the family went, they were armed with automatic weapons.

Ben Brackenridge arrived home at Rainbow's End on 9 January 1978, when the war was at its height. He and his family had gone to be with his sick mother. They were due to open the Rainbow's

End farm store the next day. It was the rainy season and the Umfuli River was flowing fast over the weir, which was close to the house. The frogs were in full song.

The Brackenridges had three children. There was Bruce, who was eleven, the same age as my future brother-in-law, Bruce Campbell. They were both keen young falconers and used to fly hawks together. Then there was Nigel, who was two years younger, and Julie, who, at the age of seven, was Laura's age. Julie was sick in bed that day. There were also two other boys from Salisbury (now Harare) visiting the family.

While they had been staying at the house a little time before, Camilla ("Cammy"), Ben's wife, had woken in the night with an overwhelming sense of an evil presence. She woke up the children and brought them together to hold hands and pray.

On the evening of 9 January, Cammy was about to lock up when she heard Julie calling from her bedroom. As she walked down the corridor to the little girl's room, she heard something. It sounded discordant, not quite right. In a time of terror, one's ears become attuned to any noise that jars, but it was difficult for Cammy to identify what it was against the thunder of the flooding river.

"What was that?" she called down to Ben, who was with the four boys in the living room.

"Stay where you are, Cammy," Ben shouted back.

With that, the air exploded. There was a shout and the staccato sound of automatic fire. Then silence. After that there were more shots. Then silence again. The silence of death. The silence that comes from the barrel of a gun.

Cammy and Julie stood frozen in Julie's bedroom. After a little while they heard footsteps coming down the passage. It was Cammy's middle child, her nine-year-old son Nigel. His leg and knee were shot to ribbons. Blood was bubbling out and flowing down his leg. He was with his young cousin, Brian, who was also injured.

"Daddy's dead," Nigel cried. Then: "Bruce was so brave."

Cammy would never know what he meant by that. Had young Bruce somehow tried to protect the others against the men with the guns?

Cammy was a nurse and she knew that she would lose Nigel if she didn't act quickly. She grabbed an eiderdown and bound it around his leg. She comforted the children and then followed the blood trail back down the passage to the living room.

The lifeless form of her eldest son, Bruce, lay on the floor. Most of his face had been shot away. He was dead. Her husband was dead too. He had died with his hand curled around his son's foot. It was a fatherly gesture, something tender in that grisly scene of horror. The other boy, Alan, was dead in his chair.

Numbly, Cammy walked through to her mother-in-law's bedroom. She knew what she'd find there. The old lady was dead too, slumped over her tray, soaked in her own blood.

The sickly sweet smell of blood and death was everywhere, pervading everything. The smell left by Mugabe's "freedom fighters".

Cammy locked the doors, knowing that they might come back if they saw that there was still life in the house. She went back to the bedroom, to the huddled band of children, to get her revolver. Her hands were shaking so badly that it accidentally discharged, narrowly missing Julie.

Mike Campbell went in as the scout for the regular force reaction unit that did the immediate follow-up. There was always the danger of an ambush and of land mines having been laid, so they used the back way in. Mike and the others tried to track the killers down but it was difficult to pick up the spoor in the darkness and by morning the terrorists had had most of the night to make good their escape. The bush was thick in the middle of the rainy season, making it easier for them to get away.

By this stage of the war Mike and Angela had had a number of close friends killed by the *terrs*. All three of their children, Cath, Bruce and Laura, had had friends killed too. The railway line that ran past the farm was often blown up. One night a man was killed when a grenade was hurled into one of the Mount Carmel farm workers' houses. Various other houses were burned down by the *terrs* that night.

They were harrowing times in which to try to work a farm and bring up a family. Many farmers were bankrupted by the looting and hamstringing of their cattle and they couldn't carry on. By the end of the war, in the year 1979 alone, the stock theft toll amounted to 92,000 head of cattle. Cattle were driven off at night and taken to the villages and slaughtered at the *pungwes* (indoctrination meetings) taking place to buy favour with the rural people who had been farming the communal land. It was impossible to keep going in the face of such difficulties, especially in a time of full economic sanctions.

By the end of the war about a third of white farmers had left their homes and farms in Zimbabwe and had gone to start a new life elsewhere. The loss of farming expertise was a serious blow to the agricultural sector, which contributed about a third to the country's Gross Domestic Product (GDP). The other key contributors were mining and tourism. In 1975 the *United Nations Food and Agriculture Yearbook* ranked the then Rhodesia second in the world in terms of yields of maize, wheat, soya beans, and groundnuts, and third for cotton. In the combined rankings for all these crops Rhodesia ranked first in the world.

After independence, when the bush war was over, and during the *Gukurahundi* massacres, more than fifty white farmers were murdered in the Midlands and Matabeleland regions – many more than had been murdered during the whole war in that area. In Matobo district, only nine out of forty-one farmers remained on their farms by the end of 1983. There was mass murder of the largely Ndebele rural population by Mugabe's North Korean-trained 5th Brigade. Nobody knows how many thousands of innocent civilians were killed in the atrocities. Even babies were slaughtered, but no one dared speak out. No one dared try to resist. People were just murdered and nobody counted the bodies. For most of the white community it was the beginning of a head-in-the-sand mentality. It was better to keep a low profile and not dig too deep.

Many years later I had lunch with a prominent lawyer who was in Mugabe's cabinet at the time of *Gukurahundi* and was a former Minister of Justice. I asked him what he knew about what was going on then and he claimed that he knew nothing until he read what had been written about it. I didn't believe him – but maybe it was true.

People living under the rule of a dictator become too afraid to talk if a few thousand people get murdered. That's why a few thousand more end up being killed. The lawyer I had met with didn't publicly call for an enquiry and prosecutions, even when he did find out. He would've been too afraid to do that. People disappear without trace under dictators. That's why almost everyone goes along with what the dictator wants. It's a pragmatic approach, directed by people's fear of losing their life. It's ironic that this very approach inevitably leads to many more lives being lost. The thousands of murders during *Gukurahundi* happened because people were too afraid to expose what was going on. Almost everyone became complicit with murder, because they simply did not want to know.

Living up in Harare, I was oblivious of all that was going on in the rest of the country. We weren't allowed down to Matabeleland. I was told it was because of "dissidents". I didn't know what dissidents were, but I discovered that they were terrorists. I accepted that and it didn't bother me. My father was in the British Army and we'd just come from Northern Ireland, where we'd had terrorists and bomb scares too. I was used to terrorists. I had never understood why people's thinking could become so warped that they would want to kill innocent people, but terrorists were part of life. I was young; I knew there were plenty of other lovely places to visit in Zimbabwe even if we couldn't go to Matabeleland.

What did affect me as a boy at that time was the Thornhill incident in 1982. Explosives were planted on Zimbabwean Air Force planes at Thornhill Air Base near Gweru, and ten aircraft were severely damaged, including four new planes. Immediately after the sabotage, many of the senior white men in the Air Force were arrested on suspicion of having planted the explosives, including the deputy air force commander, Air Vice-Marshall Hugh Slatter, and his deputy, Air Commodore Phil Pile.

The sabotage was quite obviously nothing to do with these men. None of the evidence supported it in any way. It was a victimization programme. The accused men were taken off to remote places and denied access to their lawyers while they were systematically broken. They were beaten all over their bodies and hooded and deprived of sleep. One of the torture methods that stuck in my mind as being particularly horrible was the use of high voltage electric shocks on their genitals while they were naked. The men lost an average of nearly a kilogram in weight each day during the time that they were being abused. Despite their bravery, the torture was so bad that in the end they all signed false statements.

When the airmen had been missing for some time, their lawyers went to the High Court to try to get information released about where they were. The Attorney General, Godfrey Chidyausiku, said that he didn't want the lawyers to see their clients because investigations were still underway and he'd been told by the people briefing him (that is, the torturers) that the accused were much less cooperative after they'd seen their lawyers! Soon after the land invasions started in 2000, the Chief Justice, Anthony Gubbay, was hounded out and Chidyausiku was appointed by Mugabe as Chief Justice in the Supreme Court of Zimbabwe.

The first time I ever went inside a court building was when I went to the High Court of Zimbabwe for the Thornhill sabotage case. There was a gallery up above and I could look down on the wigs of the judge and the advocates and hear the arguments.

The judge was Judge Enoch Dumbutshena. It was in the days before the judiciary had been tempted with free farms and free Mercedes motor cars.

On one occasion the defence lawyer asked a witness whether he had been in Gweru or in Harare at a particular time on a particular date, as he appeared to be telling two conflicting stories and both of them couldn't possibly be true. The witness thought for a while and eventually said that he was in both places at the same time! The lawyer quipped that if it hadn't been so serious he would have believed that it was a comedy.

I wasn't there when Judge Dumbutshena exonerated all the white airmen and pronounced them "not guilty". My mother, who'd been going every day to listen and pray, told me it was very emotional. A tangible sense of relief flooded the courtroom and everyone's heart leaped with the joy of seeing justice being handed down. But in the middle of the excitement the forces' chaplain warned everyone, "This is the time when we must really pray." He was right. Just as they thought they were free, the airmen were all rearrested on exactly the same charges as before and marched back down into prison. The new arrest warrant had been signed even before the judge had given his judgment.

There was a huge intimidation campaign after the rearrests. The lawyers were given the classic midnight knock treatment by the CIO (the Central Intelligence Organization, or secret police) and they all eventually left the country. Dictators can't abide people who support law and order.

The airmen were released in batches and banished. They were taken to the airport in handcuffs and made to leave the country immediately. They were told that if they spoke to the press, the men left behind in jail would be victimized. Mum and Dad were involved with raising the 7,000 Zimbabwe dollars needed for airfares, which was £5,000 in those days. The money poured in and, just before the time limit expired, exactly the right amount had been contributed. It wasn't luck. I know that for sure. Again and again I've known situations where the exact money that is required has come in. It's God's provision.

This was my first experience of seeing the operation of the law in combating injustice. Before that, I thought the law was a stuffy business, but now I could see how vital it was to have good judges and respect for proper legal processes, processes that would take place in the full public eye. Looking back, it was at the Thornhill judgment that the seeds were sown for my later life. I understood that the fight for justice is a vital one.

The Thornhill case resulted in most of the white and Ndebele populations in the Zimbabwean armed forces leaving their jobs. Thirty per cent of the air force had been white before that time. But Mugabe didn't want white people, or Ndebeles (President Mugabe is a Shona from the Zezuru clan), or anyone who might question his excesses, in his forces. If he was to become the untouchable dictator he wanted to be, he needed loyal stooges who would obey his orders blindly.

By 1983 the white population of Zimbabwe had fallen to 100,000, just over a third of what it had been a decade previously. By the time of the elections in 1985, Mugabe said, "Those whites who have not accepted the reality of a political order in which the (black) Africans set the pace will have to leave the country." He then continued, in Shona, "We will kill those snakes among us. We will smash them completely."

In a speech on 14 June 1986, at Rufaro Stadium in Harare, Mugabe said, "The only language that the *mabhunu* will understand is the language of the gun. The more you kill, the nearer you get to your objective." (*Mabhunu* is the racist term used for a white farmer.) It was stirring stuff, designed to ensure that the whites who were left never opposed him or stood against his excesses in any way.

But the international community still treated Mugabe as the darling of Africa. He would even go on to receive a knighthood from the UK in 1994: he was a hero. The world had decided to turn a blind eye to what was going on. Almost no one was willing to risk their life by going in to take pictures or interview survivors of *Gukurahundi*. The apartheid government in South Africa had to be overthrown and no one seemed willing to acknowledge the fact that genocide was taking place in Zimbabwe. In the words of the British Ambassador of the time, "There were 'more important things' to address." It was a shameful time for anyone who truly believed in justice and in doing what was right.

Gukurahundi was finally over with the signing of the 1987 Unity Accord between ZANU–PF (led by President Mugabe) and PF–ZAPU (led by Joshua Nkomo). PF–ZAPU was absorbed into ZANU–PF, which did not change it name. Shortly afterwards, I left school and travelled for a couple of years working on various farms around the world, then came back to Zimbabwe to get some farming experience before going to agricultural college.

CHAPTER 3

In 1994 I married Mike and Angela Campbell's daughter, Laura. I knew without a doubt that she was the right person for me. Laura is small in stature but she has a big heart. While quite an introvert in many ways, she is very insightful and doesn't suffer fools gladly, responding very fiercely when people are doing wrong to others – particularly to those weaker than themselves – or harming defenceless animals.

We'd hitch-hiked up to the Tazara Express train that runs between Kapiri Mposhi in Zambia and Dar es Salaam in Tanzania. We couldn't get seats and even the corridors between the seats were full, so we sat on our packs between two carriages. It was dark and the noise was tremendous. There were people continually pushing past us and we knew we had three days of it to come before we'd reach the end of the track at the Indian Ocean.

I had to shout through the noise of the train wheels on the rails and the grating of metal on metal between the carriages, "Will you marry me?"

I think she was slightly incredulous at first but there was no mistaking it when in the darkness Laura shouted back: "Yes!"

We got married on Mike and Angela's farm, Mount Carmel. A battered wooden cross was erected overlooking the dam in a natural amphitheatre among the rocks. The altar was made out of Rhodesian teak from old railway sleepers. Our guests sat on hay bales and my friend James played the trumpet and then the piano from the back of the Land Cruiser. Giraffe, zebra, wildebeest, impala, eland, and other animals wandered across the plain of swaying golden grasses behind us. Laura walked out of the savanna on Mike's arm in a beautifully embroidered day dress that was nearly a hundred years old. We'd found it in a trunk belonging to my grandparents in a dusty old barn in England.

Before the wedding, my friend James and I had completed the first ever successful navigation of the Rufiji River by canoe. The river runs through the Selous Game Reserve in Tanzania, Africa's largest game reserve. It was a defining trip for me, the start of a lifelong love affair with a very beautiful and tyrannical mistress. That safari, more than any other, brought the savage golden glory of Africa, with all her untamed freedoms, firmly into my heart.

James and I didn't see another human being for a whole month. At the end of an adventurous six weeks of canoeing through those wild lands with the animals of Africa all around us, we finally hitched a lift at the delta on a dhow and sailed up to Dar es Salaam, sleeping on a cargo of mangrove poles. I was so impressed by the vessels of the east coast, which continued to ply their trade by sail, as they had done for so many centuries, that I planned to convert one and sail it up through the Red Sea and into the Mediterranean for an extended honeymoon.

Unfortunately this boating adventure was my plan and no one else's. Laura was caught up in the romanticism of it for a little while, but it didn't take long for her to see the impracticalities. For me it was a childhood dream, to sail the world in my own boat. During my travels in New Zealand I had become a committed Christian and I knew that I should ask God for guidance about everything I planned to do. But I was afraid that he might say no. Mike, my father-in-law, had prayed at our wedding that Laura would have a house. Well, that would come later…

Laura and I based ourselves on the east coast, close to Bagamoyo, the former Arab slaving port, opposite the spice island of Zanzibar. We were the only white people for miles around and children often threw stones at us. We had no vehicle and the sixty-kilometre road to Dar es Salaam was a poor one that normally took about three hours to travel, lurching nightmarishly along by bus.

We lived on the beach in a cottage that we rented from the Tanzanian Government. It had been built by the Norwegians and was the remains of one of the thousands of failed aid projects that litter the continent of Africa. At the boatyard, in the nine months that we were there, the trained boat builders did nothing but drink tea all day. Once they cut one small dinghy in half to make two even smaller dinghies, but that was the sum total of their efforts for the year. Next door to us lived the second-in-command of the place, Mr Liaquipa, with a few of his wives. Every day, the wives would sit on their veranda chattering away in Swahili interspersed with numerous exclamations of "E-heyyyy!" Every evening, Mr Liaquipa's gangly figure would come weaving toward us for a chat. He was always staggeringly drunk, slurring his words and agreeing pleasantly with everything we said, using his favourite affirmation of "Eczaactlleeee!"

And so we lived as most of Africa does. There was rarely electricity. No telephones worked. If we wanted meat, we had to find a man slaughtering a goat under a tree, hacking off bits of flesh and bone with an axe among a cloud of sticky flies. If we wanted milk, we had to find a man who had a cow at milking time. If we wanted to go to town, we had to get a lift on the back of a bicycle to the main road where the bus used to stop, so crammed with a sweating, seething mass of people that there was often only room to put one foot down on the floor at a time as we careered drunkenly along.

Soon after we arrived, we went to the town of Bagamoyo, a few kilometres away from the bay where we lived. On our way from the town to the beach we meandered down a little path between the coconut palms. The flowers of a beautiful pinky-coloured creeper rambled over the old walls of Arab slave traders' houses and German colonial buildings. Two men stood by a coconut palm next to the path a little ahead of us.

I immediately tensed. I'm normally trusting by nature, but there was something about those men that set me on edge.

I continued to lead Laura forward along the path, which we wound down in single file. As I neared the first man, like lightning he pulled a *panga* (a half-metre long knife) from his trousers and attacked me.

I don't remember anything in particular going through my head, I just sprang forward to meet him and grabbed his arm so that he couldn't use the *panga* to hurt me. I charged onwards in a rugby-scrimmaging dive, pushing him out along the path toward the beach, while the other man jumped on my back, trying to tear off the small rucksack where I kept our money and passports.

After a brief but furious struggle I threw the second man off. I don't know what happened to the *panga* in the melee. Suddenly I heard Laura scream, "Help, he's got my watch!"

"I'm coming," I shouted back breathlessly, abandoning the first man right next to the beach, where I'd hoped to get some help. I ran back, past some dense bushes, to find that Laura's watch had been ripped off her arm but she was unharmed. Both of the scoundrels had disappeared.

It was a lesson to us. After that, we were always vigilant. Wherever we walked, we walked quickly, constantly watchful, never resting, always alert, summing up everyone, never trusting anyone. I now realize it was how I'd seen Mugabe behave in the rally. That way we survived without further mishap. But we knew that any mistake, any relaxation of that attitude, and we'd be victims.

In order to build my dream boat we needed a work permit. To get a work permit we had to pay bribes, but we weren't prepared to do that because we knew it was wrong. We visited Dar es Salaam every couple of days to try to get things moving, but we were fairly worn out after spending six hours a day bumping along that dreadful road, often standing on one leg for hours at a time. Dealing with petty bureaucrats in grime-covered offices that hadn't been painted since independence nearly forty years previously was a soul-destroying process, especially as each official always seemed to need yet another piece of paper that no one ever had.

Looking back, the nine months we spent on that beautiful coral sand beach were the most frustrating of my life. We eventually abandoned the whole project. As a Christian it was a big lesson to me: to do things without God is to court disappointment and disaster. It was good to learn that lesson, although it was a hard one to appreciate at the time.

From Bagamoyo, Laura and I went to Zambia, planning to build a safari island camp near Sinazongwe on Lake Kariba. But before moving into the Zambian venture, my friend James and I went on another expedition, this time a three-month walk with mules and donkeys through southern Ethiopia into northern Kenya, following the Omo River and Lake Turkana.

It was on this trip that the old Africa, the Africa of the "noble savage", presented itself to me. I was young enough to believe in the idea of the "noble savage" back then.

In those days, the Omo Valley in Ethiopia was an incredibly wild place. There were no roads and the escarpment was too steep and the vegetation too dense for any vehicle to make the precipitous descent down to the river.

The tribespeople there lived as they'd always lived, dressed in skins or sometimes in nothing at all. It was impressed upon us by everyone we spoke to in the Highlands that the tribesmen and the lions were dangerous and we'd need an armed escort to get through the Omo Valley intact.

There were no white people in the Southern Highlands except the occasional brave missionary family. James and I were given a lift to a place near our starting point by an American called Ben Skaggs. A bearded man wearing a lumberjack shirt, a pair of old jeans, and leather sandals, Ben had a voice deeper and more gravelly than the rawest cowboy from a Western. He was the only white man who knew the Ma'an language.

With him we passed beautiful, impenetrable rainforest, with huge trees towering out of jungles of dense, lush greenness. The escarpment was breathtaking – vast and wide, with awe-inspiring views that went on forever. It was truly fabulous country. The big man gazed at the scene before us and in his gravelly voice summed it up: "God made all this!" He said it in such a simple, factual way, with such plain and truthful sincerity, that it made me want to cry. Said in that place, and in those circumstances, by that good man, it made an impact on me as one of the most profound things I've ever heard. Whenever I see intense natural beauty, I hear the echo of Ben's words.

During our walk, James and I went to places where the local tribesmen had never seen white people before. Almost all of the men were armed, some with reasonably modern AKs, though most of them only had three or four bullets. Some of the men had horseshoe-shaped scars on their upper arms, one horseshoe for each man they'd killed. The people in the Highlands had told us that even if we got past the lions unscathed we'd never get through the Bumi tribe, because they were cannibals. Often we moved at night and lay up during the day.

It was wild, lawless country. Each tribe survived through vigilance, cunning, and strength. Any weakness on their part would lead to their destruction. They were nomadic, pastoral people, always on the move, playing out the ancient game of the African plains between the predators and their prey – except that sometimes they were hunters and sometimes they were the hunted.

There were no schools or hospitals, or policemen, or courts down there. The tribespeople had no knowledge of a written language, or the combustion engine, or of wearing woven clothes. The only law they knew was the law of the spear or the gun. Life was cheap, and life expectancy not very long.

As James and I walked through the south of Ethiopia, we threaded our way past famine and disaster. Ethiopia had already seen death on a horrific scale through the destabilization campaign of the dictator Mengistu Haile Mariam. This and the civil war had resulted in a quarter of a million people being killed. It had also resulted in over a million dying in the terrible 1984–85 famine, which shocked the world with its images of emaciated people. One of Mengistu's own ministers said of him, "His conduct was not limited by any moral considerations. He began to openly mock God and religion. There was a frightening aura about him."

Under Mengistu, Ethiopian farmers had had to cope with the abolition of tenure to their land when it was nationalized. After that, they'd had to sell their grain to the state monopolies at sub-economic prices. Then, in order to control them absolutely, the regime imposed a forced resettlement programme, during which another 100,000 or so people were killed and a million displaced.

When Mengistu was finally forced to flee Ethiopia in 1991, Mugabe granted him asylum in Zimbabwe. He lived in the leafy suburb of Gunhill in Harare for many years with a Zimbabwean police guard. In Zimbabwe today, Mengistu is credited with masterminding Operation Murambatsvina, when the bulldozers were sent in to "clean out the filth" and 700,000 people were left without homes in the high density suburbs of the cities. Many people also believe that Mengistu advised Mugabe to create hunger so that he could have complete control over the population of Zimbabwe. Under this strategy, there is only one thing to do to productive farms – destroy them.

As James and I continued our trek, off to the east of us lay Somalia. Three or four hundred thousand people had been killed there too in the previous few years, under the government of the warlords. That was more than 10 per cent of the entire population of the country. After the UN force had gone in and taken control, none of the warlords had been disarmed and nobody had been brought to justice. The UN was too afraid of the possibility of losing men, and this fear resulted in the continued suffering of millions of people. When the UN pulled out, the warlords reverted to their reign of terror with their guns.

To the west of us was the Sudan. General Ibrahim Abboud, who took power in a bloodless coup in 1958, two years after independence, had expelled the Christian missionaries en masse. Civil war started with the repression and mass enslavement of an estimated 200,000 people. By the end of the first ten years, 500,000 people had been killed.

In 1984, Sudan, once the breadbasket of Africa as a result of the massive irrigation scheme put in by the colonials between the Blue Nile and the White Nile, saw 250,000 people starve to death. Hunger became a weapon used by both sides in the civil war when food aid was prevented from getting to the starving people. In 1988 a further 250,000 people starved to death in the south. Many more were driven from their homes.

On our trek to the south, James and I eventually crossed into northern Kenya, where the Shifta roamed in raiding parties as they always had. Enveloped by a universe of tyranny, the Omotic tribes were suspended in a world of their own. Their lives hadn't changed for thousands of years. It was the old Africa of fierce tribal peoples living under an unforgiving sun.

Looking back, our 2,000-kilometre walk was an education. Threading our way through fear, famine, war, and tyranny was like walking through the eye of a storm. I started to understand that human beings need a system of law and order if their nations are not to degenerate into places of senseless human tragedy where hunger and poverty are imposed through the barrel of a gun.

CHAPTER 4

In the mid-1990s, when Laura and I lived there, Zambia had very little in the way of anything. We used to joke about the Zambian currency, the kwacha, as I needed a couple of briefcases full of 500-kwacha notes to pay the workers each month. Inflation stood at nearly 200 per cent and we couldn't imagine how things could be any worse. We had no inkling of what was to come later in Zimbabwe, when paying the wages meant carrying fertilizer bags full of money around with us.

After a year of trying to build a safari business on a shoestring, we were tired, and I wondered if it was time to move on. It wasn't an easy decision to make, because in my heart I knew it was a big one. I found myself wrestling with all sorts of conflicting thoughts. The Zambian experience had certainly been interesting and I'd learned a great deal about operating under difficult circumstances, with no electricity, bad equipment, and some unhelpful politicians and chiefs. But despite everything, we'd laid the foundations of a fine safari set up out of nothing much at all.

One night I went to bed knowing that Laura and I had to make our decision the next day. This time I prayed and asked God for his guidance. I spent the whole night in a tossing turmoil, but by morning I was completely at peace. I knew that we should go to Zimbabwe. It was a tremendous relief and I felt that the decision and the peace I had about it could only have come from God.

I put my papers in to the Zimbabwean immigration department and a week later Mike, my father-in-law, radioed to say that the permit had been granted. This was unheard of: obtaining immigration paperwork was known to be an extremely long and drawn-out affair. I had been given a full residence permit with no employment restrictions.

I started looking for a job and eventually heard of one with the Commercial Farmers' Union, the CFU. I had various interviews, including a long and difficult one with David Hasluck, the CFU director. I remember coming out feeling decidedly dazed and slightly disoriented and found myself wandering down the road through Harare not really knowing where I was going.

Everything counted against me. I had no experience in agricultural politics or the civil service, which at that time was very "old school". I'd come to the interview without a tie, which was unfavourably commented on, and of course I was – unforgivably – British-born. But I was given the job of Regional Executive Officer, based in Mashonaland West province. Although I knew it was right to take it, I was convinced that it would just be a filler before I moved on to something more challenging. Offices, desks, and computers have never been my thing. For me, life has always been about getting out and living it. I love wild places and the challenges of mountains, rivers, oceans, or the African *veld*. I knew that to be chained to a desk wasn't my idea of having a life. So I was fortunate that at the start of my job I was detailed to go off and visit commercial farmers, both black and white, to get to know what they did.

I began to work for the CFU in 1996. At that time, Zimbabwe was going through one of the most fascinating periods of success in the history of post-independence Africa. Thousands of hectares of irrigation were being developed by farmers each year and our economy was one of the fastest growing in the world. A new black middle class was rapidly emerging, educated men and women who were independent of the ruling party. Agriculture was booming and diversifying, and every year Zimbabwe was exporting more agricultural produce. Zimbabwe's climate means that almost anything can be grown and almost any kind of livestock thrives there. Indeed, I don't know of any tropical or temperate crop or animal that won't thrive, with the right care, in Zimbabwe. In those days we never saw aid workers in their fancy four-wheel drives, because there was no need for them. The bad old days of war and persecution appeared to be over.

During my first months with the CFU I visited many types of farm and met a tremendous variety of farmers. I was amazed by how diverse they were. Each farmer had his own story and his own unique way of farming, building, and developing his land. Most of the older farmers had bought their farms as virgin land and lived in mud huts at first. Natural selection took its toll. Not everyone is cut out to be a farmer and there were many who didn't make it. Only the best farmers survived the droughts and the difficulties that came with farming in Zimbabwe.

Farmers in those early days faced the mammoth task of clearing virgin bush to open up new areas for farming. I remember staying with Dave and Anne Boden on Devon farm in Hwedza. They told me that they'd had no house when they got married, so they arranged for a few of their newly employed workers to build a pole and dagga (mud) abode while they were on their honeymoon. Two weeks later Dave and Anne came back and moved in.

Unfortunately the house wasn't as well thatched as it might have been, and with the first rain their bed got very wet and so did they. They decided that if they were to survive the rains, they would have to go to Salisbury to buy a tarpaulin. So they hitched up the oxen and embarked on the three-day trek, which now takes an hour by motor car. On the way, David, who had evidently got the worst of the storm on his side of the bed, went down with pneumonia. They got their tarpaulin, though, and went on to spend the rest of their lives building up their farm – until they were violently evicted in February 2005 and it was destroyed.

When I went about my job and saw what had been built up on all those farms by the families who had survived down the decades,

I was intrigued and full of admiration for them. They had been through so much. My brief from the CFU was to get to know them and their problems and assist them in whatever way I could.

Despite their successes, the problems were many. There were labour matters, infrastructural and utility problems, miners coming on to their land to dig gold, water disputes, marketing and procurement problems, legal problems, poaching problems, problems with local politicians, fuel procurement problems and so it went on. But they were interesting days. No problem was insurmountable and everyone appeared to be going forward and developing. In fact, when I started the job, Zimbabwe's GDP annual growth rate was close to 10 per cent – one of the highest in the world.

In 1997 Laura and I decided to build our own house. We designed it ourselves and dug the foundations on a corner of the family farm, Mount Carmel, between beautiful indigenous woodland and open grassland, with a view that stretched away and away to a lovely hill in the northern distance.

Just as we finished the foundations, in November 1997, Mount Carmel was listed for acquisition by the government. The publication of the acquisitions list was a huge shock to everyone. There were 1,472 farms on it. When farmers saw the names of their own farms in print, they were devastated. Many of them came to my office in tears. I helped them to prepare objection letters, listing all the developments they'd made, how many people their farms supported, and what their production statistics were – all the good reasons why their farms shouldn't be acquired by the government for resettlement.

I knew what resettlement meant. I'd visited resettlement areas as part of my job. Even on prime farms with dams and irrigation and good infrastructure, resettlement was invariably a disaster and the resettled farms ended up becoming places of subsistence, supporting significantly fewer people than they had done before.

The problem was that, once the government had bought the farm, the title deeds were vested in the state president and there was no actual on-the-ground owner any longer. The people who were resettled on the farms were not necessarily farmers and they were certainly not given any kind of legal assurance that they would be able to remain. This was of course deliberate. If you can keep people reliant on your patronage you can control them a lot more easily. That is the story of Africa. There isn't a country to the north of us in sub-Saharan Africa where the state doesn't own the vast majority of the land.

The problem with not having ownership lies in the way that human nature works. What a person doesn't own, he doesn't look after wholeheartedly. There's a vast difference in the way that people look after and develop the land when they own it – and have an assured future on it – and when they don't. If you don't own the land, you just don't have the same motivation to develop and care for it. Furthermore, no financial institution will lend money to develop a commercial enterprise on land where there is no security, and so everything goes backwards and people become poorer.

Despite being listed, Laura and I carried on building our house. Early in 1998 Agriculture Minister Kumbirai Kangai delisted us. We breathed a huge sigh of relief.

In September of that year, a large land donors' conference was called at the Sheraton Hotel in Harare, facilitated by the United Nations Development Programme (UNDP). I attended on behalf of the CFU and had some input, but mostly I just listened. Most of the attendees were from the cocktail and diplomatic set and I felt out of my depth.

On one of the days, though, we went out to see things on the ground in Mashonaland Central. We visited a commercial farm, which was right next door to a communal area. The commercial farm was an oasis of irrigated crops and productivity. The communal area was dry and barren and there were no trees. The two farms had the same soils and the same rainfall and yet the communal area was a disaster in terms of its productivity.

We also visited a former commercial farm that the government had bought for resettlement some years before. It looked very similar to the communal area except there were a number of trees that had not yet been cut down. It was a hot day and the wind eddied around, lifting the dust. The place had an air of desolation and hopelessness about it.

On the way back to the conference, we talked about the importance of ensuring that people had security of tenure. The day had illustrated its value so starkly.

At the summing up on the last day, various nations pledged tractors and equipment and money to help support a land reform programme, but I don't remember any of the ambassadors talking about the value of security of tenure and the need to bring title into the communal areas. It was too thorny an issue to advocate back then.

The person who spoke the most sense, I thought, was the Israeli Ambassador. He told us that the Israelis had come to a desert with no gold or oil or other natural resources fifty years previously and that the desert was now flourishing. He said that human resources were the key to development, and it was imperative to take this into account if we wished to see the land developed.

The donors agreed that an inception phase to land reform should develop models that might be successful. I went back home and thought about it. With input from the other farmers in the region I put together a model that we all believed would make sense, a model that would bring people out of poverty and resettle more people than would be displaced.

We knew a place where we could try it out, a tobacco farm known as Chikanka, on the Biri River downstream from Mount Carmel. The owner wanted to sell up and go to Australia. There was already one dam on the property and there was a fabulous dam site for further expansion of the irrigation potential. We knew that if we could implement the schemes that we were looking at and duplicate them on a bigger scale, we could support far more families than the land reform programme envisaged by the ruling party could accommodate. And with the aid of irrigation these families could rise above their subsistence status and not be reliant on ruling party handouts during dry years. The Ministry of Agriculture maintains that there is the potential to irrigate three million hectares in Zimbabwe.

Our scheme was for a centralized company to run the main infrastructure on the farm, growing the seedlings, ensuring that the flood irrigation worked, doing the tractor work, curing and marketing the tobacco, and ensuring that the agronomic advice was good. The company would be run by us through a trust. Together with a general manager, who was an experienced and successful commercial tobacco grower himself, we would ensure that it was run at a profit so that the central infrastructure could be maintained and developed.

The people applying to settle on the farm would have to do things on time and to a good measurable standard over a five-year trial period before earning title to their property. If they failed to do this, they would forfeit their plot and someone else would be brought in.

Thereafter, once they had got title, they would still have to do things on time and to a high standard if they were to be allowed to use the central infrastructure. But those who wanted to put in their own irrigation scheme, or curing facilities, or other crops, could then do so if they wished.

We got as far as interviewing applicants for the project at the district administrator's office. I was with the chief *Agritex* officer, Bob Mubai, a good man, doing the interviews. It soon became apparent, though, that I wasn't going to have a say in who was chosen. The local politicians were going to choose politically connected people, as opposed to committed farmers who might have the right skills and credentials to make the scheme work. It also became apparent that the idea of having commercial farmers running the company in charge of the central infrastructure was unacceptable, as was the fact that the applicants would eventually get title.

We eventually shelved the scheme and the government resettled fewer people on Chikanka than the number of farm workers who had lived there originally. I've visited Chikanka a number of times since. The farm has failed to produce even a fraction of what it used to generate and the entire infrastructure has gradually crumbled into sad decay.

It was a pity that we couldn't implement our scheme. I'm convinced that it would have been a success. Unfortunately the government couldn't countenance white farmers making a success of a resettlement scheme that it didn't control.

***

Despite all the uncertainties, Laura and I moved into our new house in 1999. Some of our friends described it as a five-star mud hut. It was built around an oddly-shaped courtyard with a second storey at the back that looked over the swaying grasses of the *veld* into the distance. It was all built from the materials we had around us. We made the bricks from an anthill and the roof trusses and ceilings from the gum trees that grew on Mount Carmel and our neighbour's land. We cut the grass for the thatch from the old railway line that used to run past the southern boundary of Mount Carmel. The roof and floor tiles were made from the soil from another anthill. Laura made the colours for the internal walls by mixing pigments with whitewash; the colours for the outside walls were made from crushing bricks mixed with builders' lime. The windows and the window frames were made out of recycled Oregon pine from one of the old tobacco barns that Mike had taken down after he stopped growing tobacco.

Laura designed and planted the garden and everything grew. Visitors always said what a beautiful place it was. Even through the worst of what was to come, there was always a peace about our home.

CHAPTER 5

Soon after we moved in, there was talk about a new constitution for Zimbabwe. Mugabe's party, ZANU–PF, tried to sell the idea on the land issue, saying that the white man's land could be taken and the Zimbabwe government wouldn't have to pay for it. This was supposed to be the sweetener to allow the further entrenchment of the president's power within the constitution.

We knew that this was a critical issue, so we arranged a big meeting at my offices with all the farmers and the people who were heading up the constitutional commission. One of them was Godfrey Chidyausiku, who had been the attorney general at the time of the Thornhill trial. He was demonstrating his loyalty to the party just prior to his appointment as Chief Justice in the Supreme Court of Zimbabwe.

I made an impassioned speech at the meeting. I knew that what was being proposed was extremely serious and we needed to do whatever we could to stop it. Back then I didn't know much about law, but I knew that if the government was simply able to take the land without paying for it, and property rights were no longer recognized, we would end up with another African disaster on our hands. I'd seen enough of those in my travels.

The referendum for the new constitution was set for February 2000, and the people voted "no". It was a very significant vote. President Mugabe knew that something had to be done if the forthcoming parliamentary elections in June were not to spell the end of his long reign over Zimbabwe. He knew that even though white people only owned about 20 per cent of the land at that stage, more than 20 per cent of the total population lived on those farms and depended on them for their livelihoods. He knew that all these people had to be cowed into submission, along with the farm owners and the rest of the rural population.

Within two weeks the dogs of war were unleashed.

The first farm to be invaded in Mashonaland was Saffron Walden in the Narira hills near Norton. It had spiritual significance because Sekuru Mushore, the *n'yanga* (witch doctor) whom the president was said to consult, lived there. I'd been up to the caves in the hills where he practised.

Ross Hinde, the farmer at Saffron Walden, had asked me earlier whether he should get an eviction order against Mashore and I had advised him that he should. The *n'yanga* had been there for some time and was gradually taking over the place. Blood sacrifices and who knew what other evil practices were going on. I felt that Ross, as the owner of the land, had a responsibility not to allow these things to continue. I also believed that he shouldn't let someone simply take over the land when they had no legal authority to do so and hadn't paid for their piece of ground. Such a practice would lead to anarchy.

After the police had eventually been prevailed upon to follow the court order, I went to the site where Sekuru Mashore had practised. Animal skins, ceremonial weapons, and bones were all scattered about. I didn't stay long – the place had a hauntingly eerie feel to it.

The group that invaded Saffron Walden farm was a large one, armed with *pangas* and axes, and they were noticeably high, doped up on *mbanje* (cannabis). The group surrounded the homestead, beating drums. Liz, Ross's wife, had to escape on foot through the bush. The police refused to do anything, so the local farmers went to help, wearing their police "C" reserve uniforms. We'd encouraged farmers to become police reservists – I was one myself – and we often patrolled at night, with the regular police, manning roadblocks on small rural roads to stop theft and other crime. When the farmers arrived at Saffron Walden, the invaders ripped their police jackets off them and beat them. The regular police refused to do anything to help the farmers. It was clear right from the very beginning that the invaders had been assured that they were untouchable and could invade at will. And the police had been intimidated into allowing the invasions to happen.

It was a terrible time. Large lorries and pickup trucks were used to transport groups of invaders from place to place. In some cases army vehicles were used too. As the invaders roared along on the back of their transport, they would sing *chimurenga* songs at the top of their voices and punch the sky in the black power ZANU–PF salute, brandishing their machetes and axes whenever they saw any white people.

At first, we, as the farmers in the area, set up observation teams, parked off the road, to try to monitor where the groups were going, so that we could help farmers if they were at risk of being beaten. We tried to work as a community and some of the older generation used to come out to our positions with coffee and sandwiches for us.

The fluent Shona speakers among the farmers acted as negotiators and tried to talk to the leaders of the invasions, but this was almost always impossible as the invaders were usually too high on *mbanje*, or else were too drunk to listen to reason. They were clearly under orders and they were being paid through the party, using the district administrators, to do a job.

A couple of weeks after the invasions had started, I was on my way to Harare with Laura and our son Joshua, who was then only three months old. We decided to call in at the Whites' farm, R B Ranches (near Lake Chivero, south-west of Harare). They had been invaded and a number of their workers had been beaten up the previous night. We just wanted to give them some moral support. After entering the farm we passed a group of about thirty invaders and were then stopped at a roadblock made from cut-down trees and 200-litre drums. Another twenty invaders were manning the roadblock. I wound down my window and asked if I could see Mr White.

"Get out of the car!" commanded their leader.

His eyes were bloodshot and Laura said afterwards that they looked very evil. She's better at assessing such things than I am. The men started to raise their axes and *pangas* and it was clear that they were in a belligerent state of mind.

Joshua was sleeping on the back seat in a carrycot.

"Drive!" Laura said. That was all.

I knew she was right. I put my foot down and as I did so the first axe smashed through our windscreen. I wheeled the car through 180 degrees, dust flying, as more axes came smashing into the car. Fortunately none hit us.

We were then facing back downhill toward the main group of invaders. I accelerated fast, away from the men at the roadblock. It was a rocky place and the invaders had amassed a large stockpile of rocks by the road. Laura and I were already covered in glass from the smashed windscreen and there was nothing to protect us as I drove straight toward the main group. I saw them pick up their rocks and, as we came closer, they started to throw them.

I knew that if just one rock caught either one of us in the head, that would be the end. A number of missiles hit and dented the bonnet before bouncing over the top of the vehicle. Others hit the roof and smashed into the side of the car. One very large one crumpled the metal into a big hollow just below Joshua's window. It would've killed him if it had been just a little bit higher. Amazingly, not a single rock actually hit us.

Still at high speed, I veered to the left, past the greenhouses, to avoid any more invaders. They ran after us, chanting and brandishing weapons. Now we had to find a way out. We felt desperate. We didn't want to get cornered and we had no idea whether the track led anywhere. It was clear that the invaders meant business. A little further down the track we found a man walking. He had a bandage around his arm and I knew that he must be a farm worker and a victim of the beatings the night before.

I stopped the car. "Jump in quickly and show us how to get out of here," I said. "They're after us." He jumped in and sat next to Joshua, who, astonishingly, had slept through the whole ordeal.

We couldn't go back through the mob, so we had to go out through the back of the farm. It was a risky venture as it meant crossing two wet *vleis* and then going through the boundary fence. It was the end of the rainy season, so it would be easy to get stuck in the *vleis*. The vehicle we were in wasn't a four-wheel drive and we knew that if we didn't get through, we'd have to make a long and dangerous walk in unfamiliar countryside with a three-month-old baby and that we'd lose our vehicle. It was better than chancing the mob again, though.

We got through the first *vlei* at high speed and then there was no turning back. Somehow, bumping along with the wheels spinning, we made it through the second *vlei* as well, and then we were at the fence line. We didn't have wire cutters but the man with us found a place where the fence had been joined and he managed to undo it for us. I thanked him profusely and we then found our way out onto dirt road that rejoined the main road away from the mob.

I telephoned a report about the incident to the police but they did nothing.

A few hours later another man was stopped on the main road next to the same farm by the same group of invaders and was robbed of everything he had with him. I spoke to him a bit later. He didn't want to make a report to the police. Everyone was already becoming disillusioned about reporting anything. Any incident involving land, or a white man, was termed "political" – and political offences were condoned. The man said he was going to pack up and leave the country.

Sometime later, Mugabe declared an amnesty for all political crimes. Nobody was ever brought to justice for the thousands of similar incidents all over the country. I saw a copy of an official ZANU–PF document entitled "Operation Give Up and Leave", which stated that "the operation should be carefully planned so that farmers are systematically harassed and mentally tortured and their farms destabilized until they give in and give up".

These were times of terror and brutality. Trees were cut down, gardens were destroyed, pets were killed, and cattle were hamstrung. The dogs of a woman whose parents we knew well were beheaded and their heads stuck onto stakes. Farmers were accused of having arms caches and had their gardens dug up.

Initially we all helped each other, but as time wore on the terror spread and some farmers refused to go and help others because of the likely repercussions. It was not an unfounded fear. On all the occasions I was subsequently beaten up, it was because I was trying to help someone in dire straits.

There was some resistance to the invasions at first. In Shamva, farm workers organized themselves into "football teams" to try to take on the gangs of invaders that were threatening their homes and livelihoods. Although the farm workers outnumbered the invaders by hundreds to one, the invaders had the police and the political authorities at their beck and call. Meaningful physical resistance was a futile exercise against soldiers and police with guns.

At the CFU, we took the decision to resist the invasions through the courts. An urgent application was put into the High Court outlining the damage that was being caused and the violence and brutality that were meted out every time a farm was invaded.

Within a couple of weeks President Mugabe was reported as saying that "the ex-fighters would be allowed to remain on their farms". He said that this was necessary in order to "teach the local white community that the land belongs to Zimbabweans".

The day after this comment, on 17 March 2000, Justice Paddington Garwe bravely ruled that the invasions were illegal and the police should remove the invaders. We breathed a sigh of relief and took copies of the judge's ruling along to the police stations to get the police to act. We waited, but nothing happened. The judgment of the court was simply ignored.

President Mugabe had warned of "very, very, very severe violence against the white farmers if they took action against the invaders".

Other members of the government joined in the war of words. Joice Mujuru, who was later to become Mugabe's Vice President, said, "They (the white farmers) call themselves Zimbabweans. They are not. I am a Zimbabwean. When will you learn? Africa is for black Africans." This was racist talk. If a senior politician in the UK had said that black people could not be British and that Britain was only for white people, he would have been relieved of his post immediately. But among black nationalist states in Africa such racist talk brings promotion.

Patrick Chinamasa, the Minister of Justice, was reported as saying that the invasions were the "unfinished business" of the armed independence struggle and that "a political decision has been made to go back and fight again".

Those who were entrusted with upholding the law showed no respect for it. The power that comes from the barrel of the gun was being reasserted. It was clear that Mugabe wished to drive the white people out and to have the whole rural population living in fear. We had to prepare ourselves to face that.

***

Laura and I had arranged a holiday in South Africa that Easter, so after getting the car panels beaten back into shape and the glass replaced, we headed off. While we were away, we heard that Dave Stevens, a farmer from Macheke, had been attacked by war veterans and had taken refuge at the police station. From there he had been abducted by war veterans, beaten, forced to drink diesel, and then shot in the head and back. The police had done nothing to stop it. Soon after that, Dave's foreman was also killed. All over the place people were being severely beaten and hospitalized.

A few days later we heard that war veterans had come to demand meat from Martin Olds, a farmer in the Nyamandhlovu district, for the Independence Day celebrations. Martin refused. At dawn on Independence Day, 18 April 2000, a large group arrived at his farm. Martin had already had death threats made against him, so in the light of what had happened to Dave Stevens, he'd sent his family away.

When they arrived, Martin knew that the invaders meant business. There were lots of them and they were armed with guns.

Chris Jarrett, the Nyamandhlovu Farmers' Association chairman, spoke to Martin on the phone. "What do you want me to do?" he asked.

"Get some police here – fast!" Martin said.

Chris phoned Nyamandhlovu Police Station and spoke to Constable Ngwenya, who was manning the switchboard. "Can I speak to Inspector Sakhe?" Chris requested.

"I have just phoned his house but there is no reply," said the constable.

"Then can I speak to Assistant Inspector Hlomayi?" Chris persisted.

"The line to his house is unserviceable."

"There is a large group of very belligerent armed people at Martin Olds's house and the police need to get there immediately," Chris said desperately. "Can you send someone to run to Assistant Inspector Hlomayi's house and apprise him of the situation so that the police can proceed with all haste to Martin Olds's house as he has requested?" Chris knew that the assistant inspector's house was only about a hundred metres behind the station.

Meanwhile Mac Crawford, the CFU's chairman for Matabeleland, also managed to get through to Martin on the phone. Martin said he was peering through the window at the mob outside. "Now they're trying to smash down the gate!" Martin slammed down the phone.

When Mac managed to get through to him again, Martin said that he'd gone outside and been shot in the leg. "I need an ambulance," he said.

Chris Jarrett asked John Dudman, a farmer who had a small plane, to fly over Martin's house to see what was going on. He then called the police to update them. "Have any policemen left yet?" Chris asked.

"We have no vehicle to go to the scene," he was told.

John got into the air as quickly as he could. He counted ten vehicles about 400 metres from the house, parked at the cattle grid, and another vehicle parked at the main road. A new tractor was just arriving on the scene. John managed to count about forty men with guns in cover surrounding the homestead. When he flew over the police station, he saw a police vehicle driving from Inspector Sakhe's house to the station. What Chris had been told about the lack of a vehicle was obviously a lie.

It was now nearly two hours since the police had been informed about what was going on. It was clear that there was going to be no help forthcoming, despite Martin having been wounded and being on his own.

We only found out later what had happened on the ground. Martin had clearly held off the invaders for a long time. He was a keen hunter and a good shot and had been an excellent soldier. He was brave, too, once having dived into the water and rescued a man who was being attacked by a crocodile. For that he had been awarded the highest civilian award for bravery – the Bronze Medal of Valour – by Mugabe himself. Perhaps that was why he was singled out.

Martin tried to defend himself by shooting from inside his house, trying to keep the men who were attempting to kill him at bay. As he ran out of ammunition for one weapon, he would disable it and take up the next one, darting from window to window, despite his wounded leg, and shooting out into his garden, trying to make each shot count.

Eventually the invaders set the house on fire. The heat must have been intense, but Martin obviously realized that he'd be killed if he tried to escape. He ran the bath to try to survive the heat and flames.

While he was taking cover in the bathroom, a sniper killed him.

The private investigator who was called in later discovered that snipers were firing from four positions. They were all obviously professionals, who tried to cover their tracks by picking up all their cartridge cases, but ballistics tests showed that the bullets were .22 high power bullets, which are used in professional sniper weapons. One informer said that Deputy Commissioner Obert Mpofu was around all that day at Inspector Sakhe's house and that Inspector Sakhe had actually gone to the scene to observe the attack. Some of the vehicles from the scene were seen going unhindered to Induna barracks and others to Mbalabala barracks, despite the police roadblock at Nyamandhlovu village, which had prevented the farmers from going to the scene.

Martin was the Independence Day sacrificial lamb. His murder was meant to breathe fear into the hearts of white men, and it did.

The words of President Mugabe at Rufaro Stadium came ringing back to me: "The only language that the *mabhunu* will understand is the language of the gun. The more you kill the nearer you get to your objective." Not long afterwards, he commented that, "If whites in Zimbabwe want to rear their ugly terrorist and racist head by collaborating with ZUM, we will chop that head off" (ZUM being the Zimbabwe Unity Movement).

Mugabe's objective was now being realized. Terror was in the air. Our fellow farmers and friends were getting killed. Zimbabwe was being torn apart. Martin's elderly mother, Gloria, was shot dead in cold blood at her gate on the farm almost a year later on 4 March 2001.

When Laura and I got home from our holiday, I was amazed to see men on the sides of the roads cutting the grass with their slashers swinging high, back and forth, back and forth, glinting in the wintry blue air. It didn't make sense. The country was heading into deep chaos and yet people were still cutting the grass on the side of the road as though there was nothing wrong. It seemed inconceivable.

All rights to protection of life and property had been removed in the name of white cleansing. Mugabe's first aim was to cleanse the land of white people. If the white man was out of the way, then he could get on with intimidating the black people without any hindrance. "Skull bashing" is essential if a tyrant wants to retain his grip on power.

The whole thing was Hitleresque. Later, Mugabe said, "I am still the Hitler of our time. This Hitler has only one objective – justice for his own people, sovereignty for his own people, recognition of the independence of his people and their right to their own resources. If that is Hitler, then let me be a Hitler tenfold. Ten times Hitler, that is what we stand for."[1]

This time, though, Hitler was a black African cleansing his country of white Africans. In the black nationalist and pan-Africanist ideologies, a white man cannot be an African. This has always seemed strange to me, because, taken to its logical conclusion, it means that white people cannot be Australian either, and nor can black people be American or Australian or British. The intended aim of the extremists in the brotherhood that leads black nationalism is to drive all the whites out, whatever the cost to the ordinary black people.

This is terribly dangerous. Unfortunately, though, black nationalism is an accepted ideology that no one appears to condemn, just as no one really condemned the anti-Jewish programme in Nazi Germany. It's only afterwards that people become brave. While terrible events are happening, they hunker down.

Meanwhile, a gang of about forty belligerents arrived at Mike and Angela's house on Mount Carmel from the Musengezi resettlement area. I knew the Musengezi area quite well from various agricultural outreach programmes going on there. It had been resettled in the 1980s and the farms had been bought by the government on a willing seller basis.

Mike and Angela were away when the mob arrived but Bruce, Laura's brother, was at home. The invaders were fired up and demanding. They managed to extort twenty litres of diesel and helped themselves to fifty kilograms of mangoes and five kilograms of meat from Angela's freezer on the veranda. Then they ordered Bruce to go off and shoot an impala.

While all this was happening, Bruce had managed to call me. I contacted the police but they wouldn't help so I got Barry Lenton from next door to come along. We arrived just as Bruce was heading off in the Land Cruiser with a gun.

I phoned Webster Shamu, our local MP, and got him to speak to Shepherd Bangani, who was leading the invasion. He was evidently told he had taken enough because he left soon after.

Bruce came roaring back less than fifteen minutes later with a dead impala ram. It was the quickest hunt I'd ever seen. Bruce was furious with the invaders and I think with himself too.

Alan Dunn from Beatrice was the next to be beaten to death, just outside his house, where his family saw it all happen. But there was no accountability. The police stood by because the invaders were untouchable.

In 2001, in the middle of this countrywide chaos, we went back to the Supreme Court and managed to get a ruling, which said:

> *It is overwhelmingly obvious that the farm invasions are, have been, and continue to be, unlawful. Each Provincial Governor, each Minister in charge of a relevant Ministry, even the Commissioner of Police, has admitted it. They could do nothing else. Wicked things have been done and continue to be done. They must be stopped. Common law crimes have been, and are being, committed with impunity. Laws made by Parliament have been flouted by the Government. The activities of the past nine months must be condemned.*
>
> *But that does not mean that we can ignore the imperative of land reform. We cannot punish what is wrong by stopping what is right.[2]*

Despite the Supreme Court ruling that the rule of law should be re-established, the lawlessness continued. The attacks continued in an ongoing exercise over time to intimidate the judiciary. The most overt attack took place when the police allowed the violent invasion and overrunning of the Supreme Court in 2000 by war veterans, while it was in session hearing argument on the CFU land case. The judges, as well as everyone else in the court room, had to beat a hasty retreat through the back door.

Notes chapter 5

1. Peta Thornycroft, "'Hitler' Mugabe launches revenge terror attacks," *The Telegraph*, March 26, 2003, http://www.telegraph. co.uk/expat/expatnews/4186630/Hitler-Mugabe-launches-revenge-terror-attacks.html.
2. *Commercial Farmers' Union v Minister Of Lands, Agriculture And Resettlement, Zimbabwe 2001* (2) SA 925 (ZS) Gubbay C. J., McNally J. A., Ebrahim J. A., Muchechetere J. A. and Sandura J. A.).

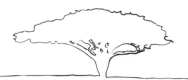

CHAPTER 6

We fished around for other options as to how to deal with the situation that we were facing. Paul Hanly, the CFU chairman for our area at the time, had the idea that we should just give all our farms to Mugabe on the condition that we could then lease them back from him. That way the rhetoric regarding land belonging to white people would be defused and we could hopefully get on with farming without interference.

Paul asked me to come with him to Zambia so we could see how the tenure system worked there. All the farms in Zambia had been nationalized under President Kenneth Kaunda and then leased back to the few farmers who were prepared to stick it out. But many decided that once the state owned the land, there was no point in trying to soldier on, and so they left. Paul and I saw farms that had been derelict for twenty-five years.

The lease-back system did work up to a point. Unfortunately it doesn't have the same security as full ownership title has, and that has financial implications. Many Zimbabwean farmers who went to Zambia when it became impossible to farm in Zimbabwe found that trying to raise finance at the banks was a lot more difficult without full title. Instead they had to make agreements with the big tobacco companies and other corporates and many got fleeced.

Of course the whole lease-back idea was naïve. Mugabe wanted total control of the people. He wanted the white people out. He didn't want them on the land at all, whether they owned it or not.

Paul Hanly eventually decided that on his own farm he would try to make a deal and go into partnership with the district administrator's wife. He managed to get an offer letter signed by the minister without too much of a problem. Unfortunately such a letter counts for nothing in a lawless situation. A little later Lourie farm was gobbled up and he was removed when some senior Air Force people decided that they wanted the farm.

We soon realized that there was no security in either an offer letter from a minister, or a government lease document that allowed the lessee to be evicted if he didn't support the ruling party. Anyway, it wasn't up to a farmers' organization like the CFU to dictate what an individual farmer should do with his land under a government in which nobody could be trusted for anything and deals were broken whenever it suited them. Property rights – full legal ownership of the land – are a non-negotiable absolute for any country wishing to see its agriculture flourish, its people fed, and its resources developed.

From my position in the CFU, I tried to keep everyone informed about what was going on. I knew that without proper information facts can get distorted in small communities and the wildest rumours fly about unchecked. Every night for months on end, without a break, I put out situation reports on the five radio networks in the district. I tried to play things down as much as possible, to stop panic. Every night I ended my report by reading out a Bible verse. I believed in the encouraging and strengthening power of God's word.

I also compiled a daily report for head office so that they would know what was going on in our area. They were busy times because so much was happening and I was in constant demand.

At first I spent a lot of time trying to reason with the local authorities and the warlords on the ground. I got to know them all reasonably well. I was always polite to them and, though they tried to intimidate me, I was able to remain reasonably aloof and unaffected as the situation deteriorated but my trust in God grew.

Often, a group of invaders and ZANU–PF politicians in dark glasses would come to see me at my office. On one occasion

Makoni, one of the very active war veterans in the area, was with them. He is a small fellow and, in order to show his mettle, he did press-ups on the lawn outside as if he was starring in some cheap gangster movie. Every week I would have CIO officials visit me. I had nothing to hide and I spoke openly to them about the things that were wrong.

The authorities tried to exclude me from their meetings with the farmers. It was easier for them to pick on the farmers individually when they were each summoned, alone, to the District Lands Committee meetings. Normally the farmer was kept waiting for hours or even days on end so that he was worn down. These meetings were kangaroo courts at which the Lands Committee members would accuse the farmer of all sorts of seditious and untruthful things, in order to warn him off. The accusations were very difficult to defend on one's own, facing a large group of hostile people who were intent on taking everything that you had. Lands Committee meetings were chaired by the district administrator, who was set up as "God" in each district. Any crime on a farm resulted in the police saying that the farmer must go to see the district administrator. I tried to impress on everyone that they must insist that the crime was recorded so that the police couldn't argue in the future that the crime had never happened, but it was often impossible.

I did manage to go to a few of the early Lands Committee "hearings". They were conducted so unjustly that it was almost impossible for the farmer to show why he should be allowed to stay in his home and continue to farm. I saw many farmers leave these meetings shaky, defeated, and without hope.

From the Lands Committee hearings, many farmers would try to get to see the governor and various ministers in Harare. They'd spend days waiting outside office doors, cap in hand, to see a single minister. One minister would pass them on to the next and then to the next, until often they did a full circle and ended up back with the first one.

It was a frustrating, wearying process. Nothing was ever put in writing and everything was always left in a state of uncertainty. The more worn down the farmers became, the easier it was for Mugabe's government to walk over them. When people become so tired and hopeless, it's easy to persuade them to sign documents giving up most of their property, on the assurance that they'll be left in peace on the other part of it.

The CFU hierarchy advised all its members to make the deals and sign the forms. It was foolishness, but dictators make people into fools through fear.

All over the country *pungwes* were being held on farmers' front lawns. Often the invaders would slaughter one of the farmer's cattle and build a big fire on the grass, using trees cut from the garden. Drums would be brought in, and all night long the invaders would beat them relentlessly, making any kind of sleep impossible. This threatening behaviour, combined with the knowledge of the murders and countless beatings that were happening all around, kept farmers and their families in a state of terror.

The police always refused to attend because it was a "political matter". Actually, it was a form of torture. To survive such relentless pressure wasn't easy and I don't blame anyone for capitulating. Some farmers were barricaded into their houses for days or even weeks at a time, unable to leave. Some were elderly, like Tom Bayley, who was in his late eighties when war veterans barricaded him and his wife in for over a month on their Danbury Park farm in Mount Hampden during 2002. None of their friends or family were allowed to visit, even to bring them food or water. Tom had a fall and broke his hip and nobody could get in to help for some time. He died shortly afterwards. The callousness of the leaders instructing the gangs beggared belief.

The anti-white campaign in the state media continued to build, particularly after the only independent daily newspaper, *The Daily News*, was bombed in January 2001 and its printing press put out of action.

In Chinhoyi, to the north of Mount Carmel, a very intimidating situation arose when a large and aggressive gang invaded one of the farms. The farmers from the surrounding area came to offer moral support. The situation got ugly when they were attacked by the invaders and retaliated, defending themselves. A few farmers were injured, as were some of the invaders.

It was what the police had been waiting for. They moved in and arrested all of the farmers. It was early August – the middle of winter in Zimbabwe – and it was cold. Each farmer was only allowed two items of clothing in jail and their heads were shaved. A white pastor from the church visited the prison to try to bring food in for the arrested men. He was promptly arrested and put inside too. The prisoners were all paraded before the press as criminals, shackled together in leg irons. It was part of the ongoing propaganda campaign against the whites to try to incite racial hatred against them for being "criminals".

Being in a Zimbabwean jail is not pleasant. There are no beds or chairs and the toilet is a hole in the ground in the corner of the cell, often overflowing with effluent. The blankets are normally infested with lice and there is rarely more than one blanket between two or three people. You're not allowed shoes and your pillow is the hard concrete. I know many farmers who weren't even able to lie down flat to sleep, because there wasn't enough floor space in the cell for everyone. Food in prison is almost non-existent, unless visitors are brave enough to come in with some (and even then, they may not be allowed to see the prisoners).

The day after the farmers were jailed, any white person seen in Chinhoyi was beaten, in broad daylight. One elderly white woman was asked if she was a white farmer's wife, but before she could reply she was assaulted. A number of white people were hospitalized. Ralph Corbett, a 76-year-old farmer in the Midlands, was struck with an axe in the head and died. His neighbour had been shot dead some time before.

The farmers remained in jail for a number of weeks. Hundreds of people, many of them women, voluntarily shaved their heads in solidarity with the imprisoned men. After several weeks it was shown that they were all innocent, and they were released.

It was a terrible time. Two days after the arrest of the Chinhoyi farmers, farm trashings began just to the north of Chinhoyi, in Doma and Lion's Den. They were part of the softening-up process.

In Doma, where the local police station had tried to uphold the rule of law, the entire staff was changed, then large gangs of looters were sent in to create havoc in the area.

The first trashing was on Two Tree Hill farm, where a mob arrived at first light. They chopped down a large jacaranda tree in order to block any escaping vehicle. Then they rattled the gates and started shouting abuse and threats at Charl and Tertia Geldenhuys and their young children. "We want to see your blood flow," they shouted at Charl when he came out and faced them. It wasn't an empty threat. Such things had happened time and again at the hands of these state-sponsored mobs.

Then they started looting the sheds and taking all the fertilizer. Charl phoned the police and the local security company and other farmers, but nobody would come. If the police stayed away, how could anyone deal with an arrogant, lawless mob who knew they were untouchable? Negotiation didn't work. Farmers couldn't protect themselves with guns because they would just be put in jail themselves, or killed. There was a feeling of complete hopelessness. Everyone felt utterly alone.

After six hours, when the mob had finished looting the sheds, they came back and broke the padlock on the gate to the house and garden. When one of Charl's dogs came toward them, one of the leaders pulled out a gun and shot the dog. It died in its own blood by the gate.

The family locked themselves into the house. Their children were terrified by the whole ordeal.

After nine hours, the Minister of Local Government, Minister Ignatius Chombo, arrived with Philip Chiyangwa, the local ZANU–PF MP, and Governor Peter Chanetsa. They came with the police and a crew from the Zimbabwe Broadcasting Corporation (ZBC).

They sat down, out in the open, on some looted sacks of fertilizer that had been taken out of the sheds but not yet carted off, and the cameras started to roll. Charl came out to speak to them, trying to persuade them to restore order and put an end to the looting and lawless behaviour. In the charade that followed, Minister Chombo publicly accused Charl of shooting his own dog and being aggressive toward the invaders. Inside the house, Tertia was praying and Charl didn't rise to the bait. He kept his cool.

When the dignitaries left, no one was arrested or cautioned. The mob was allowed to continue. The episode was shown on the ZBC news purely and simply to give groups of looters the confidence to carry on and mete out the same treatment to other white farmers.

Charl and Tertia packed a few possessions and managed to escape with their children in two cars – but that was all. Within a couple of days the looters had stripped everything out of the house. There was no furniture left, or clothes, or beds. The window and door frames were hacked out and the whole roof was taken off. Even their tame eland, Em, was slaughtered. When I managed to get over there a few days later, there was nothing left. It was eerie to see how quickly a place could be destroyed. It had taken Laura and me two years to build our house, and many more to furnish it. When I looked at the remains of Charl and Tertia's home, I realized that my house could be destroyed just as quickly as theirs had been.

Tertia later wrote that revisiting the place where her home had once stood showed her the destructive nature of evil. "While I was walking from one empty room to another demolished room, this vast empty nothingness dawned on me – it's as if we no longer have a past, as if we no longer existed," she said.

It was as though the mob wanted to rub out all the white farmers. They wanted to erase us as a people and return the land to the way it had been many years before – a place of insecurity and hunger and escaping from invading, looting tribes.

As the looting spread from farm to farm and the police still refused to react, most farmers in the area decided to evacuate, realizing that if they stayed to defend themselves or their properties, they would either be killed or put in jail.

Then the access road for the Doma farming district was sealed off by the looters. The gangs moved in in greater numbers.

Some farmers managed to get a light aircraft to fly overhead and try to assess what was going on. Everywhere it was the same story as on Two Tree Hill. The state-sponsored party mob had free rein to do what it liked. In each place the looting was done with such an impassioned, demonic fervour that it left nothing behind. Clothes, pictures, curtains, and other furnishings were all taken. Security fences around houses were rolled up and taken away. Roofs were taken off, doors were wrenched away, window and door frames chipped out. Plugs, light fittings, and wiring were all pulled out, taps and plumbing pipes were dismantled, and toilets and basins were smashed. Everything was stolen or destroyed.

Many barns had their tin roofs ripped off. The invaders mostly left the asbestos ones alone as they break up too easily. Any bales of tobacco that hadn't already been sold were stolen. The workers at one place told us that a truck with ZANU–PF emblazoned boldly on the side had come in and taken away load after load of tobacco.

I saw diesel tanks that had holes punched into them. Thousands of litres of diesel had been allowed to simply run out onto the ground in a river that had gradually been swallowed up by the thirsty earth. I saw state-of-the art tractors and combine harvesters that had had all the wiring ripped out of them. Fertilizer, chemicals, and seed for the coming season had all been looted. Maize had been taken and was spread around everywhere. The whole area was a mess. In just four days, about fifty-four homesteads and adjacent tobacco barns were ruined.

When it was plain that there was to be no accountability, the mob coerced the farm workers to help them in the destruction. This hurt many of the farmers more than anything else. How could the people they had looked after, and housed, and taken to hospital, and whose children they'd built schools for, turn and loot from the very people who had helped them?

It was a bitter betrayal, and that – more than anything else – ate away at the farmers and made them, through clenched jaws, feel like leaving Africa to its own awful, self-destructive fate. Many had had enough already. It's not easy to take such sustained pressure and find that everything important is destroyed at the hands of the state.

But a number of those farmers bravely tried to start all over again.

CHAPTER 7

Back on the home front, things were also difficult.

We'd had our first sustained invasions on Mount Carmel in 2000. A group of invaders picketed Mike and Angela's house, brandishing their axes and *pangas*. Andy Ferreira, the Selous Farmers' Association chairman, came over and managed to negotiate for them to move to a large hay shed on the other side of the river and wait there until things were clearer on the legal front. It wasn't ideal, but at least it would save thousands of trees from being cut down when the invaders decided to build huts. It also contained them a little way away from Mike and Angela's doorstep.

The group waited in that shed for some months. I had a small irrigation scheme nearby, growing horticultural crops, so I saw them often and tried to talk to them. I wanted them to understand the consequences of their actions. But they were being paid for what they were doing. They were there to ensure that there was no campaigning for the opposition party on any of the farms. The invaders' reward was to get the farms for themselves.

In August 2001 the invaders were officially resettled. First, the farm was divided up into little plots. It was a haphazard, ill-considered exercise. A man from the Ministry of Agriculture arrived in a beaten-up pickup truck with a paint pot and a paintbrush. He got the people who wanted the farm into a group and they walked around together, simply painting numbers on trees and fence posts every 400 metres or so. No survey was done. No thought was given to the consequences of this piecemeal distribution of the land. The system regarding who got which plots was mostly done on a lucky dip basis with people pulling out numbered bottle tops from a hat. The number that the invader pulled out was the number of the plot that he was allocated. The whole process was finished in a few hours.

They'd divided up the orchards into little plots too. I knew the trees would all die because the irrigation system was centralized and couldn't be run on a piecemeal basis.

When it came to the resettling, they suddenly decided to put everyone on Carskey, the next-door farm where Laura's brother Bruce lived, presumably to reserve Mount Carmel, where the orchards were, for a *chef* (a senior party official).

Carskey was one of the few white-owned farms that had escaped being listed. That didn't worry the government. They resettled it anyway. The officious man with his paint pot was rushed in again and before we knew it there were fifty-seven plots, with people cutting down the trees and building huts and killing all the animals in the wildlife area.

Cattle were systematically rustled, snares were put up everywhere and fences were stolen. It was a free-for-all. Bruce, who is a strong and good looking person, is a great bushman. He's always looking after orphaned or injured birds of prey and nursing them to be released back into the wild. He can sometimes be taciturn, but he's effusive when talking about the bush that he loves so much. He's also a very good cattleman and an ardent environmentalist.

He ran the cattle on the Savory system, where the *veld* is grazed hard with a high density of cattle and then monitored minutely while it recovers. The cattle are only allowed back to graze there again when there has been sufficient recovery. Pioneered by Allan Savory, a Zimbabwean ecologist, it's a system that copies nature: buffalo group together in large herds for protection against lions, and hammer the *veld* as they move, allowing the areas behind them to recover ungrazed. But in a conventional paddock system, cattle spread out and go back to the good grasses again and again until bad grasses take over. In *mopani* areas the grass is grazed so hard that eventually there is none left and there are big bare patches that get eroded. The net result is that over time the topsoil is washed away, the environment deteriorates, and the number of cattle that can be run on a particular farm diminishes.

Bruce was busy reversing this trend by using electric fences that were moved constantly throughout the day.

It was a huge problem to try to manage the *veld* once the invaders arrived. They came with matchboxes. Normally there might have been a couple of accidental fires a year on the farm that needed putting out. But when the invaders arrived, there were a couple of fires most days. It was demoralizing for everyone.

As soon as smoke is seen on a farm, everyone has to drop everything and go out with tractors and sprayers and knapsacks to fight the fire. When the wind is strong, a fire can jump even big fire breaks fifteen metres wide, so there has to be back burning to make wider breaks to stop the fire's onward march.

I often thought that the fires were symbolic of the invasions. They swept on, relentless, fierce, hot, and angry. The flames leaped up into trees and galloped through the dry winter grasslands, making the whole *veld* crackle. In their wake, there was nothing – just smoking black ground that was devoid of life. The difference was that at least we could extinguish bush fires. The invasions just carried on and on, seemingly inextinguishable.

We compiled reports and wrote letters to the police and to the Minister of Tourism, pointing out the illegality of the actions being taken – but it was to no effect.

The Supreme Court had previously prohibited "any officer or employee of the state, or persons acting on its behalf from causing, facilitating, participating in or giving sanction to any entry or occupation of property". Mike pointed this out in a letter to the district administrator in August. He also quoted from the Bible, from Deuteronomy 27:17, which says, "Cursed is anyone who moves their neighbour's boundary stone." He continued quoting from the next chapter, which predicts what would happen to those who move boundary stones on a whim. It says, "You will be cursed in the city and cursed in the country. Your basket and your kneading trough will be cursed. The fruit of your womb will be cursed, and the crops of your land, and the calves of your herds and the lambs of your flocks… until you are destroyed and come to sudden ruin…"

Mike's letter was prophetic. It didn't matter that Deuteronomy had been written more than 3,000 years before. The curse still holds true. Where boundaries are moved and there is no respect for private property, hunger will result. History has shown this to be the case over and over again. Where property rights are respected and people are allowed to develop in peace and security, there has never been hunger.

In the following month, in September 2001, Mugabe signed the Abuja Agreement. This stated that there would be no new invasions and that the human rights abuses would stop. There would be firm action against violence and intimidation and a restoration of the rule of law. People who were living on farms illegally would be moved to legally acquired farms, and farms that had been listed contrary to the five government-stated criteria would be delisted.

We were very hopeful, but the agreement turned out to be a meaningless bit of paper. Before the ink was even dry, the illegal invaders had been officially settled on Carskey, although it was an unlisted farm that had not even had the first step taken toward its acquisition. We wrote to inform the authorities of this. It was clear that the fact that Carskey was owned by a white man was what made the resettlement legal in their eyes.

A few days later, while Mike was sorting out a problem with a delegation of police and war veterans who were claiming that our cattle had eaten a bit of thatch on the chairman's new hut, the other settlers drove the whole herd of 550 cattle into Angela's garden. She is a wonderful gardener and her garden is always beautiful, but trampling cattle are very destructive. As it was lunchtime there was no one around to help, so when Mike came back, he and Angela had to try to drive the cattle out themselves. About 1,500 new citrus trees, which were due to be planted out in the orchards, were destroyed. The settlers stood at the gate, ululating with glee. Of course no one was arrested or cautioned for that act of wanton destruction and the police never even came out.

Then they started a bush fire, which burned the plastic pipes in Bruce's irrigation scheme on Carskey. While Mike and Bruce fought it to try to stop Bruce's house being engulfed in the flames, a group of six invaders arrived and started laughing at them.

It was chaos.

Fences started to disappear and cattle were chased out of the paddocks. Bruce spent much of his time trying to recover cattle that had been stolen. They would be driven off, often as far as a hundred kilometres away from the farm. Sometimes it took days to track them down. It was a wearing process. About 120 cattle were stolen from the farm without being recovered – about 20 per cent of the breeding herd.

The settlers burned the grazing as soon as they moved on. They smashed the gates and brought in a few of their own cattle, without any movement permits or veterinary clearance. The police weren't interested in prosecutions. Foot and mouth and the various tick-borne diseases could go ahead and spread as far as they were concerned.

In October fifty farmers went to a meeting at the Selous Club. The gang who had been filmed sitting on the looted fertilizer sacks at Two Tree Hill farm was there: Minister Chombo, Governor Chanetsa, and Philip Chiyangwa. Webster Shamu, our local MP, who was later to become Minister of Policy Implementation, was also there, with the district administrator and police.

The Abuja Agreement was discussed and it was agreed that the illegal settlers on Carskey and some other farms would be removed. The district administrator was instructed to do it.

Mike and I felt a little more hopeful as we drove home. But when we passed our neighbours, the Reochs farm, we saw that while we'd been at the meeting, listening to assurances that the rule of law would be respected, the main house and the cottage had been burned down. There was just a glow coming from the remains of the two buildings.

It soon became apparent that what we'd been told by Minister Chombo and his gang was not sincere. No one intended to remove any of the illegal settlers. It was the classic game of raising hopes and then dashing them again.

Throughout October and November of 2001 there were constant incidents on Mount Carmel and Carskey. Cows were stolen and slaughtered, locks on gates were smashed, and fires were started, often in the early hours of the morning. Once we heard five shots and discovered that the settlers had killed an eland calf. Mike and Bruce arrested three of the men and took them to the police station with their rifle and the dead calf as evidence, but the men were released immediately.

One of our dogs, Ginger, was very good at warning us about poachers. He was gun shy and when he heard a shot, even several kilometres away, he would come very close to us and stand there shaking, his teeth chattering. If he heard a shot during the night, he'd wake us up and let us know. When this happened, I'd climb up to a little eyrie that we'd built on the top of the house and look out to the north for spotlights. Often Ginger would wander over to Mike and Angela's house and, when he was there, he would warn them of shots too.

Once, Bruce went out in his vehicle after hearing shots at two o'clock in the morning. He discovered a hunting vehicle being driven around with a spotlight, so he fired a warning shot. The poachers took off in an open pickup truck, firing three shots at Bruce from a shotgun. He heard the pellets shredding the leaves in the branches near his open window. Eventually, Bruce caught up with them and managed to arrest four of them, although the fifth one escaped with the weapon. A trophy wildebeest and three oribi were lying in a pool of blood in the back of the vehicle.

Bruce took them to the police together with the animals and all the evidence, but they were immediately released on free bail. It made a mockery of the law. Bruce had risked his life trying to stop the animals from being killed, but he was getting the message that, "They can kill all your animals and there is nothing you can do about it." For somebody brought up to protect and conserve wildlife, this callous message was very disheartening.

Of all the professions, I am convinced that farming is the closest to the laws of nature that God set in place at the beginning of time. If you don't take account of those laws, things go wrong very quickly. I believe that God created everyone and everything to be loved. All life responds positively to love. Nature – or God's creation – needs to be loved and cared for if it is to thrive. But where the right kind of love and faithfulness are lacking, life begins to ebb away.

The farm invasions in Zimbabwe are phenomena that are far from God's laws. They are fuelled by jealousy, hatred, and greed. These things are the antithesis of what brings life and peace – and so life breaks down and people and plants and animals die.

***

Some of the settlers had brought with them a virulent strain of malaria. Before they came, none of us on Mount Carmel had ever had the disease, but now many of the farm workers fell ill. Nine died in a month and the funeral drums beat through the night.

Bruce's wife, Heidi, who was pregnant with twins, also fell ill. Although she was treated, septicaemia set in and she and the unborn babies died. We were all devastated, especially Bruce and his five-year-old daughter, Megan. Heidi had been so full of life – a laughing, bubbling, effervescent Christian who shone in those dark days.

The day before Heidi died, some Ministry of Health officials finally came to do a spraying programme because of all the malaria deaths on the farm. Mike put them up in the safari lodge. He was driving down in the morning to check how they all were when he came upon an improvised roadblock. He drove around it and carried on.

On his way back Mrs Nyembesi, one of the settlers, threw a large rock with both hands at the windscreen of Mike's vehicle. The windscreen shattered. Mike stopped the vehicle and got out. Mrs Nyembesi ran at him with a crowbar. Fortunately Mike had a large knife under his seat. He reached for it and held it toward her. "If you come any closer we'll both go down," he growled. She backed off and Mike slowly got back into the vehicle. What else could he do? He drove off and, as he did so, Mrs Nyembesi attacked the vehicle with the crowbar, denting it in several places. The dents are still there today.

It took many months and an awful lot of effort to get Mrs Nyembesi to court. The docket went missing a number of times. She eventually got off with a suspended sentence and was allowed to continue living illegally on the farm.

The harassment and death threats were continuous. The settlers would meet every week outside Bruce's house. They didn't want him around. On the day he got back from Heidi's funeral, they demanded that he get out. It was a callous, heartless thing to do.

On one occasion Bruce had been out shooting doves for his falcons when he heard the settlers outside on the veranda, beating one of his dogs, a pointer. As he ran out to stop them, he grabbed the loaded .22 rifle that was lying on the dining room table. At the same moment, the settlers came in through the door with their sticks. Bruce raised the rifle. The settlers turned around, and Bruce shot above their heads so that the bullet passed just below the top of the doorframe and lodged in a wall on the veranda in front of them. After that they didn't come back into his house.

Early in the morning of 18 March 2002, just after first light, my telephone rang. Terry Ford, the owner of Gowrie farm in the Norton district, had been murdered on his farm. One of his staff had come in early and found him lying outside, shot through the head.

I got straight into my car and drove over. It was a horrible scene. Terry was lying on the ground near the fence, covered in a blue cotton blanket that was soaked in blood. His dog, Squeak, a Jack Russell who used to go everywhere with his owner, was lying cuddled up next to him.

Terry had had a volatile situation on his hands because his local MP, Sabina Mugabe, the president's sister, wanted his farm. Terry had decided to back off and was helping out at a school in Harare, but he came down to the farm periodically to check that everything was all right. A gang had trashed four houses in the vicinity that week and had moved into the second homestead on Terry's farm. But now that the elections were over, I guess Terry decided that it would be safe to come back.

When Terry arrived everything seemed OK, so he decided to stay the night and get back to the school in Harare early on Monday morning. But sometime during the night the gang entered the house. Terry managed to call the police but he was told that the driver of the police vehicle was asleep and couldn't be woken. Terry frantically phoned around, trying to reach a neighbour who could help.

It must've been a terrible time for him, all alone in the dark, apart from Squeak, with the mob baying for his blood. I can only surmise that when things got too threatening, he decided to try to make a break for it. He'd obviously managed to get out of his house and into his vehicle. I could tell from the spoor that the gang's vehicle had been blocking the gate. It looked as though Terry had tried to crash his way through the fence, because that was where his vehicle had come to a halt.

Terry must've realized that he was trapped. One of his shoes was stuck in the mud near his vehicle. Whether the gang had ripped him out of the vehicle after he'd tried to smash through the fence or whether he had tried to make his break on foot, I suppose we'll never know. They caught him, though, and they beat him badly before putting him against a tree and shooting him in the head with his own weapon – the weapon that he had obviously made a conscious decision not to use against them. His body was a mess of mud and bruising and blood.

Squeak wouldn't leave him. When the police eventually arrived, quite a long time later, with their black boots and guns, he wouldn't let them anywhere near Terry's body. It was a pathetic sight – a little dog keeping those big men with guns away from his dead master. Tears came to my eyes as I watched.

At Terry's funeral there wasn't a dry eye. Hundreds of people had come, too many to fit into the church. The hardest part of the whole service was the song composed and sung by Cecile Ferreira, a farmer's wife from close by. The song was written from Squeak's point of view. I saw strong men shaking as they sobbed uncontrollably. It was a time of overwhelming grief. So many people had borne so much.

Laura and I needed a break. We went to visit my mum and dad in England that Easter. One Sunday morning we went to a new church that my parents had just started attending. During the service, a lady in the music group had a vision. She said that she could see a farm in Africa. It was a very flat farm with some hills in the distance. I immediately realized that Mount Carmel fitted that description very well. Chegutu is perhaps the flattest farming district in Zimbabwe, and Mount Carmel is one of the flattest farms in that district. Laura and I had built our house to look straight toward a hill in the north about fifteen kilometres away.

This lady read us a passage from Psalm 121. It says:

> I will lift up mine eyes unto the hills, from whence cometh
>   my help.
> My help cometh from the Lord, which made heaven and
>   earth.

He will not suffer thy foot to be moved: he that keepeth thee
will not slumber.
Behold, he that keepeth Israel shall neither slumber nor
sleep.
The Lord is thy keeper: the Lord is thy shade upon thy
right hand.
The sun shall not smite thee by day, nor the moon by
night.
The Lord shall preserve thee from all evil: he shall preserve
thy soul.
The Lord shall preserve thy going out and thy coming in
from this time forth, and even for evermore.

Dad had given me the very same passage only a week before. I knew it was confirmation that we should stick it out and trust in God. And so it was that with renewed courage we were able to go back and face it all again.

CHAPTER 8

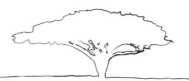

They called it revolution – the Third *Chimurenga*. It was an excuse to complete unfinished business from the First and Second *Chimurengas*. The spirits of jealousy and greed were in control.

Murenga means "resister". The First *Chimurenga*, in 1896–97, was named after Kaguvi, who was one of the main spirit mediums at that time. Kaguvi lived in the Mhondoro communal area, near where Mount Carmel is today. The Mhondoro is a lion spirit that is associated with chiefs and national issues. Many years later, it was next to the Mhondoro that Gilbert Moyo, one of the leaders of the violence in our area, had his base camp.

Kaguvi's real name was Gumboreshumba, which means "the foot of the lion", but he claimed to be the *svikiro,* or personal spirit medium, for the *mudzimu,* or ancestral spirits, of the historical Kaguvi who was said to have been involved with founding the Rozwi empire in the late seventeenth century.

His spirit was said to speak through the rocks and the trees. One eyewitness of the First *Chimurenga* reported that Kaguvi dressed himself in striking feather caps and fastened horns to his head. He would then "rush into the centre of the people… then, falling into a trance, presumably possessed, give out orders".

After the First *Chimurenga* had started, it became plain that the spirit mediums were coordinating the attacks on the white people. About 10 per cent of the whites in the country were murdered. Kaguvi worked with the paramount Chief Mashayamombe, by the Umfuli River near Hartley Hills, not far from where I was subsequently beaten on two different occasions. Interestingly, and perhaps not insignificantly, gold was first discovered there by the hunter Henry Hartley in 1867, sparking the curiosity of the early pioneers to seek their fortune in the fledgling colony in the years to come.

Fort Martin was built beside Chief Mashayamombe's *kraal*. The chief, the most effective secular leader of the rebellion, refused to surrender and died in battle. Kaguvi managed to get away and joined another spirit medium, Mbuya Nehanda, in Mazoe. He later surrendered, and with that the First *Chimurenga* came to an end.

Fort Martin became the name of a farm in our area. Over a hundred years later, Fort Martin farm was the subject of one of the first overtly state-sponsored takeovers. Pete Ziegler, the owner, had run a model farm and a model workers' village, and was winner of the prestigious tobacco grower of the year award. He was also very community minded and served on the rural district council, building and maintaining the rural infrastructure of roads and health clinics. But because the farm happened to have Fort Martin on it, from which Chief Mashayamombe had been defeated, Pete didn't stand a chance of keeping it. The army was brought in. Fiona Barry, one of Pete's neighbours, was made to run barefoot, along with her workers, in front of an army lorry while uniformed soldiers beat them with hosepipes.

At one point an army helicopter hovered over Pete and his workers for half an hour while they were trying to get on with their farming activities. He knew then that the threats were serious and that he would be the next murder victim if he resisted, so he surrendered, and packed up and left.

Not long after Pete left, I heard about the abduction of Hennie Bezuidenhout from Farnham, another farm not far from the Mhondoro communal area. Hennie and Sissy, his wife, had already been beaten once that week. This time the invaders took Hennie away from the house and into the bush. I kept calling the police, urging them to do something, and we got people praying. Hennie was beaten with sticks for about four hours, most of the time while he was lying on the ground. The beating was directed by a CIO man waving a pistol.

I was worried that Hennie's feet would be beaten. Everyone knew that this was the torture method used by the militia. Hennie had diabetes and had to wear slippers because if his feet were rubbed or bruised, gangrene could set in.

In the middle of all the violence, Hennie later told me, a man came to him and talked quietly into his ear. This man seemed different from the rest of them. He told Hennie, "You'll be OK." Hennie was sure that the man was an angel. His feet were left untouched.

After much persistence, I eventually persuaded the police to respond. They went out and stopped the beating, allowing Hennie back into his house.

When the police said that it was now sorted out and safe, I drove over intending to take Hennie to the hospital, but when I got to his gate a young boy of about fourteen was guarding it.

"Please could you open the gate?" I asked.

"Where are you going?" he responded.

"To see my friend, Mr Bezuidenhout," I replied. The boy refused to open the gate.

Then, from nowhere, a number of other people arrived.

"Where are you going?" their leader demanded.

"I'm going to see my friend," I explained again.

"We need to search you for weapons. Get out of the car," the leader commanded. He was a dark, stocky fellow with a big gold chain around his neck. About twenty-five other men were milling around him.

In retrospect it was a silly thing to have done. But the police had just been there, and they had assured me it was all right. And I knew if I were to get to see Hennie, I had to get out of the car. I'd been in many such situations before and had negotiated my way through similar groups without a beating. I decided to get out of the car, leaving the keys in the ignition to show that I trusted the men and had nothing to hide. I had a second set in my pocket, just in case.

I was immediately grabbed and beaten with sticks over my face and across my back. Two men pulled my feet from under me and in an instant I was on the ground, rolling in the dust. I put my head down so that they couldn't beat the front of my face any longer, and then I managed to leap up.

"I'm just going to see my friend," I remonstrated. "I don't even know you and I have no argument with you."

They grabbed me again and shoved me back down on the ground. I felt boots kicking me in the ribs, while blows from sticks continued to rain down on my head and body. I scrambled up again. "Please," I said, "what have I done wrong?"

I was only twenty metres from the car. The blows stopped for a brief minute; I saw a gap, dived through it and sprinted forwards. The keys were still in the ignition and I started the car in one turn as two of my pursuers yanked the door open.

I thrust the vehicle into reverse and put my foot down. The two men hanging on to the door were thrown off into the ditch as I accelerated backwards. I turned around and sped back toward Chegutu, leaving the gang behind me in the dust.

My back and face were covered in red stripes but the internal bruising wasn't too bad. I'd got away in time.

I made another report to the police, but they didn't investigate and no one was ever arrested or charged.

The next day Hennie, Sissy, and I all went for a medical examination. Both Hennie and Sissy had been badly beaten and had deep bruising, but they were tough and they both recovered well.

The CIO operative who had beaten us subsequently erected a monument to the spirit mediums of Kaguvi and Mbuya Nehanda, by the side of the road near where I was attacked. He also built a house there. One day he had an altercation with his wife and shot her six times, I was told. He then shot himself twice in the head and staggered outside the house before collapsing in a heap. He survived as a cabbage for a month after that and then he died.

It got me thinking much about the spiritual forces of darkness and light that were at work in the region.

Sometime later, Heidi Visagie, of Wantage farm in our district, was parked close to the Harare Central Police Station one evening, waiting for her husband, Dirk, who had gone into a government office nearby. Heidi saw a police truck go past with a lot of black people in civilian clothes riding in it, and she suddenly felt the urge to pray, knowing that many people were abducted at night, never to be seen again.

As she looked toward Harare Central Police Station, she saw above it a great battle raging. There were no people involved; it was a battle depicted in fierce light and colour and movement in the sky. Within the red and blue and silver and yellow lights Heidi could see two distinct forces clashing against each other. It was clearly a battle between good and evil, she told me.

In the modern Western culture, people try to reason away the forces that are work in the supernatural realm. But if the problems of Africa are ever going to be really solved, I believe that we need people of understanding to face the problems in the unseen world that have such a hold on the lives of the majority of Africans.

The farm invasions had only recently started when I heard Langton Gatsi speak at a Farmers' Association meeting. Langton is a Zimbabwean, but he spent much of his time in Zambia during the war years and went on to be the first black lecturer at Stellenbosch University in South Africa. His mother was a spirit medium but Langton became a Christian and, eventually, a Christian pastor. He is a statesman in the church and has met many African presidents, trying to bring them around to making righteous choices so that their people are not harmed. I consider him a great friend, and I've learned much from him about the spirit world.

Langton spoke about the demons in high places, and the totems and ancestral spirits that feature so prominently in the lives of the majority of black Africans. He talked about spiritual bondage, and especially about the water spirits that, throughout Africa, have had a malevolent influence, from the beginning of its history.

Langton is an insightful man and a gifted speaker, and he opened my eyes to many things. One of his subjects was the crocodile, Mugabe's clan totem. I remembered my trip with James to the Rufiji River and the crocodiles that we'd encountered there. Once we were paddling quietly along a wide open stretch of water, filled with golden sandbanks, when we saw the most enormous crocodile making its way straight toward us from the right bank, over 200 metres away. Even from a distance we could see how massive it was. As it came closer we could see that its head, which it held high out of the water like a grotesque sea monster, was broad, gnarled, ugly, and evil looking. It surged along effortlessly toward us, its head making a bow wave through the water. The distance from its eyes to its snout was nearly half a metre, so we knew that the beast was at least as long as our canoe. Its great body was hidden below the surface, vast and powerful.

I'd had a touch of sunstroke over the previous couple of days and had been feeling rather sorry for myself, letting James do most of the paddling. The night before, I'd dreamed that I was a snowflake on the bank of the river, melting under the searing sun. I was nauseous and weak, feeling dizzy, uncoordinated, and in an almost hallucinatory state.

The sight of that crocodile's head, close up, brought me back to the reality of our precarious situation in a moment. Suddenly I was able to think clearly and act decisively. Our strokes were fast and strong as we frantically made our way downstream, looking back over our shoulders as we went. The crocodile swam ten metres behind, sailing silently and effortlessly along like a clipper in the trade winds.

We tried to outpace it but it kept up, surveying us. Our strokes became a little panicked.

Rarely have I been so afraid. It wasn't so much the size and ugliness of the beast as the cold, brazen way in which it fixed its eyes on us, travelling coolly and calmly just behind us, ready to pluck us like dainties from a fruit basket at any second.

James and I veered to the left, taking a course toward the bank. As we neared it, the gigantic head slipped silently below the surface of the water with hardly a ripple. We rammed the shore and leaped out of the canoe in terror.

As we made the fire and drank our tea we kept looking out to see where that crocodile had gone. After some time it still didn't reappear. So we packed the live coals into the tin that we carried them in and emerged cautiously out onto the river again.

As we got a little way from the shore the head reappeared from beneath the water, those wicked slit eyes surveying us once more.

To the crocodile, we were prey, and it was only our strangeness and unfamiliarity that kept us from being flipped and rolled into the murky depths of the river. We hugged the shore, ready at any moment to bail out. Finally, after a few hundred more metres, the crocodile veered away, sank beneath the water and disappeared. We remained uneasy for some time after that, our eyes everywhere, looking for it to reappear – perhaps underneath us this time.

There's no doubt that that great bull crocodile was king of the river. When I think of evil African dictators, I think of the crocodile, because crocodiles are absolute tyrants. They lurk unseen, then strike at the moment when they know that victory is theirs. Nothing can survive their attack.

Back in the meeting, Langton went on to talk about the tyrants in recent times who had appeased the water spirits. He told us that, at the start of his reign of terror, President Idi Amin of Uganda had sacrificed 3,000 bullocks at the source of the Nile, so that their blood could run throughout the country. He went on to murder hundreds of thousands of his own people.

I thought about it a lot. Africa has always been known as the "Dark Continent", and it's not hard to see why when you realize what's going on here. At the beginning of 2001, only fourteen out of Africa's fifty-four countries were democracies.[1] One third of the world's 21 million refugees were in Africa.[2] Because of war, famine, and civil strife, there were a further 30 million displaced people within individual African countries.[3] The security forces within thirty-three African countries regularly used torture on their citizens, and in twenty-seven African countries people were regularly incarcerated without charge or trial and left to rot in prison.[4] War and civil strife rock the continent and almost half of the world's child soldiers live in Africa – until they are killed in battle or at the hands of the captors who have abducted them from home.

Disease also bedevils the African continent, with AIDS being the most crippling of all. Figures vary considerably as to the extent of the problem, but at the turn of the century there were thought to be 8 million AIDS orphans in sub-Saharan Africa alone.

It's not as though nothing is ever done to help. Every year, billions of dollars are poured into the continent to feed the hungry, house the homeless, and cure the sick, but all the time new wars, new famines, and new disasters continue to take their toll. Over a trillion dollars of Western aid has flowed into the black hole of development aid in Africa during the last sixty years. Everyone seems to know the answer for Africa, but when those answers are put into practice, they fail – time and time and time again. Africa is littered with failed aid projects. Well-meaning organizations and individuals come in, full of enthusiasm, to try to help, and within a couple of years leave disillusioned. Their project may thrive while they are there managing it, but as soon as they leave, it's doomed to failure.

Larger organizations and governments try to bolster the institutions that promote justice and democracy and a free-market system. They try to make sure that the central bank, the judiciary, and the media, are independent. They also try to promote neutral, professional armed forces, so that property rights can be upheld, and the country can thrive under the rule of law and a free flow of information. But the long trail of African disaster stories continues.

So why doesn't it work? I wondered. Why are there so many hungry people in a continent where there is the potential, over much of it, to get double the annual grain yields per hectare of the best farms in Europe? A continent that has more agricultural land, more mineral wealth and other natural resources than any other? A continent where, only half a century ago, before "liberation", there were food surpluses and almost every country was self-sufficient in grain?

I came to the conclusion that the answer is simple. Every country, every institution, every enterprise is made up of individuals. And it's the individuals within each business, or organization, or government, or country that make them tick – or stop ticking. The problem in Africa lies with individuals and, more specifically, the spiritual forces within or behind those individuals.

The Bible teaches that, "Our struggle is not against flesh and blood, but against the rulers, against the authorities, against the powers of this dark world and against the spiritual forces of evil in the heavenly realms" (Ephesians 6:12). Throughout history there has been a continual tussle between the spiritual forces of good and evil, whether or not we choose to recognize it. In Africa today, these spiritual forces are working very powerfully. Witch doctors, spirit mediums, spells, even human sacrifices, are not uncommon in Zimbabwe, which is (or has been) a relatively civilized country, with a well-educated population and a literacy rate that once topped 90 per cent, the highest in Africa. But often in Zimbabwe, an individual who is doing well will suddenly fall sick for no apparent reason, and actually die.

In my limited understanding, this is because of the spirit of jealousy, coupled with the spirit of fear, that rules African society. The spirit of jealousy comes in first and then, with the aid of spirit mediums and *n'yangas*, the spirit of fear finishes the job.

These spirits – particularly the spirits associated with water – have a huge hold over peoples' lives. *Nyami Nyami* is the name of the water spirit or great river god on the Zambezi. It has the body of a snake and a fish-like head. During times of need, *Nyami Nyami* (literal meaning: meat meat) allowed the people to cut meat from his body. It is the traditional role of tribal elders and spirit mediums to intercede on behalf the inhabitants of the river valley when *Nyami Nyami* is angered. The Tonga people believe the building of the Kariba Dam deeply offended *Nyami Nyami*, separating him from his wife. The regular flooding and many deaths during the dam's construction were attributed to his wrath. After the dam was completed, the Tonga believe that *Nyami Nyami* withdrew from the world of men.

The crocodile and the serpent, "who is the devil" (according to Revelation 20:2), are spoken of together in Isaiah 27:1: "the Lord will punish with his sword… Leviathan the gliding serpent". Although we always think of the snake as the symbol of the devil, the crocodile is often used as a picture of evil. It has no natural enemies, is able to survive for over six months at a time without eating and, according to palaeontologists, has remained virtually unchanged since the age of the dinosaurs.

Today the crocodile, and the symbolic chevron design that is associated with it, are still much in evidence in Zimbabwe. Until the currency completely collapsed, the chevron crocodile pattern appeared on all the bank notes. Outside the Reserve Bank of Zimbabwe is a statue of the Zimbabwe Bird from the Great Zimbabwe ruins, with a pool underneath. This particular bird was the only one found at the ruins, with a crocodile creeping up the plinth. The Zimbabwe Bird is believed to be an ancestral link to the heavens and is sometimes called Shiri ya Mwari, the Bird of God. The stone eagle became the country's emblem and symbol of freedom because it linked the Shona to their ancient ancestors.

So in the pool at the Reserve Bank, the crocodile, the great consumer who knows no real enemies, symbolically lurks. The bird (as spirit of the skies) is displayed on the flag, stamps, number plates, and many other things. Behind it, always, lurks the crocodile.

In 2007 Webster Shamu, the Member of Parliament for the Mount Carmel area, who was at this point the Minister of State for Policy Implementation, gave Mugabe a five-metre stuffed crocodile for his eighty-third birthday. Shamu was quoted as saying that the crocodile "symbolized maturity, distilled and accumulated wisdom and majestic authority, attributes that have been characteristic of the President's leadership…". His words were a lie. At that time, life expectancy in Zimbabwe was already the lowest in the world – thirty-four years for women and thirty-seven years for men – and the country had the world's fastest declining economy with the highest inflation rate in history. Death stalked the people of Zimbabwe. But while his people suffered and died, it was reported that Mugabe was unveiling a plan to build a monument to himself, the Robert Mugabe Museum, at his home area of Zvimba, at a cost of £1.6 million. His clan totem, "Gushungo" (meaning "crocodile" in Shona) was to take pride of place. The Mugabe farming empire includes Gushungo Dairy Estate, formerly Foyle farm, in the Mazowe district. The former white owners were forced off their land.

I don't believe it's coincidence that the first gang to start killing white farmers in 1964, led by Ndabaningi Sithole, was known as "the Crocodile Gang". On Saffron Walden farm, where the first farm invasion in Mashonaland took place, and where the *n'yanga* Sekuru Mushore lived (whom Mugabe was said to consult), Ross Hinde's son was killed by a crocodile. The crocodile has always had symbolic power. The body of the first white martyr in Zimbabwe, Father Silveira, was given to the crocodiles in the Musengezi River by the Munhumutapa in 1561.

President Mugabe isn't the only African leader to use the crocodile as his totem. At his coronation, the king of Lesotho was covered from head to foot in a huge robe with a crocodile printed it. General Babangida of Nigeria was known as the prince of the

Niger River. Langton Gatsi told me there were many others who revered the crocodile and water spirits.

President Mugabe's Zezuru clan, who were part of the Duma people, moved from north-eastern Zimbabwe in 1820 and colonized the ruins of Great Zimbabwe, the heart of the former Munhumutapa kingdom, which had long since fallen. The ruins are said to be the "guardian spirit of the nation". But there is great significance in the name: Munhumutapa, or Mwene Mutapa. It means "master pillager" and was the praise name for the dictator of that time. The spirit of the master pillager lives on in Mugabe and his henchmen, the judges and policemen and parliamentarians who allow the pillaging to continue unchecked today.

In Shona tradition, the effortlessly soaring Bateleur eagle is the messenger of the ancestral spirits. It oversees the observance of all the sacred laws in the land and plays host to the ancestral spirits. Many of our farm workers live in fear of black birds that swoop down from the sky. "If they hit you, it won't be long until you are dead," they say. I remember going to pray for hours on end with a woman who had been perfectly healthy a few days earlier but who had become unable to walk or talk or do anything. She had been "hit" by a black bird. She wouldn't accept that she could choose life, and she died soon afterwards.

The other bird that is often used as a totem is the *hungwe*, the fish eagle. Some say that the earliest totem in southern Africa was the *dziva-hungwe* (pool of water and fish eagle). The fish eagle and the crocodile are closely linked by the pools of water that they are both associated with.

I believe that, to a greater extent than most people understand, it's the malevolent spirits of the dark underworld, represented by the bird and the crocodile, that have allowed the leaders of Zimbabwe to cause much of the people's suffering. Peoples' minds have been deceived and clouded by their fear of these spirits. Meanwhile, the world outside has little or no knowledge of the spiritual forces that are at play in the hearts and minds of the people of Africa, or of the evil influence that the spirit world has on the interplay between the corrupt authorities and ordinary men and women.

Africa is in such a mess today, I believe, because the spirit of the crocodile has been roused by many of its leaders. A covenant with death has been formed. The result of entering into a covenant with death is that everything that you touch simply dies. One of the clearest illustrations of this is in agriculture. The war veterans who have invaded our farms always claimed that our land was far better than theirs. Their crops, however, look pitiable standing next to our crops, although the same rain falls on theirs as falls on ours and both crops share the same soil.

The reason that Africa is hungry is not because of physical factors; there is absolutely no physical reason why Africa should be hungry. Africa is hungry because of the covenant with death and the web of lies in which it has encased itself. Where there are lies, there is no reason, no logic, no justice, no God, and no goodness. Without faith, it's easy to get ensnared in the tangle of lies. It's also very easy to compromise one's principles out of fear.

I wrote an article about the water spirits and the "monster of the waters" and shortly afterwards was chatting to the then Selous Farmers' Association chairman, Roy Fuller, at my offices. I could tell that he'd just about had enough. As a boy he'd left the Congo in dramatic circumstances. His mother had gone to Mass one Sunday morning but returned home shortly afterwards absolutely horrified. All the nuns had had their heads chopped off. Their gruesome bloody remains had been posted up on stakes around the mission compound. The Fullers had packed what they could carry into a few suitcases and left their home and the farm and everything on it and driven to the railway station. They left their car by the platform and squeezed onto a train with the other refugees and never went back. Everyone remembers the bewildered looks of all the refugees from the Congo and other countries that pitched up at railway stations with nothing but the goods they could carry at the different times of independence in the rest of Africa.

I left the office musing about the battle in the spiritual world that was raging over Africa. In the Democratic Republic of Congo (DRC) they'd tried to wipe out anything to do with Christianity, as they had in a number of other countries. Human rights and the rule of law were clearly inconveniences to the new breed of dictators that ran most of the continent.

It was dark, and while I was driving over the Mupfure River, the largest river in our district, and where the water spirits are believed to reside, a car came toward me with its lights on full beam. Unbeknown to me there was another car full of war veterans crawling along just ahead of me, with no lights on. I saw the vets' car too late and tried to cut in on the inside to avoid the oncoming car. The whole right side of my vehicle was ripped and the pillar of the windscreen narrowly missed chopping off my right arm. I ended up smashing into some concrete pillars with my back wheels hanging over the edge of the bridge.

My car was a mess and none of the doors worked so I climbed out of one of the broken windows feeling a little bit dazed. I recognized some of the farm invaders and they immediately tried to beat me up. I was saved by some municipal workers who were trying to fix the pumps in the river.

Several hours later, when we had sorted things out, I couldn't help feeling that there was a strong element of the spiritual in the accident…

Notes chapter 8

1. *The Wall Street Journal,* 19 January 2001.
2. Reuters, 29 May 2000.
3. International AIDS conference, Zambia, 1999.
4. Amnesty International, 17 June 1999.

CHAPTER 9

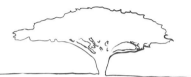

In the year 2000, through my job with the CFU, I was invited to a rally in Kadoma, which included having lunch with President Mugabe beforehand at the Kadoma Ranch Motel. I arrived at midday, but Mugabe and his star team were nowhere to be seen. After three hours of hanging around, all the guests were told that lunch would be delayed and we should go to the rally first.

As usual, all the schools had closed for the rally and school children lined the roads, having waited for many hours through the heat of the day to cheer on the passing politicians. When the cars ahead of us in the convoy passed, the children all gave the black power clenched-fist salute. My car was right at the end of the line. I didn't give the black power ZANU–PF salute. I'm not partial to any black power – or white power – salutes. I merely gave a friendly wave. The children, very excited, immediately responded with the open-palm MDC (Movement for Democratic Change – the main opposition party) salute and there was much cheering as the car that I was in drove past.

At the stadium we were chaperoned by war veterans wearing T-shirts emblazoned with AK-47s dripping red blood. Mugabe had wanted to use this emblem in the 1980 elections but the British hadn't allowed him to. The war vets led us from the car into the tent and we were seated on a little wooden bench down on the right-hand side of the stage where Mugabe and his entourage were sitting.

The stadium was full. I estimated that about 40,000 people had been bussed in. They were now all sitting on the ground inside a concrete durawall. I had never been to such a large rally.

The master of ceremonies, Stanley Majiri, introduced each speaker from a microphone on the lowest part of the stage.

Higher up was a lectern with another microphone. Several cabinet ministers were at the rally, and they each had to be called upon to give a speech. The crowd sat through it all stoically, until the president was introduced and given the floor. He'd barely got going when I saw a man in the centre of the crowd stand up and turn his back. As he got up, others around him all began to rise and turn their backs too. In a few seconds, everywhere I looked people were getting up and turning away from the stage where Mugabe was speaking.

Stanley Majiri leaped up and screamed into the microphone, over the top of the president's voice, "If you are children of ZANU–PF, sit down!"

It was as though he was talking to the wind. There was no response, only more people getting up and turning their backs and starting to walk away.

"If you are children of ZANU–PF, sit down!" Majiri commanded again, in a shrill, high-pitched scream.

But, like a great army, the crowd was on the move. The stadium's gates were barred to prevent them getting out, but, almost in slow motion, the durawall collapsed outwards, as though hit by a great ocean wave. The crowd continued to walk on, spilling out of the stadium, not running, merely moving patiently away.

"Let them go. They have buses to catch," said the president. He'd sized up the situation and realized that there was nothing he could do. The people had had enough. And so they walked away.

Mugabe delivered the rest of his speech to those of us who were left and then we went back for lunch. By this time it was about 6 p.m. and nearly dark. The president and his wife, Grace, sat at the centre of the top table in the dining room, with various ministers on either side of them. The other tables were set at right angles, stretching down into the room. I was led to a table directly under the gaze of Mugabe and Grace, just a few metres away from them. The war veterans with the bloody AK-47 T-shirts sat around us.

I tried to make conversation with the man next to me.

"What do you do?" I asked him.

"I am the mayor of Chinhoyi," he said.

I'd read about the mayor of Chinhoyi in the *Herald* (state-owned) newspaper. He'd been found with a severed human head in the boot of his car in 1994. The head had been used for a ritual of some sort.

Without thinking I asked, "Are you the one with the head?"

"I am the one," he replied.

I had never had dinner with someone who would transport a human head around in the back of his car and I couldn't think what to say next. Our conversation ended.

I contented myself with watching the top table. I didn't see either the president or his wife utter a word to each other or to their neighbours throughout the whole meal. They weren't given the same food as the rest of us, but ate healthy-looking fruit, which they peeled themselves, staring straight ahead in stony silence.

At the end of the meal, we all got up when the president and his wife were ready to leave. As Mugabe passed me on his way to the door, I put out my hand. Out of some weird kind of fascination I wanted to feel his hand again. He grasped mine unseeingly. It felt the same as it had the first time I met him – cold and clammy. There was a huge distance between us.

***

As a result of all the difficulties that farmers were facing, a strong movement toward appeasement began to gain momentum within the CFU. I argued strongly in favour of continuing court action against the government. We couldn't allow the lawlessness to carry on without challenge. If no one was held to account, evil would keep flourishing.

Tim Henwood, the CFU president at the time, was already moving into appeasement mode, laying the foundation for his successor, Colin Cloete. It was under Colin's leadership that the organization finally came under Mugabe's heel.

At a special CFU congress in March 2001 an expensive PR firm put together a snazzy presentation for the farmers. The hall at ART (Agricultural Research Trust) farm, where we held the meeting, was full to bursting. I sat behind former CFU president Nick Swanepoel, who had put an advert in the paper accepting the government's target at that point of 5 million hectares for redistribution, including 100,000 hectares of arable land for immediate resettlement, with free tillage, seed, and fertilizer. He also advocated a change in the leadership of the CFU, on the basis that the current leadership was perceived to be opposed to land reform and was associated with the opposition party. Nick assured us that if we followed his plans, money would come pouring in, law and order would be restored and security of tenure would be guaranteed. Just like waving a magic wand.

Nick sat by himself in the meeting. I watched him try to light a cigarette, but his hand was shaking so badly he could barely manage it.

His ideas were naïve wishful thinking. I'm not sure who he thought was going to make the 5 million hectares of land available. Or why money would pour in, as he suggested. It was in effect a hostage situation and would set a terrible precedent, opening farmers up to worse intimidatory tactics in the future.

The strange thing about that meeting was that, although Nick's plan was rejected, the PR presentation was accepted. It amounted to much the same thing. We had to be "part of the solution and not part of the problem," apparently.

The problem, as far as I could see, was that we were living in a country of state-sponsored lawlessness. But we farmers were not part of that lawlessness. If we stood by the law and God's principles, we would be part of the solution. The presentation had said that there was a need for national consultation, constructive engagement, and dialogue. While there is most definitely a time for all those things, that time had long gone. What was required now was continuous and strong legal representation with as much press coverage of the violence and injustices as possible. I knew that if we went down the dialogue route and stopped publicly challenging what was going on, there would be no good faith on the government side.

Nelson Takawira from the ZANU–PF central committee was at the Congress. He summed up the situation well, saying that we needed to be part of ZANU–PF, because the party would remain in power whatever happened. He said that no external pressures would change the government, so we should stop exposing things in the press. He also said that because some leading farmers had supported the opposition, there was much suspicion and the CFU needed a new leadership who would always support ZANU–PF.

Sure enough, the change in leadership took place a few months later.

Colin Cloete became president of the Commercial Farmers' Union in August 2001. By then, the ZIJIRI – Zimbabwe Joint Resettlement Initiative – was in full swing. This was in effect a rehash of Nick Swanepoel's plan, which aimed to give the government a million uncontested hectares from farmers.

It was my job to find suitable land in our area. We managed to get agreement that the names of the farms would not be divulged in advance, because if it got out that land on particular farms was to be uncontested, it could lead to all sorts of problems for the owners. Only once the money was on the table would the names of the land holdings be divulged.

But Vice President Joseph Msika wanted to know the names of the farms that were being put forward before the money was found. Dave Connolly, who was later to become a very good friend of mine, had found 200,000 hectares in Matabeleland that farmers were happy to sell. He was told by Olivia Muchena, who was in the Ministry of Agriculture at the time and was heading up negotiations from the government side, "You have to realize that this is a controlled revolution." Dave couldn't get his head around such an apparent contradiction in terms. And Vincent

Hungwe, the Director of Lands, said to Dave, "If we can't get what we want, we will take every brick off every brick." It was the talk of a spoilt child. Hungwe's father, the governor of Masvingo, had taken David Dobson's Bryne farm in my area. Dobson was an old man and he was found wandering around his scrap heap in a total daze, unable to decide what to take with him. Scrap is valuable on any farm, as it's used so often when things go wrong and parts are unavailable.

Dave Connolly refused to divulge the names. Nick Swanepoel told him that he must. Dave said that there was clearly no good faith on the part of the government. This was at the time of the Chinhoyi farms arrests and farm trashings. Nick said that the Chinhoyi farmers had made their beds and they must sleep in them. Dave realized that ZIJIRI wasn't going to go anywhere – there was no possibility of any joint resettlement – because Mugabe wanted everything. He wouldn't leave the tobacco farms alone, because they employed so many people, all of whom Mugabe wanted to control.

Vice President Msika told ZIJIRI that "dirty washing should not be hung up in public". This meant that there could be no court cases and no publicity about the injustices. With intimidation at such a sustained and high level, the farming leadership grasped at appeasement as their best bet. They would stop publicizing violence and injustice and stop trying to get justice in the courts. They would do just as Mugabe wanted.

Some people were prepared to do anything in order to survive. Kobus Joubert, who was President of the Zimbabwe Tobacco Association, which produced 40 per cent of Zimbabwe's foreign currency reserves, told us that he was prepared to "deal with the devil". He said that's what we'd have to do too.

When I picked up *The Herald* on 11 October 2001, I was appalled to see on the front page a large picture of eighteen white farmers and various government ministers, all crouching down before Chief Svosve, who had led many of the invasions. The caption read, "Government Ministers, commercial farmers and settlers crouch as they go through a ritual of appeasing the ancestral spirits at Rapako farm in Hwedza yesterday." Among them were Kobus Joubert and former CFU president Nick Swanepoel, various other agricultural leaders, Minister Ignatius Chombo, Minister Joseph Made, and other senior party men.

I was incensed. I spoke to both Kobus and Nick and they told me that they hadn't been appeasing the spirits. I pointed out that a large picture of them crouching down, with a caption saying that they were appeasing the spirits, had gone out to hundreds of thousands of people. If that wasn't what they were doing, then they needed to let people know, publicly, because, in the perverse world in which we live, lies that are allowed to continue unchecked become the truth. It appalled me that our leaders could be appeasing the spirits represented by the chief. I believed that such actions would give the spirits of evil a greater hold on the nation.

I waited a month to see what would happen and then decided to write a letter to the director of the CFU, David Hasluck, knowing it could be shared with the full CFU council. It wasn't easy, because I knew I'd probably be fired from the CFU and come under considerable personal attack once the letter was read.

I described the article and the picture and then went on to write:

> As a Christian I feel it is important and my duty to point out that whatever was done at the ceremony, however innocent it may have appeared, was wrong and will lead the country into further chaos.
>
> In Ephesians chapter 6 verse 12 it says, "Our struggle is not against flesh and blood, but against the rulers, against the authorities, against the powers of this dark world and against the spiritual forces of evil in the heavenly realms." The land issue is not a struggle for land. It is a struggle (politics aside) for the control of the spiritual places, the

"High Places", the places of the water spirits and the ancestral spirits that are part of the land. It is a struggle of good against evil "in the heavenly realms".

There are some excellent characters in our farming leadership. They work night and day trying to sort out problems, trying to get people to be allowed to farm and build our country for the future. They spend hours sitting outside the offices of important people, pointing out the problems and the injustices and creating the solutions. They are resourceful people with complete dedication of purpose in wanting a good outcome for us all.

But the word of God is described as "a double-edged sword" and it cuts to the quick. There are no twilight zones between right and wrong and good and evil. God's word is strong, forthright, and uncompromising. God created order out of the chaos and darkness and if we mix with chaos and darkness only chaos and darkness can result. We can't "do evil that good may result" (Romans 3:8), however innocent it may appear. The Bible is extremely clear regarding this and I feel it is my duty to point some of the verses out.

In chapter 28 of the first book of Samuel, Saul, in desperation, consulted a spirit medium at Endor, because everything was going wrong. His land, Israel, was being overrun by the Philistines and his kingdom was divided within itself. He was "in great distress" and believed "God has turned away from me". So he disguised himself and went into the dark alleys looking for a medium to consult, despite the fact that he himself had previously ordered mediums to be purged from the land. When he found one he asked her to bring up the spirit of Samuel, which she duly did. Saul "prostrated himself" before Samuel and was told that because he had not obeyed God he would be killed, with his sons, the next day. This duly happened.

The Bible says, "Do not turn to mediums or seek out spiritists, for you will be defiled by them" (Leviticus 19:31). It continues [in Exodus 20:5] "you shall not bow down to them".

It also says, "[God sets] before you today a blessing and a curse – the blessing if you obey the commands of the Lord your God… [and] the curse if you disobey" (Deuteronomy 11:26–28). God pleads with us, "Who will take a stand for me against evildoers?" (Psalm 94:16).

Jesus Christ did not come, as many believe, to bring tolerance and a wishy-washy twilight creed. He preached love but he also preached judgment. He preached forgiveness; but he also preached repentance. He never preached being all things to all men. He had the audacity to call the religious leaders "sons of hell" (Matthew 23:15). He said, "I did not come to bring peace, but a sword" (Matthew 10:34). Christ's mission was one of truth, and the truth very often brings persecution and even death, as it did for him. But Christ didn't take up the sword – the sword was used against him, because he spoke the truth with authority. He did not retaliate with the sword, but with more truth, in love. The darkness hates the truth, as we all know so well; but this must not stop us from speaking the truth and standing up for it, regardless of the consequences.

I believe that as Christians we will win in the end against the evil that has descended on the land. But we need to be vigilant. We need to cut through the lies, the deception, and the wickedness with the word of God, which is the truth. We need to walk toward the light, not back toward the darkness. We need to walk toward life and not back toward death and the spirits of the dead.

I was right about the effect of the letter as I received various threats. Kobus threatened to sue me for everything I had.

Other moves were made to stamp out openness and opposition. Colin Cloete, the new CFU president, put a stop to the daily situation reports – known as Sit-Reps – we'd been compiling. These were crucial in informing other farmers about what was going on, and in letting the world know about the injustices that were happening. The problem was that the publicity was embarrassing the government. The CFU leaders were told that they must hide the truth if they wanted to survive. It was a moral dilemma that was conveniently glossed over as a pragmatic business decision.

Then, one day, *The Farmer* magazine arrived in the post with a stark black cover. It was the last issue. No one had been consulted and no one knew that the magazine was being closed down.

I couldn't keep quiet. I brought up the closure at the next CFU council meeting. Colin explained that the magazine wasn't financially viable. But if that was the case, why hadn't they put out an appeal to the readership and the wider public for funds? Why didn't they downsize it in order to keep it going? What had we got to hide? Why were we suddenly hushing up everything that was going on?

The magazine's editor, Brian Latham, a former Reuters correspondent, who had always described incidents as they happened, and published pictures of beaten-up farmers and farm workers, wrote in his final leader column, "History will judge critically those who believed, for whatever reason, there was merit in burying the truth. Critics [of the magazine] said we made it difficult for the Commercial Farmers' Union. Well, for us the Union is its members – the people who are being intimidated, beaten, threatened, extorted, chased from their homes, robbed, and murdered. To us, victims like Terry Ford are far more important than the people in Agriculture House."

Then there was silence.

We had no forum in which to express our views or publicize the terror that was unfolding around the country. No information was able to get out openly about all the various agricultural issues. Rumours abounded. Everything was just like that final magazine cover – black darkness.

In essence Colin and the CFU hierarchy had followed orders from their political masters. They had quietly rolled over and capitulated, becoming complicit in the destruction of the country by refusing to stand up against evil. Fear had won, as it so often does in the face of tyranny. The farmers' leaders felt that if they appeased the evil aggressor, they would be left alone. I can only believe that they didn't understand the full extent of the problem. The alternative scenario is that they did understand and were given assurances that they would save their own skins if they followed orders. I don't want to believe that this was the case. I hold on to the belief that they followed orders because they thought that maybe government might relent.

It was plain to me that it was naïve to think that government might relent. The problem was that we farmers employed too many people. Approximately 20 per cent of the entire population of the country lived and worked on our farms. If the government let up on the pressure, the opposition MDC party would be able to come and visit the farms, and the farm workers would be free to vote against Mugabe. But as long as intimidation levels remained high and intense fear was in the air, this couldn't happen. In his battle for total control, Mugabe had to continue on his course. There was too much blood on his hands already for him to change tack.

Under Colin Cloete's leadership, the CFU also put a complete stop to any legal actions. Vice President Msika told the Zimbabwe Joint Resettlement Initiative (ZIJIRI) that they couldn't "dialogue" with each other as long as there were pending court actions. Rather than tell the government that an impartial court was by far the best place to "dialogue", Colin told the farmers that they were now on their own. If they wished to fight in court, they would have to find their own lawyers and money and take the flak themselves. We were told that we had to compromise and negotiate for ourselves and that the best way forward was to downsize. We had to feed the crocodile and hope that we would be the last to be eaten. The CFU was bowing out. It was a bitter betrayal of all the people that we represented.

When recourse to the courts was taken away, it was as though the carpet had been ripped from under us. We were in a totally different world, without any idea of how to operate in it. There was no foundation any longer and there was nothing to hold us together. We were like a building in which great gaping cracks had suddenly appeared. Our leaders had allowed our foundations to be undermined.

Our two greatest tools were now closed to us. If justice was to prevail, we needed access to both the courts and the press. The government knew that, and hated them both, bristling and spitting and threatening whenever they were mentioned.

In normal times, people like to think that they would never bury their principles in a time of crisis. But it's only in those times that a person's true nature is revealed. During a period of tyranny, leaders need to be visionaries, with prophetic voices, who are able to rise above the present crisis and take a principled stand. But nobody in the farming leadership dared to draw a line in the sand and say, "So far and no further!"

CHAPTER 10

As a family we made a choice to base our actions on the foundations of the law that was given by God on Mount Sinai and fulfilled in his Son, Jesus Christ: the law of love, of justice, and of truth. I have never once regretted it.

We lived from week to week, checking "the list" that was published every Friday in *The Herald*. This was the list of white farmers' land that was up for acquisition. Our homes and our livelihoods depended on that list. If our farm was listed we had to act, otherwise we would lose everything by default.

The law wasn't complicated. The government first had to issue a preliminary notice of acquisition, known as a Section 5. This was published in the newspaper and had to be delivered to the farm as well. When that was done, the farmer had thirty days in which to object. Then the government could issue a Section 8, which was an acquisition order. This had to be confirmed through the administrative court, in what was known as a Section 7.

If the acquisition was confirmed, all that the government had to do was to pay fair compensation within a reasonable time. Then the farmer had to move out.

Back in the 1980s and 1990s, lots of communities had got together to make blocks of land available for resettlement. Twenty-four farms to the north-west of Mount Carmel were resettled in this way. In total, 3.6 million hectares were bought and resettled.

All this time, the government had been issuing "certificates of no present interest" to farmers who were selling their farms on the open market. This meant that the government had the first option on any sale. If they didn't want the farm, they issued a certificate. When you had the certificate, a private sale could go through. We'd had two certificates issued in 1999, when both Mount Carmel and Carskey were transferred from Mike's own name to the family company name.

The law was changed on 8 May 2002. The new legislation said that anyone who had a Section 8 acquisition order would be arrested and could spend up to two years in prison if they were still in their homes, whether or not the Section 8 order had been confirmed in the administrative court. It was the beginning of institutionalized dictatorship – *rule by law* as opposed to the rule of law.

It was this legislation that made me realize that there were no good guys in the ZANU–PF parliament. They all voted for the new law, knowing that almost all the white farmers had Section 8s by that stage. Every single MP had become complicit in the destruction and hunger that were overwhelming Zimbabwe. I knew that it was the end of the road if we didn't do something about it.

I was asked to put together a questionnaire regarding the current situation, for all the members of the CFU to fill in. The last question I included related to whether members wished the CFU to go forward with legal action in the courts to protect their rights; or to continue in dialogue. This final question was mysteriously struck off the questionnaire before it was sent out. No explanation was forthcoming.

Three weeks after the Section 8 legislation came into effect, the CFU council met. I opened the meeting in prayer and quoted from a verse in Deuteronomy 30, which says, "This day… I have set before you life and death, blessings and curses. Now choose life, so that you and your children may live."

The debate was directionless and without substance. The leadership got sidetracked into talking about restructuring the organization. I couldn't believe it. Here we were, talking about restructuring the CFU, while everything was going up in flames around us. For the first time in my six years of service I wrote to the director and said how disturbed I was by the directionless debate and the inability of those taking part to get to grips with the core issues.

David Hasluck, the director, called me but said he wasn't willing to discuss my letter.

Eventually, on 12 June 2002, a statement of CFU policy was published, under Colin Cloete's name. It hadn't been agreed by the council.

The statement read:

> *There is a mounting sense of desperation precipitated by Government statements that white commercial agriculture will be destroyed by August this year. The most obvious instruments for achieving this are the provisions of Section 8 under the recently amended land act…. The CFU policy revolves around 3 main principles:*
>
> *CFU is a politically neutral organization that works with the government of the day.*
>
> *CFU will continue a non-confrontational approach, seeking to resolve issues through dialogue.*
>
> *Notwithstanding the obstacles and cognizant of the risks, CFU continues to advocate a production-orientated approach.*
>
> *We recommend that each individual should relinquish land that is not essential to core business. Official Government forms LA 1–LA 5 have been gazetted (made available from the regional offices and the head office) and the Land Acquisition Act has been amended to facilitate offers and subdivisions.*

I was shocked by this statement. How did Cloete think he could resolve the effects of an adverse law by dialogue? If parliament had voted the law in, it was quite clear that they intended to use it. It would be naïve in the extreme to believe otherwise. The Third *Chimurenga*, the one that we were living through, was all about getting anyone with a white skin off the land so that the government could skull bash the black people into line at will.

One of the CFU's key objects, from its inception, was to "sponsor, oppose or support any legislation, the introduction of which is likely to affect beneficially or otherwise as the case may be, the interests of its members or the agricultural industry generally". The current legislation had been brought in with the specific aim of breaking commercial agriculture. Clearly it needed to be challenged, but the CFU hierarchy was being drawn like Odysseus toward the singing sirens of destruction. I couldn't see what I could do to prevent them from abandoning organized agriculture to its final end.

The next CFU council meeting was closed to everyone but the inner core. Closed meetings are a feature of tyranny. When people don't know what's happening, fear begins to take hold. Victims begin to believe that they too have things to hide, and so they start to act as though they're the ones who are the criminals. One of the things I found really distressing was that some white farmers, who were the victims here, began to cosy up to the tyrants and do things in the same way as the oppressors. Bad company corrupts good character. What is right disappears in the face of what is expedient, when honest men become corrupted by constant intimidation and threats to life and property. Paranoia and fear become entrenched, and the tyrants know then they are unassailable.

I was told that the council had met in closed session because of me. I had apparently compromised the president, Colin Cloete. I was formally reprimanded and told that I was running out of friends in the CFU.

I wrote back, informing the leadership that I wouldn't compromise on what was right, and suggesting that the CFU needed to unify its members through taking on board those who were intent on taking a principled stand. I received no reply, but understood that my point had been noted.

On 16 July I went to a meeting with fourteen lawyers in Harare to discuss the Section 8 legislation. I was the only person there from CFU. Farmers were beginning to realize the folly of the CFU's failure to challenge a law that enabled them to be jailed for up to two years if they remained on their own farms. It was an unusual meeting. We stood around the edge of the boardroom in a large ring while the lawyers sat around the table in the middle. The meeting went around in circles, discussing the political ramifications of taking certain actions. I was frustrated, and something was burning inside me. So I spoke up.

"I have a legal problem," I said. "We have a Section 8 on our farm. We'll be on the wrong side of the law and may spend two years in prison if we're still in our homes and still farming in three weeks' time. All of us white farmers have the same legal problem. I want a legal solution to my legal problem."

One of the lawyers said in response that the only way to solve the legal problem was for the CFU to challenge the legislation on constitutional grounds. No other organization had the *locus standi* to do so, and lawyers wouldn't have the time to put together thousands of individual cases. The other lawyers all agreed.

I phoned David Hasluck, the CFU director, on my way home. I was driving through the centre of Harare at the time and it was dark. David was angry when I told him what had been advised. He was very short with me and was clearly very disturbed by what the lawyers had advised.

I was confused. I thought David was a good guy. At the beginning of the invasions he'd been very strong on the law. He told the CFU council that the law went back to what God had told Moses in the Ten Commandments and that all good law was based on those principles. He said we must stand by it. It was a revelation to me at the time. I realized that something must now be very wrong if he was angry that the lawyers had advised us that the CFU should challenge this unjust law.

It became clear that a clique had been formed to keep the CFU from challenging the law and thereby allow what was known as the "legal revolution" to take place unhindered. Colin Cloete was flown with Nick Swanepoel on a secret mission to Maputo to meet President Joaquim Chissano of Mozambique, as though dialogue might get them somewhere. We had nothing to hide, so why were things done in secret? Why were there hushed conversations in corridors? Secrets are part of the world of darkness. They come about because people feel important and powerful if they know things that other people don't know. Secrets spread when everyone is engulfed by a climate of fear. Value systems get turned upside down and the victims start to believe that they need to keep secrets in order to survive. Solzhenitsyn wrote in his masterpiece of life under dictatorship, *The Gulag Archipelago:* "Secrets, that was our problem."

I sent out a résumé of the meeting with the lawyers, pointing out that all of the fourteen lawyers present had strongly urged that CFU should take representative action.

Shortly afterwards, I was called into David Hasluck's office. I felt like a naughty schoolboy being summoned by the headmaster, but my conscience was clear. I had complete assurance that what I was doing was right, so I knew I had nothing to fear. I wasn't afraid of unjust punishment.

Nick Swanepoel was in the office with Hasluck when I arrived. I had to wait outside for nearly an hour. When I was finally called in, Hasluck had tears in his eyes. He'd just been told about the secret mission to Maputo and was distressed that he had been excluded and knew nothing about it until after the event. It appeared to me that he was being blackmailed into keeping quiet. Although he never told me as much, I believe that the appeasement men knew that if Hasluck was strongly in support of the CFU taking up the legal challenge to protect its members, then that's what the CFU would have to do. And if the CFU went to the law, the legal revolution wouldn't happen as easily. It gave the violence and destruction on the farms an air of respectability. The government desperately wanted the legal revolution. The big money and the powerful players close to government wanted to keep the government happy, even if it meant the eventual destruction of commercial agriculture and the resultant suffering of the white farmers and nearly two million farm workers and their families.

David Hasluck wanted me to pray for him. I did so, but I believe that the blackmail he was facing was too big for him to stand against. He was afraid. And so he never advocated that we should go to the law. He allowed Cloete and his inner circle to be led by the nose by those in government who had duped them into believing that the Section 8 legislation would never be used to put farmers in jail. It was a triumph for evil. All those who hadn't resisted had in effect sided with it.

Hasluck asked me to write a letter to Cloete. In the letter I expressed my concern regarding the deal that I was convinced must have been made with government regarding whether or not they were going to use their new law to destroy us. I said: "History has shown that what is good and right always prevails in the end. The end never justifies the means if the means are underhand. Please take these words as constructive – it is too easy to fall into the traps of evil and devious men who corrupt decent men too often."

***

In the meantime, I was helping to put together another organization, called Justice for Agriculture (JAG). Our first meeting was at Antelope Park in Gweru. Lion cubs were wandering around on the way to the room in which our meeting was to take place, which seemed to me to be very apt. Symbolically, lions were circling and we were not in a happy position.

It went against all my instincts to believe that there was nothing we could do about the situation we all faced, so we put together a case to challenge the Section 8 legislation off our own bats. We couldn't use the Justice for Agriculture name, as JAG didn't have *locus standi* to bring a case to court. So we had to find and support brave individuals who were willing to look at their own cases for procedural irregularities and try to get their own Section 8s nullified. George Quinnell from Banket, near Chinhoyi, was willing to have a go.

There was very little time. The due date for the legislation to come into force was drawing very close.

I was driving to the CFU congress on 7 August when I became convinced that I should try to get permission to open the congress in prayer and to read out a passage from the Bible, Deuteronomy chapter 8. I prayed about the idea, and spoke to David Hasluck when I arrived. I wasn't in his best books by then, so I was amazed when he said that I could.

The morning session was interesting. The farmers voted the CFU legal advisor out because he'd done nothing about challenging the adverse legislation in the courts. He'd even said it would be better to wait until it came into force and farmers were in jail before mounting a challenge. The farmers didn't agree, however, even though the hierarchy had apparently decided that the advice was good.

Ray Passaportis was proposed as the new legal advisor. He was in favour of challenging the new legislation. There was an open vote and everyone raised their hands until the room looked like a forest of waving arms. As well as being a strong vote for Ray, it was also a clear vote of no confidence in the CFU leadership and their official appeasement policy. Almost all the delegates from the farmers' associations voted for Ray. The majority of the CFU council voted against him. It was a telling moment. It was clear that only the views of the CFU inner circle mattered. The farmers whom the CFU was meant to represent were considered to be irrelevant.

When I took the podium at the beginning of the afternoon session, there were over 700 people present. At the front sat senior members of ZANU–PF, including Vice President Joseph Msika, Minister Emmerson Mnangagwa, Minister Ignatius Chombo, Governor Peter Chanetsa, Minister Olivia Muchena and others. They had all been very involved with the Third *Chimurenga* and the active destruction of white-owned farms.

I opened my Bible and began to read from Deuteronomy 8. I was reading it to all the farmers who were present. I knew that some of us were arrogant and we all needed to learn humility.

I read:

> *When you have eaten and are satisfied, praise the Lord your God for the good land he has given you. Be careful that you do not forget the Lord your God, failing to observe his commands, his laws and his decrees that I am giving you this day. Otherwise, when you eat and are satisfied, when you build fine houses and settle down, and when your herds and flocks grow large and your silver and gold increase and all you have is multiplied, then your heart will become proud and you will forget the Lord your God…*
>
> *You may say to yourself, "My power and the strength of my hands have produced this wealth for me." But remember the Lord your God, for it is he who gives you the ability to produce wealth…*

The passage continued with a dire warning: "If you ever forget the Lord your God and follow other gods and worship and bow down to them, I testify against you today that you will surely be destroyed."

It was a prophetic word. If we didn't return to God and stand up for his laws and his principles, we would be destroyed.

I prayed that we would learn to come back to God:

> *Lord God, thank you for the situation we now face. Thank you, not because we enjoy being dispossessed or assaulted, or because we enjoy having friends or family murdered or abandoned, but thank you that through this situation we are being taught to learn, and as we heard this morning: "The learners will inherit the earth."*
>
> *Lord God, help us to learn what you want us to learn, and to learn to be "content in all circumstances".*

When we are angry, calm us.

When we are bitter, cut that bitterness out.

When we are hateful, replace that hate with love.

When we are racial, teach us to know that all people were created in your image.

When we are hopeless, give us your vision.

When we are fearful, give us faith in you.

When we deal with the darkness, bring us into the light.

Most of all, Lord God, let us learn that when we are proud, when we are arrogant, we will learn what it is to be humble just as you, Jesus Christ, creator of the universe, humbled yourself here on earth.

Help us to repent of the selfish attitude that concentrates on "me, myself and I". Help us to read and learn from your word that teaches us that "blessed are the meek, for they will inherit the earth".

I finished with these words:

Finally brothers, whatever is true, whatever is noble, whatever is right, whatever is pure, whatever is lovely, whatever is admirable – if anything is excellent or praiseworthy – think about such things. In the name of the Lord Jesus Christ, Amen.

It was a big prayer. I could see that Vice President Msika and his group were angry, but when he took the podium and spoke, he hid his anger. He assured us all that whatever the law said, everyone would be left with their home and one farm and that we did not need to be concerned. "Through this process everyone will be accommodated. Nobody will be left homeless," he said. The words rang in our ears.

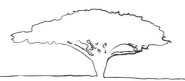

CHAPTER 11

On 16 August 2002, just a week after the CFU congress, I was called by Merv Jelliman from Battlefields, about seventy kilometres from Mount Carmel. He said he had a delegation of army, police, CIO men, lands officers, and others telling him that he had to be off his farm otherwise he would be arrested.

I jumped into my car straight away and drove over.

Merv Jelliman's father had opened up the farm, starting it up from nothing. When he bought it, he built a mud hut for his family to live in. He was a very good farmer and his two sons became excellent farmers too. They were hard workers and always got their hands dirty. The Jellimans developed a substantial irrigation scheme and had recently bought large centre pivots for it. They were predominately grain farmers and their crop yields were some of the best in our area, with several thousand tons of grain going into the silos each year.

When I arrived, I was told that the delegation that had confronted Merv wanted to do an inventory of what was on the farm. So we spent most of the day going around with them, getting them to write everything down. When we arrived at Merv's house, the officer-in-charge of Battlefields Police Station started to joke about how much she was looking forward to sharing the house with another senior member of the delegation. It was clearly meant for us to hear.

Merv's was the first farm in the country to be hit by the application of the new law. Merv complied. He was up against too much pressure to resist. Minister Paul Mangwana wanted the farm and he could get Merv locked up for years if Merv objected.

I arranged for other farmers to come with their lorries to help Merv and his family move their household possessions.

At that stage the settlers did allow us to remove tractors, seed, and fertilizer, although Merv wasn't allowed to take any fixed assets or irrigation pipes.

Not long afterwards, I got a call to say that Merv's house was on fire. It burned to the ground after the window frames had been hacked out and everything else that could be carried away had been looted.

The day after Merv's eviction, army personnel roared in to see Mike and Angela at Mount Carmel. We were given twenty-four hours to pack up and leave. They visited farm after farm and there was a frenzy of packing all over the district.

I got on to all five radio stations in the area.

"All stations! All stations! All stations! I advise you not to pack up. It's as though we're in a dust storm right now. Let's wait until the dust settles and the storm ends. Then we'll be able to see more clearly what's going on. Sit tight and don't panic."

But people had had enough. The thought of two years in jail was too much for most of them to contemplate. Everyone knew that once the farmers were in jail the settlers could loot at will.

Laura and I had a discussion with Mike and Angela as to what we should do. I said that if we were going to pack a few things, we might as well pack everything. My feeling was that we should pack nothing. Why should we capitulate now, after fighting for so long? If they saw us packing, they would think we were weakening and would put more pressure on us. I believed that we had to get to the place where our desire to do what was right was stronger than the hold that our material possessions had over us. As far as I was concerned, if we lost everything, so be it. There wouldn't be a lot we could do about it. If we were chucked in jail, we would fight it.

The arrests started on Friday 16 August, 2002. Arrests were always made on Fridays, because people had to be held in jail until Monday morning, when the courts reopened. The jails were packed. Everyone had to sleep on the concrete, with only a few inadequate, flea-ridden blankets to share between two or three people. Mrs Baldwin was the only woman in the cells. She was seventy-two. Her husband was bed-ridden and too sick to be taken in, so she was arrested instead. Mr Baldwin died two weeks later.

I went to visit the Chegutu prisoners, to try to help with food. I fully expected to get arrested myself, but I was left alone for the time being. When I called David Hasluck at head office to give him a report, all he did was sneer, "You're so cool." I can still hear those words today. It was very hurtful.

The farmers and their families had been through so much, but they were coming through it remarkably well. People had time to think about the important things in life while they were in jail and some of them were able to define in their own minds what it was that they believed in.

On 22 August I wrote to all the farmers on my email list:

> *It is what you believe that will determine how you live your life.*
>
> *It is what you believe that will determine the society that you live in.*
>
> *If you do not live out what you believe, your life and the society that you live in will become unacceptable to you.*
>
> *If you believe in truth, speak it! Live it! Do not compromise.*
>
> *If you believe in justice, use all just means to attain justice! Do not compromise.*
>
> *If you believe in a society without corruption, do not pay out money under corrupt circumstances! Do not compromise.*
>
> *If you believe in a society without patronage, don't allow yourself to be patronized! Do not compromise.*
>
> *If you believe in freedom of speech, speak out! Do not compromise.*

*If you believe in a happy family life, do not chase
after other people! Make time for your family. Do not
compromise.*

*If you believe in a community that helps each other, be
the first to offer your own help! Do not compromise.*

*If you believe in God, do everything to seek him! Don't
put him aside. Do not compromise what you believe.*

*If you compromise any of these things, the person
that you are, and the society that we live in, will become
compromised.*

It's an ironic truth that the compromise of fundamental Christian principles creates conflict, not peace. Standing up and refusing to compromise is what will bring about a peaceful solution in the end.

The following day, I was called into the CFU head office and told to moderate my stance. My email hadn't been helpful and my prayer at the CFU congress had "adversely affected dialogue". Colin Cloete said that if we put up any opposition, we'd be steamrollered, and all the farms would be trashed.

Fear had reached the heart of the organization. When that happens, it's better to resign, or dissolve the organization and run it on a guerrilla-type basis with a cell phone and a computer. Any organization that's been compromised by fear becomes a tool in the hands of the aggressor. "Fear of man will prove to be a snare," said King Solomon in the Bible. So it was proving. The fear of being steamrollered or trashed was the very thing that allowed the steamrollering and trashing to happen.

I remembered driving through the bush on Mount Carmel with Mike one day. We saw a small tree in a dense thicket suddenly start shaking violently, its leaves flying up and down. When we got out to investigate, we found an impala ram caught with a copper wire snare, which had been made from our stolen telephone lines, around its neck. It was plunging up and down in the undergrowth.

We went in to try to release it. I grabbed its horns while Mike got his Leatherman knife out and managed to loosen the snare and release the impala. So many of our animals had been snared like that – hundreds of beautiful antelope just on Mount Carmel alone.

The trouble was, our own agricultural leaders weren't prepared to risk the horns and step in to fight for freedom and release. We'd become trapped, like the animals on our own farms that were being picked off, one by one, in fear, at night.

I told Colin Cloete and David Hasluck that if things were fundamentally wrong, I would continue to speak out about what was right. David told me that the CFU was democratic but I obviously didn't believe in democracy. They gave me two days to resign. Then they went back to looking at some files, as though what they had just said was commonplace and of no consequence to anyone.

I walked out sadly.

When I got home, I decided that the democratic thing to do was to email farmers in the area to ask them whether or not I should resign. After all, they were the ones who employed me. Within forty-eight hours I got a response from over a hundred farmers. Not a single one wanted me to step down.

The Chegutu Farmers' Association called a meeting and gave me a unanimous vote of confidence in my absence. They also passed a resolution asking that a referendum be called regarding the course of action the CFU was taking. And they asked that I should remain in the position until the referendum took place.

Their resolution was completely ignored.

On 2 September I was handed a letter, dated 30 August, suspending me from my position in the CFU, without pay or benefits. I was told to give up my phone and car, leave my office forthwith and not return. The reason for my suspension was that I had allegedly "refused to faithfully represent and promote the policies enunciated by the council of the Commercial Farmers' Union, as instructed by the president Colin Cloete".

However, I knew that the post of vice chairman of the Mashonaland West/South region was vacant, so I immediately filled out a subscription form to become a member. Up until then I had been an employee of the CFU, rather than a member. I met the other Farmers' Association chairmen in the area and explained that I wished to continue to serve them, but as I was not wanted as a member of staff, I would represent them as an elected member if that was their wish. I was voted in unanimously as the new vice chairman of the region.

The next CFU council meeting was only a few days later, on 9 September. Colin had circulated a memo before the meeting, stating that, "It is certain that this land reform process is irreversible. The legality of Section 8 compulsory acquisition orders is not being challenged by the Union at this time as the Council has preferred to mandate the CFU president and vice president to enter into dialogue with the government to ameliorate the effects of the Section 8 orders… group or class actions that are seen to attack the fundamental principle of the programme will simply not be tolerated."

I was angry when I went to the meeting. The CFU leadership appeared to have learned nothing, despite all the arrests. I couldn't understand why they didn't want people to try to protect their rights. Those with title needed to stand on that title and not accept that the whole thing was irreversible. How would the country ever grow in the future without property rights? How would the people be fed?

There was much consternation when I walked in. David Hasluck asked me to leave, but I refused. I had every right to be there. Then Hasluck stood up and demanded that everyone except CFU elected councillors should leave. His voice was menacing and everyone except the inner circle shuffled out obediently.

Hasluck looked me in the eye. "Ben, if you want to stay, you must resign as a member of staff."

The air was heavy with tension. Many of the council members were glaring at me as if I were the problem, not Mugabe. They didn't seem able to see the bigger picture. All they were focused on was me. A great black cloud seemed to hang over them. I felt like a criminal in the dock with a jury of angry men glaring at me accusingly.

I held my ground and refused to resign. I didn't know of anything that stopped me from being both a suspended member of staff and an elected member of the CFU. I was told to leave while the rest of council discussed the issue.

I walked out and waited in the corridor. It was dark outside and the corridor was dark too. I felt a real sense of evil in that place. Cloete and Hasluck got their way and I wasn't allowed back into the council meeting. I drove home to the farm in the dark. What had been done was wicked. The back of commercial agriculture had been broken. The farming leadership had been complicit in allowing it to just happen, and now they were entrenched in their position and were too proud or too scared to change.

That night I couldn't sleep. Sometime after midnight I saw a black dog-like creature with great powerful jaws down on the floor by my bed, looking up at me with its mouth open. It looked much like a Tasmanian devil – squat and strongly built but not overly large. It was panting, and with each breath that it exhaled I felt as though a wall of flames was leaping up around my heart trying to burn it up. I was terrified. I couldn't move a muscle. I didn't know what to do – it was as if my mind was frozen. I felt that if I moved I'd be burned up, consumed by the dog's fiery breath. Suddenly, as I lay there, paralysed by fear, I knew what to do.

"Go, in the name of Jesus," I commanded the dog.

Immediately, it fled out of the open bedroom door and away. A great sense of relief flooded over me and I was able to get to sleep.

I've spoken to a number of people about the incident. Many of the black people I asked about it said that they sometimes get evil visitations from a black dog too. I can only conclude that it's demonic, something from the realm of spiritual darkness. I have never had an experience like it before or since.

***

With no salary coming in, money was a real issue, so I contacted the chief accountant in the CFU. He told me that he wasn't allowed to pay my medical aid and I couldn't draw my pension contributions, which were 8 per cent of my salary over the previous six years. I had more than a year's worth of leave stored up and I wasn't allowed any payment in lieu. Inflation was running at frightening levels already and the CFU hierarchy clearly knew that by the time everything was settled, the money would be worth nothing.

Colin Cloete offered me two million Zimbabwe dollars in cash if I resigned. When I asked him where the money was coming from, Colin told me that he had access to a special fund but he couldn't divulge its source. I told him I wasn't interested in the money if it wasn't above board. I knew it would be madness for me to compromise. If I gave in just once, I could be blackmailed in the future and made to keep quiet. A little while later, I was offered three million dollars. It was a lot of money – the equivalent of nearly three years' salary. And we were hard up. We would've had no income at all if Laura hadn't started a linen business about two months earlier. She was making hand-embroidered bed and table linen and teaching the wives of some of the workers how to embroider. It was God's providence.

Instead of taking the money, I wrote another letter, demanding that the CFU leadership apologize to the farmers in the region who were imprisoned and thrown off their farms as a result of being on the wrong side of the law. A law that the CFU was constitutionally obliged to challenge, but had meekly accepted. I also asked for an apology to myself, pointing out that I had stood by the constitution of the Union and had faithfully represented the views of the membership. I knew that my suspension was unjust.

David Hasluck could see the writing on the wall. Most of the farmers had had enough and were packing up. Hasluck resigned shortly afterwards, along with many of the CFU's senior staff.

It didn't change anything. Eight years later there still has been no apology and I remain suspended, having never been paid a cent.

After that, it was a busy time in Justice for Agriculture. I drove around the country speaking at different venues, trying to put heart into people and advise them on what they should do to protect themselves legally. I remember going down to the sugar estates in the *lowveld* where seventy-two white families with all their household effects and farm equipment had moved into town the day before. Several families were living together in each of the town houses, surrounded by absolute chaos. I slept on the floor in a house with a number of other families. Everywhere farms were being abandoned, left as weekend retreats for senior ZANU–PF men.

Farm workers were pressurized by the party to help with the eviction of the white farmers. Statutory Instrument 6 (SI 6) was signed in September 2002 stating that anyone leaving employment on a farm could claim a massive redundancy package, amounting to two months' salary for each year worked and a further three months' salary on top of that. The older farmers, who had looked after their workers well and had employed them for many years, were the worst affected. The CFU didn't challenge this legislation either.

Party operatives would come onto a farm and mobilize the workers to make the demands, sometimes beating them first. The farmers were then put under siege until they paid out the notorious SI 6 payments. It broke many of them. The monthly wage bill was a major item of expenditure on most farms in any case. Many farmers had to sell their possessions to try to pay the redundancy packages. And many of the workers, who weren't used to managing so much money in one go, went straight to town and spent it. Those who didn't saw it eaten up by inflation. So then the workers had nothing either.

The "new owners", as the propaganda machine called them, then evicted the farm workers, who had run out of money and weren't being paid any wages, to make room for paying tenants. Many farm workers were told that they could only stay in their houses if they worked for the new owner for nothing. It was slave labour, a return to the dark ages of patronage and complete feudal control of men and their families.

Teams from Justice for Agriculture continued to travel the country, addressing meetings. One particular meeting stands out in my mind because our team was so unusual. I drove up to Karoi in the north with Wynand Hart and Wilfred Mhanda.

Wynand Hart had lost his farm after being pulled around the garden by his hair in front of the police, who did nothing to help. He had had a serious back injury following a parachute accident in the bush war, and he realized that it would be bad for his health to stay on, but he was determined to fight the invasions in whatever way he could.

Wilfred Mhanda was at one stage second in command of ZANLA (Zimbabwe African National Liberation Army). He told us how much Mugabe hated anyone with any kind of initiative. Everyone around him had to be "yes" men or they were removed. Mugabe had arrested Wilfred and 600 others, including fifty top men, and had incarcerated them for the last three years of the bush war.

While Mugabe himself had been under lock and key in Rhodesia, he was treated well. He had been able to study and get several degrees. But his own ZANLA commanders were less fortunate. Wilfred told Wynand and me that for the first six months they were kept naked and packed like sardines on cement floors with no blankets. They had hardly any food and they were eaten by lice. They had no toilet and had to sleep in their own filth, which only got cleaned out once a month. It was so inhuman it was hardly believable.

Wilfred drove us to the meeting – very fast. Wynand and I hung on to the edges of our seats as we chatted, and the journey passed very quickly as our conversation was so fascinating. When we arrived, we found the meeting was packed with farmers, all of whom looked surprised to see an Afrikaner veteran of the bush war, who fought for Prime Minister Ian Smith, walk in together with a Shona war veteran from Mugabe's side, and me, the descendant of a long line of British Army officers.

We spoke about property rights and the rule of law, and the need for people to stand up and ensure that our rights were protected and the rule of law was upheld if Zimbabwe was to be a great nation again and everyone was to have a future. All three of us spoke the same language. Wilfred in particular spoke very well. It was so heartening to hear from a senior war veteran who was brave enough not to follow the party line. Wilfred had defied orders and had refused to lead farm invasions. He understood only too well that the invasions would result in the nation degenerating into hunger, economic disaster, and hopelessness. He knew what this sort of so-called "land reform" was really about, because he had been trained by those who were now practising it. Later Wilfred was to say, "If I knew what I know now, I would never have gone to the bush to kill people."

Land reform is about controlling the land in order to control the people on it. People need to eat, and in hard times they rely on the land to be able to grow food so that they can survive. Dictators – like Stalin in Russia and Mao in China, Pol Pot in Cambodia and Mengistu in Ethiopia – all knew that once they controlled the land, they could control the food supply and nothing could then stand in their way. They could stamp out all opposition by using food to control people, just as Pavlov used food in his experiments with dogs and got them to do anything he wanted. It has happened in country after country in Africa. Property rights have been usurped in the name of land reform and tyranny reigns unchecked. According to Genocide Watch's 2010 statistics, more than twelve million people have died in genocides and politicides in Africa since 1945. This is double the number of Jews who died during the holocaust.

CHAPTER 12

The test case in the Supreme Court regarding the amendment to Section 8 of the Land Acquisition Act was set down for 27 May 2004. It had been a long time coming, and while we'd been waiting, the government had continued to take over thousands of homes and livelihoods. We hoped to get the legislation struck down or, failing that, we hoped for a stay on all acquisitions until the administrative court had heard the cases, and given reasonable notice to wind down operations if the acquisitions were confirmed.

I like to read a passage from the Bible every morning, and the morning before the case the reading seemed particularly apt: "The Lord is a God of justice. Blessed are all who wait for him" (Isaiah 30:18). I wondered how long the farmers and their workers would have to wait for God to act.

The Supreme Court of Zimbabwe is a small building. The chairs for the five judges are set up on a platform at the front. Below them to the left sit the applicants, with the defendants on the right, separated by a central aisle. Behind the advocates are a few wooden pews in which the public can sit. It seats fewer than forty people in all.

Our advocate, Wim Trengove, had come up from South Africa to represent George Quinnell in this test case on behalf of Justice for Agriculture. Trengove spoke clearly, quietly, and respectfully and his attack didn't seem like an attack at all. Listening to him was like listening to the purr of a powerful and very well-made engine. There were no knocks or whines or grating roughness. He argued for fairness, gently teasing out the reasons why the new act was so unreasonable and unjust.

The Government's advocate had little to say in response and it was clear that, given an impartial bench of judges, our days as people who had been criminalized by the law should be numbered.

At the end of the hearing we were led to believe that the judgment would come out about six weeks later. I drove Wim Trengove to the airport. Although we felt that our case had been well put, he wasn't optimistic, believing that justice was subservient to power politics in Zimbabwe.

Sure enough, when the judgment was published, six months after the hearing, it was an adverse judgment. Only one judge, Justice Wilson Sandura, gave a minority opinion striking down the Section 8 legislation as unconstitutional. The other judges all supported Mugabe's legal revolution.

The vast majority of farmers had already been evicted from their farms by then. Not a single farm had been vacated through a bona fide eviction order from a court, and nobody was being compensated. All the evictions were implemented in a lawless, chaotic manner.

I took a drive from Chegutu up to Chakari and then down to Kadoma to take a look at the places in my region that I'd come to know well. It was a nostalgic drive, for I knew the farmers and their families and what crops they grew and the struggles they'd had to build up their farms.

Now I saw wretched huts, clustered in haphazard groups in the middle of those red soil lands. I waved at one of the occupants, but he shook his fist at me. I suppose it was because I'm white and he had been indoctrinated to hate me because of the colour of my skin.

Around the huts the ubiquitous maize patches looked miserably unkempt. The maize was mostly a yellowy green colour, half choked by weeds, growing in haphazard patches rather than in organized fields, as though nobody cared. Settlements like these are scattered all over the country. I find them full of dark despondency and despair.

Areas that had been beautiful, lush bush the last time I'd seen them were now just forests of stumps – angular ugly things to

Above: Ben Freeth meets a Mursi woman during an early expedition in southern Ethiopia

Below: Ben and Laura Campbell with their bridesmaids (from left) Jane Skovgaard, Heidi Campbell, Michelle Middleton, Jessica Train, and Cathy Kirkman (Laura's sister) on Mount Carmel farm in 1994.

Left: Stephen and Joshua on the road leading to Mount Carmel

Above: Ben's parents, Zach and Claire Freeth (left), and Laura's parents, Mike and Angela Campbell (right)

Below: Ben and Laura, with their children (from left) Anna, Stephen, and Joshua, and Ginger the horse, on Mike and Angela's veranda

Right: Ben and Mike among some of the Mount Carmel workers

Below: Laura set up a linen business with some of the workers' wives

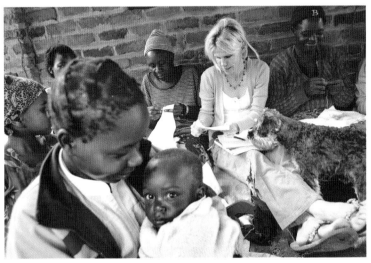

Above: Mike and Ben at the SADC Tribunal hearing in May 2008

Left: Their lawyer, Elize Angula, as the Tribunal ruled in favour of Mike

Right: Their advocate, Jeremy Gauntlett, SC

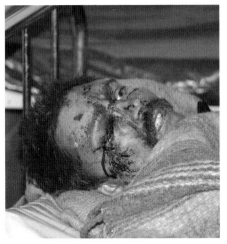

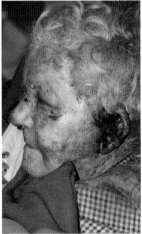

Above: Ben, Mike, and Angela (left) after being beaten by Mugabe's thugs

Below: Encounter with Peter Chamada at Mount Carmel

Above: Ben and Laura's Mount Carmel farmhouse ablaze

Bottom left: Laura watches in horror as her home burns

Bottom right: Some pages of her Bible survived

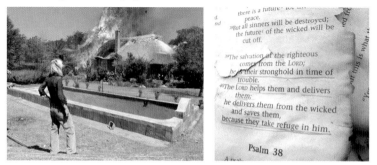

Distress among the farm workers after the fire on Mount Carmel and the destruction of their homes

SOUTHERN AFRICAN DEVELOPMENT COMMUNITY TRIBUNAL
IN THE SADC TRIBUNAL SITTING IN WINDHOEK NAMIBIA

Form 1

RULE 33

Matter No.SADC (T)......02...../.2007.

MIKE CAMPBELL (PRIVATE) LIMITED	FIRST APPLICANT
WILLIAM MICHAEL CAMPBELL	SECOND APPLICANT

VERSUS

ROBERT GABRIEL MUGABE, N.O.,
IN HIS CAPACITY AS PRESIDENT OF
THE GOVERNMENT OF THE
REPUBLIC OF ZIMBABWE   RESPONDENT

TO   THE REGISTRAR
            SADC Tribunal
            P.O.Box 40624
            Ausspanplatz
            Windhoek
            Republic of Namibia

AND TO

            ROBERT GABRIEL MUGABE, N.O.
            In his capacity as President of the Government
            Of the Republic of Zimbabwe

Certified a true copy of the original.
11/10/07

Nghivahangela Pelyeunime Salma Nambinga
Legal Practitioner
Windhoek, Namibia

Mike Campbell versus Robert Mugabe: a historic encounter

people who love trees. The harsh light, now unfiltered through the tracery of leaves and branches, brought their forms out all the more starkly.

I drove past the farms one by one. I felt as though I was paying my last respects to them and their owners – as though they were casualties sprawled on a battlefield. One by one I remembered them. I remembered their crops, their beef herds, their fence lines, their well-kept machinery. I remembered the standards of excellence and the sheer hard graft that had seen them succeed against all manner of difficulties.

Their degeneration into the listless mediocrity I now saw all around had been so quick. I've seen people die from cancer and I suppose this is much the same. The cancer, in the form of the squatters, appeared overnight and choked the farms to a standstill. And now the weeds were choking the squatters' maize patches. The cancer had broken peoples' lives. I had seen many broken people; I'd tried to comfort them. I had seen big men and strong women choked and crying as their life's work was destroyed before their eyes. I'd seen them weep as they were forced to leave the homes that that they'd built with their own hands.

As I drove, grief hit me like a towering wave.

All that sorrow. All those despairing faces.

Superimposed on the miserable landscape I was driving through I saw again all the unshaven faces I'd visited in prison, all the houses I'd watched being stripped of furniture, roofs, and window frames. I saw Terry Ford, lying in his own blood, guarded by his little dog, Squeak. I saw farm workers thrown out of their homes and left by the side of the road with their belongings. It was all too much.

As I carried on driving all round what should have been sixty kilometres of thriving farm land, the road and landscape blurred as the tears ran hot down my cheeks.

I thought of the evil men who'd made this happen and I was angry. I thought of all the people who could have done something to stop it but had chosen to appease the evil men. I thought of all the people who had carried on with their lives as though they didn't care, because the evil hadn't reached them yet. I thought of all the people who had run away and hadn't tried to help from their places of safety. I thought of all those who had washed their hands of Zimbabwe's unhappy plight.

But deep down in my heart I knew that justice was coming and that those evil men knew it would too. I knew that there was a far bigger wave building, a little way off, which would sweep over our land and cleanse it. I knew that we all had a part to play, but it would only begin to happen when we all started to act with honesty and courage – and with God in our hearts.

***

Meanwhile, back home, Bruce was facing a large group who gathered at his gate and lit a fire before breaking the locks and forcing their way in. Biggie Magorimbo, the leader of the gang, stole a motorbike from Bruce's cattle foreman. Tapiwa, one of Mount Carmel's tractor drivers, was grabbed, stripped, and beaten by the settlers. Some of the other workers were so frightened that they went into hiding and slept in the bush. The settlers caught some of them and paraded them around the house.

When Bruce removed the fire, the settlers barricaded him inside his house.

I went to the police station and eventually, after nearly two hours, managed to get two constables to come out to the farm with me. When we arrived, we could see that the situation was volatile. Nearly a hundred men were making a lot of noise and looking very intimidating. About forty of them were wielding sticks. They looked like they meant business.

Bruce came out of the house to meet us and one of the mob shouted at him, "We will kill you!"

"What did you say? Say it again!" I asked the man to repeat his death threat, but he refused. We were standing right next to the policemen. "Did you hear what he said?" I asked one of them.

The police did manage to defuse the situation after a few hours, and they retrieved the motorbike and Tapiwa's clothes, but there were no arrests.

"It is political," they told me in the car afterwards. Anything is permissible if it is "political". The notorious Public Order and Security Act (POSA) laid down dire consequences for people who formed gatherings without written permission from the police. If the law as it stood had taken its course, the whole gang would've been locked up. But it was led by militia from the ruling party, and they could get away with murder.

On 29 September 2004 a big black Jeep Cherokee drove in through the gate of Mount Carmel farm. With a feeling of some trepidation, I went out to meet the occupants.

"Good afternoon. Where are you from?" I enquired.

"We have come to take the farm," said one of them.

"Who are you?" I asked.

"I am the Provincial Lands Officer for Mashonaland West," he replied, getting out of the Jeep and looking around casually.

"And what is your name?"

"Ephraim Makaza," he told me.

"But there is no acquisition order for Mount Carmel," I informed him.

"There is!" Makaza claimed.

"When did it come out? I know nothing about it," I said.

"On 23 July," he responded.

"Then please show it to me," I asked. I knew that no new Section 8 notice for Mount Carmel had been issued. Mike and I made a point of buying every newspaper to make sure we didn't miss anything.

"I do not have it with me," Makaza continued, "but you have to be off this land by 23 October. The new owner will be sending his security guards next week."

"Who is the new owner?" I queried. There was a silence. "Is there an offer letter for the new owner?" I continued.

Makaza made an impatient gesture and a hand emerged from inside the Jeep waving a sheet of official-looking green paper.

"Can I please have a copy?" I asked.

"No!" The paper was withdrawn and the window rolled up.

"If this is official, you have nothing to hide. Please at least show me the offer letter," I persisted. Eventually Makaza did show me the paper. It was in favour of Nathan Shamuyarira of 68, Deacon Drive in Harare.

"Is this Cabinet Minister Nathan Shamuyarira?" I asked.

"Yes. I work with the Minister. Security will be sent next week to make sure you don't take anything off the farm."

The black Jeep drove off in a cloud of hot September dust.

Makaza and his men went straight from me to Mike. They asked him to provide accommodation for their new security team. Mike declined. He tried to tell them about the specialized production and marketing system for the fruit on the farm, explaining that if we were forced to leave, it would all break down.

"We will chop down the mango and citrus trees and grow maize," Makaza replied. At that stage Mount Carmel had over 40,000 productive fruit trees. Threatening to cut them all down showed up the resettlement programme for what it was – a complete and utter sham. Mike was then threatened with arrest and imprisonment if he didn't get off the farm within three weeks.

"I have no other home and I am not leaving," Mike told Makaza and his men.

"You are very arrogant," Makaza replied, before roaring off.

I went for a walk that evening. The sweet scent of the mango flowers wafted through the air and a great moon, yellowed by the smoke of bush fires, rose over the eastern skyline. The mufuti trees were just coming into leaf and the leaves looked like large pink prawns, all curled up. Whenever I have seen mufuti trees coming into leaf in subsequent years, I have thought about that day.

"It's just another day on a farm in Africa," I thought to myself. But it seemed more significant than that. I had a feeling that things were really starting to hot up. Then I remembered a verse from the Bible: "Be still, and know that I am God" (Psalm 46:10).

It was hard to sleep at night after the visit from Makaza and his men. Laura and I kept waking up with a sick feeling in the pits of our stomachs. Mike and Angela felt the same. It wasn't a new sensation for any of us, we'd lived with fear for so long, but we knew that the noose was tightening. We didn't know what each new day would bring. If only we could get the settlers to stick to the law, even their own bad laws, we would know where we stood and could plan accordingly.

I found out a bit about Mount Carmel's new "owner", N. Shamuyarira. He was a former Minister of Information and had held other cabinet posts, too. He was also the official ZANU–PF spokesperson, Mugabe's close confidant, and his official biographer. I was curious to see where he lived, so I went to find his house in Harare. The property was surrounded by large cypress trees and looked very dark. I couldn't get rid of the feeling that it was like a graveyard. There was a secure wall all the way around. It seemed ironic that we lived with no security among the people on the farm and yet this man, who was supposedly a man of the people, lived in such fear of them.

I saw the two eyes peering at me through a hole in the wall. A voice accompanied the eyes. "Who are you?" it asked.

"I am Ben Freeth and I would like to see the Minister," I responded.

The voice came back, "You can't see him." In one sense it was a relief. I didn't really want to see him.

I was worried about what the knowledge that a ZANU–PF heavy wanting to take over the farm would do to the family. Up until then, we'd all been strong, but I'd seen so many families buckle under similar pressure. In the interests of buying more time, maybe to harvest the next crop, or retrieve some equipment, it was all too easy to compromise and try not to rock the boat. This meant not going to the courts and not exposing injustices in the press.

I was still convinced that we shouldn't give in. We'd come so far. We had stood up for justice all the way. We couldn't give up on issues of principle now. We had to stand firm, and keep on standing. I believed that God had everything in hand, but that our faith was going to be severely tested.

My son Joshua was nearly four. He'd had his first run in with the farm invaders when he was only a baby. I felt moved to write a letter to him for his birthday, explaining why we had decided to stay when most people were leaving. I hoped that in future he would understand our decision.

My dear Joshua,

You were born on the eve of the farm invasions and you are now four years old. As your Daddy I have important decisions to make for you – decisions that will affect the rest of your life. As a family we live in a country where 85 of every 100 white farmers have been removed from their homes since you were born. We live in a time when inflation is higher here than in any other country in the world, and our economy is the fastest shrinking. We see our friends and our skilled people leaving all the time and they say, "We are leaving for the sake of our children."

Maybe it's stubbornness, maybe it's the inherent fighting spirit passed on to me by your grandfather, but deep down I believe that it's God's will for us to stay put. I say, "We are staying for the sake of our children." It may sound perverse, given what I say about the country that we live in, but I wish to explain.

At only three months old, you had your first run-in with darkness. Bad men smashed up our car with axes and rocks and tried to kill Mummy and you and me, but God got us through that. Your Daddy has been beaten with sticks and kicked in the dust by a CIO man and a crowd, and you were worried about that, but God got us through it. Your Daddy then had another smash-up in a car with war veterans and by a miracle God got him through that. Your Daddy's been shot at and abused; he's dealt with beaten farmers and beaten farm workers, and looted properties and butchered animals and even bloody, butchered farmers murdered in the name of land reform. He's had his job and his car taken away from him and the farming hierarchy has shunned him, but God got us through that. He has been arrested and he has seen broken men coming out of prison and broken families spread out across the continents but I still say, with your Mummy, "We are staying for the sake of you children."

We have undoubtedly been more fortunate than most. We still have our home – for today. We still have our family around us – for today. We still have an income – for today. And for today, when I see you go off in the morning with the shepherd – your hair the same colour as winter grass, head bobbing down behind the sheep; a little wild figure at one with the veld – I feel so privileged to know that you are growing up in such an environment, learning to know and appreciate the real things away from the invasive world of TV screens, computer games, city streets, and shoe-box flats.

When I say we are staying for your sake, I say it because as you grow up you will face challenges of a nature that you will not face in other places and you will know hardships, which, so long as we face them right, will make you real. You have seen death and heart-felt grief already and you have felt dust and wet earth and sun and rain and you know already the joys of growing things and hunting things and of being part of real life – the raw life that comes from being a son of the African soil.

For some, this impassioned reality that we are such an integral part of is simply too much. After a time they *grow tired. The harsh extremes become just too much. The constant fight for our very survival, which is so all consuming, eventually wears them down. "Goodbye," they say, "Goodbye to all that. We would rather not be a part of it." And off they go, to a land of security and progress, and hardly ever come back because they know they have left their hearts behind, and it would be painful to become reacquainted with them.*

From the cosy world of material security, it is an unthinkable madness that anybody should choose to stay here; but as one octogenarian couple said to me while in the process of being forcibly evicted out of their home of fifty years recently, "We do not deserve to have our home or our country if we are not prepared to fight for them."

So our decision to stay has not been taken lightly. We have taken it knowing that things are going to get worse; that the people in power will continue to persecute us because of the colour of our skins; that when the storm is passed, it won't take long for the next one to brew up; that our decision to confront evil and fight it will continue to have consequences.

Our decision is made knowing that when we become tired, God will give us the strength to go on, and that somehow in the darkness that the storm has plunged us into, we have a responsibility before God to not be overcome by it, but to rather be a beacon of light if ever we can. I write this with a prayer that you will someday understand.

With all my love,

Daddy

***

A white twin-cab arrived at Carskey emblazoned with ZANU–PF on the side. Bruce was handed a letter from the district administrator telling him he had to get out of his house by the following Monday. He'd only just obtained a High Court order nullifying the Section 8 order on Carskey, but that seemed to make no difference.

It was 2004 and the government was clearly in eviction mode. On 2 September, they'd evicted about 10,000 people from the Porta farm squatter camp near Harare. Ten people had died from tear gas – a number of them were little children.

A new Section 8 acquisition order was issued to make way for Minister Shamuyarira to take over Mount Carmel. But there was a mistake in the order: it was listed for "urban expansion". The farm was sixteen kilometres from the nearest town. We had always prayed for confusion among those trying to steal what was not theirs, and so we regarded this as an answer to prayer.

On the Monday, Bruce hadn't moved a thing out of his house. No one arrived to evict him. There had been some rain earlier, and in the evening, when we took the dogs for a walk, the flying ants started to take wing. The sun was setting behind the rocky crest of Gadzema Kopje and the ants looked exactly like a mass of large snowflakes on a still day, drifting silently upwards on their lacy wings.

Minister Shamuyarira arrived one Sunday a few weeks later, just as we were all sitting down for the weekly family roast. We heard cars hooting outside so we went out to see what was going on. A policeman carrying an AK-47 got out of the black Jeep, followed by the Minister. Mr Shamuyarira looked surprisingly fit for someone in his eighties and was wearing a pair of running shoes. Bruce, Mike, and I greeted him politely.

The conversation was not a long one. Shamuyarira came straight to the point and asked Mike if he was prepared to go into partnership with him. Mike simply replied, "I haven't worked my whole life to become your 'boss boy'."

Mike left no room for doubt. He knew that other people, under duress, hadn't been able to say no. Some people called it "boxing clever", but it never turned out to be very clever in the end. We knew many people who had agreed to go into partnership with

137

the settlers and had assisted ruling party officials in all sorts of ways to try to save their own skins. It never worked. Going into business with a ZANU–PF politician whom you don't know, who has no farming experience, at a time when there is no rule of law, is a recipe for disaster. If and when any money comes in, the partner who has forced the partnership takes it all and the business collapses very quickly. We had seen it happen time and time again. The problem in Africa is that people are always too afraid to say no.

Mike made it quite clear where we stood regarding the law. "If you want us out, please make sure you do things legally," he told the Minister. "We will hold you accountable for anything illegal that happens."

Shamuyarira drove away and spent the next couple of hours visiting the squatters. Two days later the hay barn was burned to the ground, with over 2,000 bales inside. We followed the spoor heading back toward the squatters' huts, but eventually lost it.

Thefts on the farm increased after the Minister's visit. A pump was stolen from the pack house. The motor for the main borehole for Mount Carmel house was stolen, as were the wheels from one of the trailers.

Various delegations arrived to try to intimidate us into leaving. One arrived in a lorry, which parked by the diesel tanks near the workshop. Chief Ngezi got out. He told Mike that he was the chief and Mike must get off the farm. Mike said to him, "Only Jesus will decide what happens on this farm."

Chief Ngezi thought for a moment, then said, defiantly, "I am Jesus!"

Mike told him not to make false claims, explaining that, "There was another man who made a similar claim and he was struck down by lightning."

The Chief looked up at the sky for a moment and eventually left with his entourage. He never came back, and he did in fact die not long afterwards.

Another group consisting of more than thirty senior policemen and army personnel as well as senior civil servants and CIO operatives arrived. The task force was led by Didymus Mutasa, the Permanent Secretary in the Ministry of State Security, Lands and Resettlement – although he wasn't there in person that afternoon.

We met them under the bauhinia tree outside Mike and Angela's house. They were clearly nervous. At one point Bruce put his hand in his pocket to get his cell phone out and a CIO man standing just behind him grabbed his hand. He thought Bruce might be bringing out a gun.

Like all such meetings, this one was designed to intimidate. None of our visitors introduced themselves. When I started to take notes with my pencil in my notebook, a senior policeman grabbed the notebook from me.

"You are a journalist," he said accusingly. Being an unregistered journalist in Zimbabwe is a serious offence, punishable by imprisonment. I told him that I was from the farm. The policeman handed my notebook to the district administrator, who leafed through it. Eventually I was allowed to have it back, but only after agreeing to rub out the registration numbers of the vehicles, which I had written in pencil. I had to do it while they watched.

The point of the meeting was to tell us that we all had to get out of our houses and off the farm.

It's hard to resist a group consisting of the army, plus the police, plus the CIO, plus senior government officials. We all felt, "What's the point?" It is a hard psychological barrier to get through and believe that there is any hope of staying – or any point in staying put.

But I was pleased that they had made me rub out the registration numbers. I was pleased that they refused to give their names. It showed that they had much to hide. It showed that they knew that what they were doing was unlawful and wrong.

We did nothing to effect compliance. We sent an official letter to the Minister saying that we were doing nothing illegal by remaining on our property.

CHAPTER 13

Justice for Agriculture (JAG) continued to hold meetings to advise people about what the law said and to encourage them not to back down.

One day I had just opened a meeting by reading the same Bible passage from Deuteronomy chapter 8 that had got me into trouble at the CFU Congress. Suddenly the door burst open and a group of policemen rushed in and arrested us for holding an illegal meeting. Before we were carted away, I was able to read Psalm 24 out to the meeting: "Who may ascend the hill of the Lord? ... He who has clean hands and a pure heart..."

"We have nothing to hide and we have done nothing wrong," I said, as we were taken to Borrowdale Police Station.

Most of the leadership team from JAG had been arrested: Dave Connolly, Wynand Hart, John Worsley-Worswick, and me.

We managed to make some calls and get hold of Beatrice Mtetwa, a fearless human rights lawyer. Not long before, she herself had been badly beaten up at Borrowdale Police Station while trying to defend one of her clients.

Then we were parcelled off to Harare Central Police Station. We were led up steps and down steps and through long twisting dark corridors with paint peeling off the walls. It was like a maze and I knew I would never be able to find my way out on my own. The place was dingy and smelly and felt distinctly creepy. Eventually we were taken to a room that was below ground level and allowed to sit around a table as we were questioned.

After a while we were left alone.

When the policemen returned, they took us off, one by one, to be questioned separately. I was led down a corridor past a row of little rooms. I sensed that they were torture rooms, but none of us was physically harmed. We were just being intimidated, and we knew it. We got the message: "Don't have any more meetings. We're watching you. We will put you inside and hurt you. Keep out of trouble. Let us get on with what we need to do in destroying you people. Give up. Don't hinder us."

Beatrice Mtetwa eventually managed to force her way in to Harare Central. She knew everyone there and she was not afraid of them. She had overcome fear, and that was why she was so effective. She has won several prestigious awards for her bravery in the face of tyranny. We were fortunate to have such an indomitable tigress on our side.

After several hours Beatrice managed to get us all released and we were led back through the dark corridors. As we were walking down the steps, she greeted an officer by name and quipped amicably, "Who have you been torturing recently?" There was no reply.

Suddenly we were out in the open. It felt good to see daylight and movement and open spaces. Even after a short spell in Harare Central, you appreciate the outside world more.

***

At Justice for Agriculture I'd been busy putting together the "rule of law" case with Ray Passaportis. I tried to collect affidavits from all the different provinces to show how the police – the people who were supposed to be protecting life and property and upholding the law – were allowing, and in many cases promoting, a culture of lawlessness, where heinous crimes were allowed to be committed. It was an uphill battle. The CFU did not want anything to do with it.

In Midlands Province I couldn't get a single affidavit. There was clearly a protection racket going on there. One large-scale dairy farmer had gone into partnership with Emmerson Mnangagwa, a close confidant of Mugabe and one of the most powerful men in ZANU–PF for the last few decades, who played a prominent role in *Gukurahundi*. At that time he was Minister of Security and in charge of the Central Intelligence Organisation. He became known as "The Godfather" because he brokered protection deals for other farmers too. Nobody from Midlands was encouraged to make anyone accountable. Their own CFU leadership had said that the courts and the press were out of bounds. There were some notable exceptions – people who were willing to break the rules – but on the whole, Midlands Province had become part of the CFU collaborators' consortium. Not a single person was prepared to write an affidavit confirming that the police had encouraged the breakdown of the rule of law.

It was a ground-breaking case that JAG was trying to get together, and we had no money to do it. Without the support of the CFU, it became very difficult to get people to contribute their experiences. Farmers still inherently trusted CFU and didn't believe that what CFU was advising them could be wrong.

It was a sad situation. People didn't seem to understand that if we wanted an end to Mugabe's tyranny, we had to face it and expose the things that were wrong. If nothing was said and nothing was exposed, the tyrant would be able to ratchet up the abuses. Situations like Somalia or Rwanda or the DRC were just around the corner unless we did something to stop the lawlessness and human rights abuses from happening. The best way to do this was to expose them and show people what was really going on.

What made it more difficult was that farmers are notoriously bad with paperwork. Most of them had never needed a lawyer in their lives and they had no idea how to put a proper statement together. Most hadn't kept records of what had happened to them – they didn't have the dates and times and details of how the rule of law had been systematically broken down.

It wasn't surprising that farmers felt hopeless regarding any kind of legal remedy. Police refused to handle complaints. Court orders, where people had had the courage to try to get them, were almost entirely ignored and some people had been made an example of for going to court. As a result there was no interest in pursuing justice. Many farmers felt that justice was a lost cause in the environment in which we were trying to operate. They felt that if we wanted to survive, it was better to make deals with the leaders of the people who were committing the crimes, giving them cattle, doing their ploughing for them, and supplying them with fertilizer and money.

Unfortunately Ray Passaportis became ill and was off work a great deal. He didn't have the time or the energy to keep calling the farmers and work with the statements to build a proper case. He eventually died at a very young age of a brain tumour. There were so few lawyers brave and tenacious enough to take on land cases like Ray; he was a great loss. Looking back, I should have driven things harder and I should have got the farm workers involved. I regret not having done so. I owe everyone an apology. I'm sure that with the International Criminal Court coming into being in 2002, we could have had a chance to have our case eventually heard as a crime against humanity.

Within JAG we were all cash strapped. Nobody had the money to pour into expensive legal cases. The donor community wasn't going to support us and most of the farmers themselves were bankrupt.

The Farm Equipment Statutory Instrument was the next blow. This new measure allowed the government to seize all our tractors and other equipment as well as fertilizer, seed, and chemicals. The threat to our private property was clear and real. I immediately sent an email to the trustees of JAG to get their agreement that we should challenge this new law. I then went to see Dave Drury and asked him to get stuck in with putting together a new challenge, as there was a significant threat to hundreds of millions of US dollars worth of movable private property.

Dave is the most unlawyer-like lawyer I've ever met. In the stereotypical shark-like world of mercenary law, he stands out as a humble man who does what he does because he cares about others. He often has his jersey inside out and some of his shirt collars were designed for men twice his size, but his heart is gigantic and the untiring work he has done for farmers and farm workers beggars belief.

But Dave was warned off by John Worsley-Worswick, who was also part of JAG. According to John the CFU would definitely be challenging the new law, so there was no point in duplicating time and money with a similar challenge from JAG.

The messages we were getting were confusing. I spoke to people in CFU who weren't convinced that CFU would follow through any legal challenges. I knew they were right. Unfortunately an internal battle began within JAG and dragged on for some time. We wasted a lot of energy on it. The upshot was that neither CFU nor JAG challenged the new legislation, and millions of dollars worth of equipment was stolen under cover of the new law.

The situation was made even more difficult because the government had already put a total ban on the export of farm equipment. Farmers were in a triple bind. They couldn't use their equipment in Zimbabwe because they'd been kicked off their farms; they couldn't sell it for what it was worth because there was no market for it in Zimbabwe; and now they couldn't take it to Mozambique or Zambia to start up farming operations there either. My former CFU offices already looked like a sale yard packed with farmers' equipment. It made me angry to see it like that. We'd tried, at a huge personal cost, to keep people on the land. Now the very same offices that we had used to try to do that were being used to sell off the farmers' equipment so that they would never farm again.

I think what upset me the most was the fact that the equipment was being sold mostly to the people who were stealing the farms, at ridiculously low prices. I remember looking at a big tractor-drawn four-wheel farm trailer that was being sold for twenty US dollars. Just one of its tyres should have been worth five times that.

The farmers were desperate. They'd had enough. They just wanted to sell up what they could, and go and start their lives again somewhere where they had a hope of being allowed to continue without harassment, beatings, and jail.

***

In 2005 there was another election in Zimbabwe. We dreaded elections because they were times of terrible fear, intimidation, and violence.

Our local farming community came together to donate diesel and other things to the ZANU–PF election machine in the hope that they would be left alone. Nobody approached Mike, Bruce, or me to donate anything. They knew we'd taken the decision not to feed the evil that was destroying everything. As a result we were never invited to farmers' meetings in case, by associating with us, they were deemed not to be supportive of the party.

After ZANU–PF won again, the Selous Farmers' Association chairman wrote a fawning letter to Webster Shamu, the local MP and Minister of Policy Implementation. "Our community had to dig deeper into their pockets to raise the donations that you requested for the successful implementation of your election campaign… we are proud that our donations helped you win the elections."

It made me sick. When they're outside the situation, many people believe that they would never be party to aiding and abetting tyranny. The reality is that the vast majority are so overcome by fear that they do. When the law gives no protection, people will pay for protection unless they have very strong and principled leadership. Unfortunately we did not have that.

Jesus said that "the thief", that is Satan and his demonic powers, comes to "steal and kill and destroy". Jesus, on the other hand, came so that we "may have life, and have it to the full". The Bible teaches that if we resist evil, it will "flee" from us. Almost everyone in Zimbabwe could see that what was going on was satanic and evil. The violent taking of life and property can't be anything else. But where were the people who were prepared to resist?

It was tragic. In the first eight years of invasions, not a single farmer or farm worker was evicted legally. Of all the people and organizations affected, not one, for whatever reason, successfully completed a civil challenge against the police and the authorities for allowing all those illegal evictions.

Many who have never lived under the cloud of fear that characterizes dictatorship will not believe this. It is a sad facet of human nature that people can be so easily cowed and driven to hopeless despair.

In my family we took heart from the teachings of the apostle Paul, who faced terrible situations of persecution, but was able to discover the secret of being "content whatever the circumstances". God gave us strength for each day. That isn't to say that we were never afraid. Often my stomach would tighten and I would feel sick when I heard people arriving on the farm, knowing that another group of invaders were threatening to destroy all that I held most dear.

***

After Mugabe had "won" the 2005 elections, the ruling ZANU–PF party was able to change the constitution at will, because it now had the two-thirds parliamentary majority that constitutional change required.

As a direct result, Amendment 17 to the constitution sailed through parliament. This evil piece of legislation effectively nationalized all white-owned land. No one had any right to appeal – no court was even allowed to look at appeals against land acquisitions. Not only did it mean the complete abolition of property rights, it also criminalized all white farmers and their farm workers if we stayed on our land. Through the coming into law of the Consequential Provisions Act in December 2006, we were liable to two years in prison if we didn't leave our farms.

It was the end of the white man on the land in Zimbabwe. It

was also the end of commercial agriculture and, as a result, there would be more hunger, further destruction of the land and the environment, even less investment and jobs and money to keep education and health care going, and a further loss of skills. We were facing the breakdown of the economy and the country as a whole, and we knew that it would lead to terrible suffering for the vast majority of the people of Zimbabwe.

Before President Mugabe signed the new legislation, I wrote an open letter to him entitled "The Lie of the Land", which was published in *The Independent* (see Appendix 3 for the full text of the letter). In it I summed up the history of land ownership in Zimbabwe and called on the president to make a new start and refuse to sign the legislation.

He signed.

We knew that unless we did something ourselves, nobody was going to do anything for us. The CFU was badly compromised, its leadership was weak, and there was no other organization with the *locus standi* to take up an appeal against the legislation. Was it possible, legally, to challenge the constitution? We didn't know. What higher law could we use to do so?

I went to see Dave Drury and asked him to look through the case histories of all his clients and come up with the farmer who had the best chance of mounting a legal challenge to the Amendment 17 legislation.

I got a call from Dave a while later.

"Ben, can you come over?"

When I arrived at his office, Dave handed me a piece of paper. I unfolded it and read "Mount Carmel". It was us. Out of the whole of Zimbabwe, we on Mount Carmel were the people with the best chance of challenging Mugabe head-on in the courts. I thought of Elijah taking on King Ahab and the prophets of Baal on the biblical Mount Carmel, around 2,500 years before. I also thought of what King Ahab and his wicked wife Jezebel had done to Naboth when Naboth refused to let them take his vineyard.

Mike and I knew that this was serious and we had to consider it very carefully. In dictatorial Africa the ruler is absolute and anyone challenging him normally pays with his life. Being "taken out" was a very real possibility.

I believe that God spoke to me and assured me that we were right to take this on and that we must not count the cost. The following Sunday I was due to preach in church and I read the Bible story of Shadrach, Meshach, and Abednego (Daniel 1–3). These three men had refused to bow down to their king and were willing to take the consequences. The king gave them a second chance but they still refused to bow down to him and his evil law. Eventually they were thrown into a furnace – and it was then that a fourth "man" appeared and walked with them in the flames. They survived without a single burn. They didn't even smell of smoke.

Just as Shadrach, Meshach, and Abednego had refused to obey the king's evil law and had publicly disobeyed and challenged it, so we needed to do the same. We might go through the fire too, but if we did, we must be willing to take the consequences. If we lived, we lived. If we died, we died.

Mike signed the founding affidavit. On the front of it was written, "William Michael Campbell versus Robert Gabriel Mugabe."

Tears came to my eyes when Mike signed his name. It was a momentous act of tremendous moral courage.

Not long afterwards, I was coming home from a brief visit to England. There I'd met a Romanian pastor who had been at a prayer meeting that had resulted in a letter being written to Nicolae Ceausescu by church leaders. The dictator was overthrown by the people of Romania a few weeks later.

I arrived at the airport more than two hours early for my Air Zimbabwe flight, but I was the last passenger allowed on board. We took off an hour earlier than scheduled and landed as soon as it was dark. I didn't know where we were – we'd only been flying for a few hours.

After a little while the captain made an announcement: "Welcome your Excellencies Comrade Robert Mugabe and Comrade Grace Mugabe! Welcome Honourable Ministers. Welcome ladies and gentlemen!"

I started to think. I knew this was an opportunity. I called the stewardess and asked, "Can I go through to the front of the plane to speak to the president?" She looked at me as though I was mad and said, "Nobody is allowed."

The plane took off again, nothing further happened and I began to drift off to sleep. Suddenly I woke up with a start and began to write, a poem forming in my mind.

> *The blood cries out from a thousand graves*
> *And justice must be done.*
> *But mercy cries through Him who saves*
> *By sending His only son.*

The poem went on to talk about God's grace and the chance for forgiveness for those who repent and change their ways.

I enclosed it in a copy of a daily Bible reading booklet called *Every Day with Jesus* and called the stewardess again.

"I have a booklet here for the president. Can you give it to him?"

She looked at the booklet and said, "I can't give it to him but I can give it to his chief of protocol."

After that I dozed off again. Sometime later the stewardess returned.

"Are you the one who wrote the letter?" she asked.

"Yes," I said simply.

She stared at me for some time and said nothing more. Then she walked away. I said a prayer.

When we landed, I knew I had to get out and through immigration and customs as quickly as possible. When everyone stood up, we were told that we must all sit down again and wait for the president and his wife and the other comrades to leave the plane first.

On the apron beneath the window I counted twenty-nine vehicles arrive – mostly Mercedes. From out of the belly of the plane spewed vast quantities of trunks and suitcases, which were loaded into the waiting cars. The comrades got in too. Then off they sped, clearly without having gone through any of the formalities of customs or immigration.

I was the first paying passenger off the plane and through immigration. I was relieved when I got out and away from the airport.

CHAPTER 14

Our case was the most important human rights-based challenge regarding the rule of law in Zimbabwe for over forty years. The previous major challenge was the case of Stella Madzimbamuto v. Lardner Burke in 1966. Stella's husband had been incarcerated under emergency powers for three months and was then kept behind bars while the constitution was changed to allow him to be held longer in custody. It was the same legislation as had been used to detain Mugabe himself without trial.

Stella Madzimbamuto's appeal argued for the effective existence of a higher law than a sovereign country's own constitution. She failed in the Rhodesian courts, but Sir Sydney Kentridge then led the case in the Privy Council, which declared the Rhodesian Constitution illegal. In a foreshadowing of things to come, the Solicitor-General of Rhodesia then stated that the Rhodesian government would not recognize the jurisdiction of the Privy Council.

Our case was going to create a conundrum for Mugabe similar to the one that Madzimbamuto had caused for Ian Smith. Would the president and his judiciary accept the existence of laws that were higher than the laws his own parliament had made? Professor Jeffrey Jowell QC, son-in-law of the late Helen Suzman, who was renowned for her lone fight against apartheid in South Africa's parliament, provided invaluable assistance. He said that the case had

> *huge implications for Africa and elsewhere. Because, what the Mugabe Government are saying is… "we've altered the Constitution, by popular vote… and now we can do anything". But democracy is not only about popular will, we know that through the European experience. The*

*German Government in the 1930s was elected popularly
and then they went on to do terrible things.*

*Democracy is not only about what the majority of
the people think, it's also about protecting fundamental
human rights, making sure that you can't do certain
things to individuals. Cases such as this have a resonance
not only in the region but across the world. They can
set examples and they're important, incrementally,
in establishing what the fundamental principles of
constitutional democracy are and should be all about.*

Mike and I knew that we had to have the best legal advice possible. We had no idea how we'd pay for it, but we couldn't risk messing it up. It was too important. And we had to get as much publicity as we could in order to turn the world's spotlight on the breakdown of the rule of law in Zimbabwe. So it was to Sir Sydney Kentridge QC that we now turned.

Sir Sydney is recognized as an elder statesman of English law and has served widely in Africa as well. He was the community counsel for the Sharpeville Massacre trial in South Africa in 1960 and he also led the inquest into the murder of Black Consciousness Movement leader, Steve Biko. He was a man with an impeccable record of fighting for human rights in the face of tyranny.

I wrote and asked if he could come out to Zimbabwe to fight for us. He wrote back a very endearing letter saying how much he would love to come, but on account of his age, his family had banned him from taking on any cases abroad – by then he was eighty-three. He offered all the assistance we required though. I also contacted Cherie Booth, Tony Blair's wife, but she said that she wasn't prepared to come to Zimbabwe.

Mike spoke to an old friend, Johann Kriegler, who had chaired the Independent Electoral Commission in 1994 in South Africa and who is a champion of human rights, and asked who the best advocate would be. "Jeremy Gauntlett is your man," he said.

Gauntlett, who had fought MDC leader Morgan Tsvangirai's treason trial, was independently recommended to me too.

Now all I had to do was find the money. Top advocates don't come cheap. Part of the problem was that the case involved the issue of racial discrimination. I soon discovered that organizations are generally very happy to finance fighting discrimination when black people are being severely discriminated against, but when white people are the victims, nobody wants to get involved. It's too controversial. The fact that white people had been discriminated against in post-independence Africa for nearly fifty years didn't appear to make a difference.

The CFU didn't want to know about our case because they feared it would destroy the effect of their years of dialogue. Justice for Agriculture had no money, so they couldn't help. The Zimbabwe Legal Resources Foundation didn't want to assist us at all because of the racial issue. Zimbabwe Lawyers for Human Rights made the right noises, but that was all. The various embassies and other foundations were the same.

The bill for our legal team would be thousands of US dollars a day. It was a real step of faith to engage them. So we prayed. As the case progressed, I often felt that it was as though we were at the top of a cliff and were taking a step out over the abyss with nothing beneath our feet. As we took the step, though, it was as though the ground came up to meet us and we had a solid place to stand on – the money came in as it was needed.

People told us we were mad to take the case to the Supreme Court of Zimbabwe. Everyone knew that the judges were political appointees and had mostly been given farms themselves, which they had a vested interest in keeping. I only knew of one Supreme Court judge who had not taken a farm. But Justice Wilson Sandura was highly unlikely to be chosen to sit on our case, especially as he'd had the courage to hand down the only favourable judgment in the Quinnell case.

We went to the Supreme Court because we had such a compelling case under international law. We felt convinced that if we lost, as we surely would with a stacked and corrupt bench, a way would open for us to appeal against the decision to an international court. But for the time being, all we could see ahead was a cul-de-sac. There was nowhere for us to appeal to. No higher court had any jurisdiction over Zimbabwean affairs. Mugabe's parliament could make whatever laws it wanted. Legally, it could make a law to say that all whites, Ndebeles, Indians, coloureds, or people without ZANU–PF party cards should be sent to concentration camps and then exterminated. There would be nothing, legally, that anyone could do to stop it. That is the power of a sovereign tyrant. To challenge it was a big step for an individual to take.

Our challenge rested on three issues relating to: *Amendment 17 of the Zimbabwean Constitution, discrimination,* and *compensation.*

The first issue related to Amendment 17, which had come into force on 14 September 2005. This states that, "A person having any right or interest in the land shall not apply to a court to challenge the acquisition of the land by the State and no court shall entertain any such challenge." It goes on to formally cancel the title deeds and register title over all land in the state where land has been acquired by decree.

This law affected all farms previously gazetted. It also had the potential to affect any farms that had escaped the net, plus any property that had been situated on agricultural land within the previous fifty years – which included most private houses in the towns. From that time on the government had sweeping powers to take away homes and livelihoods at the stroke of a pen without any challenge in any court being permitted. All they had to do was publish a notice in the newspaper and allocate the land to anyone they chose – including themselves.

If we won on this it would also strike down the Consequential Provisions Act, which came into force in December 2006. This made it a criminal offence for farmers to continue farming and live on their land, irrespective of whether or not they had crops in the ground or livestock to care for. This new offence was punishable by up to two years in prison. It didn't matter that the owner hadn't been compensated.

The second issue that we were challenging in the Supreme Court was discrimination. Amendment 17 effectively removed all the land from white owners – except for a few farms that escaped the net by pure chance – and none of the land belonging to black owners.

I spent days going through old newspaper cuttings, finding records of racist comments made by Mugabe and his senior policy makers. While I was still working for the CFU, I'd put together a map of the Chegutu and Kadoma districts that showed all the land and the farm boundaries and who owned what. It was one of the few things that I managed to get out of the office when I was suspended. I'd colour-coded the map to show communal land, small-scale commercial farms, black-owned land, and white-owned land. Now I updated it to show how all the farms owned by white people had been listed for acquisition and were now in state hands through Amendment 17. None of the black-owned farms had suffered the same fate.

I tried to get hold of similar maps that had been done for the other areas of the country, but the CFU didn't cooperate. What I did manage to get hold of, though, was a revealing statement from a farmer called Dana Nell regarding a meeting that he'd had with Didymus Mutasa. (Mutasa was the man in charge of the resettlement programme after the Ministry of State Security was combined with the Ministry of Lands and Resettlement.) Dana had been evicted from his farm in Karoi and was living on a farm belonging to the Municipality of Chegutu, which he farmed in a partnership agreement. He'd originally come to Zimbabwe from South Africa and had invested in an agricultural enterprise through the Zimbabwe Investment Centre. After losing most of his investment when the state settled invaders on his land, he was advised by the then Governor of Mashonaland West, Governor Nelson Samkange, to see Minister Mutasa.

155

He was finally given an appointment with the Minister on Thursday 18 January 2006. After waiting for three hours, Mutasa emerged from his office and Dana approached him.

"May I speak with you?" Dana asked.

Mutasa declined but asked what the problem was. Dana took out his Zimbabwe Investment Centre agreement and explained that he was a foreigner who had come to the country to invest. He had had approval from the administrative court to continue farming but was now finding it increasingly difficult to do so. He told the Minister that he needed paperwork from him in order to continue, and asked him to honour his country's own laws. These laws had granted Dana permanent residence in Zimbabwe and had sanctioned the capital investments he'd made on his farm.

Mutasa appeared angry and said, "A white British man used to sit under a tree and eat sadza with my father, but when that white man died that was the end of the good whites… the only good white man is a dead white man." He concluded his tirade by saying, "I will not go to the grave with any white man still on the land."

Dana remonstrated and pointed out that as a foreigner he wasn't part of that history, at which point Mutasa asked him directly, "Are you an Arabian?" Dana has a dark skin with a large nose and a black beard.

"Definitely not," Dana replied. "I'm not British either. I am a *mabhunu*, a white African."

Mutasa declared, "If you were Arabian I could give you ten farms of your choice, but because you are a *mabhunu* you must go and get your land back in the Transvaal."

Dana had never had land in the Transvaal. He told the Minister, "I am a South African. I do not want another farm."

"Do you know what my nickname is?" Mutasa asked. "It is *nyati*. If you want to fight *nyati* you must be prepared for a big fight."

The conversation ended with Minister Mutasa referring Dana back to Governor Samkange – the very person who had told him to go and see Mutasa in the first place.

Dana had approximately ten meetings with Governor Samkange but was never able to get a clear answer and his house and land were eventually taken over by senior members of the armed forces.

The discrimination issue in our court case also addressed who the beneficiaries of the land reform programme were. Almost all land that had been taken over during the previous three years had been given to the *chefs*. I spoke to as many farmers as I could and put together a list outlining who had received what, but even that was difficult. Nobody really wanted to give me the names of the people who had taken their neighbours' farms.

The *chef* list was made up entirely of ZANU–PF politicians and their lackeys – people who had the power to take a farm and were unable to resist the temptation. Cabinet ministers, MPs, senior judges, and people in the army and police and civil service all appeared on the list. I've often wondered at the morality of a whole people who accepted all that stolen property, knowing that it hadn't been paid for, and then pursued our illegal evictions with so much thuggery. Over 70 per cent of white-owned farms had changed hands since independence, with the government issuing "certificates of no present interest" when they did.

The third issue that we were challenging was compensation. Despite the government's acquisitions, no moves were being made to comply with their own laws of compensation. This meant that many people were struggling to survive. Older people were particularly badly hit as their whole pension was usually tied up in their farm. In other African countries white farmers had tried to externalize 10 per cent of their income each year, but this had not happened in Zimbabwe. At the time it had had a very positive effect: through the money the white farmers reinvested in their farms, Zimbabwe became one of the fastest growing economies in the world.

At independence in 1980 Zimbabwe was the biggest exporter of white maize in the world and the largest exporter of beef in Africa. Major cash crops of cotton and tobacco were also grown on a large scale, Zimbabwe being the biggest exporter of both in Africa. We also produced significant amounts of irrigated sugar cane, fruit, soya beans, wheat, barley, tea, coffee, flowers, vegetables, and other crops for export.

The development of commercial farms in that post-independence period was phenomenal. In 1988 Mugabe was awarded the Africa Prize for Leadership for the Sustainable End of Hunger. This US-based project had conveniently forgotten that the Ndebele people had been starved during *Gukurahundi* just prior to the award, but the rest of Africa was in such a mess that I suppose they had to find one country that was self-sufficient.

Now all the dams and irrigation schemes and facilities and equipment that had been used to grow so much over the years had been stolen, virtually overnight. The theft ran into many billions of US dollars but no compensation was ever paid.

Many of the farm workers, jobless, and homeless, had drifted to the towns, adding to the growing number of squatter camps. After analyzing the results of the 2005 elections, the government clearly saw these camps as hot-beds of opposition. On 19 May 2005, Operation Murambatsvina ("Drive out the filth") started. Police came in with bulldozers and simply flattened thousands of homes in the high density areas of the cities and towns. According to UN statistics, an estimated 700,000 homes were destroyed and 2.4 million poor people were affected. The Commissioner of Police, Augustine Chihuri, said that the aim of the operation was to "Clean the country of the crawling mass of maggots bent on destroying the country."

It happened so quickly. We were all caught flat-footed. Whole areas where people had once lived and worked were razed to the ground. Everything was being destroyed in the quest for control.

***

As a family, we knew that we needed to stay on the right side of the law if we were to avoid being evicted while we were preparing our challenge to Amendment 17.

Mount Carmel is close to a mining area called Gadzema, which means "shining place". It's a run-down ramshackle slum now, with all the buildings in various states of collapse, but it used to be one of the most active gold mines in the country. Thirty tons of gold were mined from Gadzema over the years. Gold is a curse for farmers, as mining law makes it very easy for people to come and dig legally on a farm. Fortunately Mount Carmel was a few kilometres out of the gold belt, although one miner was digging on the farm at the time.

I realized that if I put in some mining claims myself, it would make it more difficult for Minister Shamuyarira, who now "owned" the farm, to evict us. So I bought some prospecting licenses and found a registered prospector and we put in the beacons for some gold claims. In order to keep the claims open, we had to keep digging prospecting trenches. It was an enormous waste of time and energy, but it was what we had to do to stay on the right side of the law.

But even this didn't stop the invasions from continuing. Peter Chamada, Minister Shamuyarira's nephew, kept coming to try to move us off, in a different car each time, and with a new group of officials.

One afternoon he arrived with several vehicles containing Senator Jamaya Muduvuri, an enormously fat man who had taken several farms for himself already; the chief war veteran for Chegutu, whose name was Mataniki; the Chegutu Lands Officer, Clever Kunonga; Nathan Shamuyarira's brother; a policeman; and a number of others. They said they wanted to take up residence in the house with us.

Laura was in the garden when the invaders arrived. She took a photograph of them and there was immediate mayhem. The situation became very threatening. The men ran into the house after her. When they reached our bedroom, Laura shouted defiantly, "If you want to come into my bedroom, you must kill me first!"

The policeman told the other men that he didn't want an incident, so they satisfied themselves with confiscating Laura's camera and erasing all the pictures. I asked them what law we were breaking by taking a picture, and an argument ensued. Eventually it was agreed that we should go to the police station in Chegutu, together with the camera. When I arrived, the leader of the invaders was already there, talking to Chief Inspector Gunyani, who told me to get out until he had finished. I waited in the charge office.

When it was my turn to go in, I laid the Supreme Court application on the inspector's desk.

"Chief Inspector, what is going on is wrong," I said. "We have found the courage to challenge these things in the Supreme Court. You need to find the courage to stop what is going on because it is illegal to evict us while the matter is still to be decided by the court."

While I was at the police station, Mike had stayed with Laura and the children. One of the invaders wanted to take Anna, who was a tiny baby, from Laura's arms, but Laura managed to hang onto her. Laura asked them if they knew Jesus, because they needed him to show them that what they were doing was wrong. The invader replied, "We do not need Jesus, because he is the God of the white man. We have the ancestral spirits."

By the time I got back home the invaders had settled down in the garage that was attached to the house and was only ten metres from our bedroom. They were crouched around a fire and some of the younger men had gone into the orchard to steal mangoes. I managed to make a report to the police about the mango theft over the telephone.

I walked outside and started talking to them.

"What is the one thing that you and I, and everyone who has ever lived, have in common?" I asked.

They had no answer.

"It's very simple," I said. "Please tell me."

I kept them guessing for a while, then said, "We are all going to die. Death is the only certainty in life. Do you know where you are going when you die?" I asked. "Do you know what is going to happen to you? Each of us is responsible for our own life and the

160

choices we make. We can choose to do things that are wrong, or we can choose to do things that are right. At the end, though, we need to plan on things that are certain."

I went on, "If you were to die tonight, where would you go? I know where I'm going. I'm not afraid of death. You can kill me tonight but I believe the Bible when it says, 'To live is Christ and to die is gain…'"

They were quiet after that.

It was amazing that neither Laura and I, nor Mike and Angela, felt afraid. Neither did our children, Joshua, Stephen, and Anna. God gave us all peace despite the situation we were in. The children were playing on some cushions in the courtyard, piling them up and jumping onto them. Suddenly I heard crying and I saw that Josh had hurt his arm. I ran over and had a good look – it was clearly broken but it didn't look too bad. I knew that if we left the house to go to the doctor in Harare, the whole place would be looted and we might never be able to get back in.

Laura calmed Josh down and I went out past the invaders to get a chisel and some wood from the workshop. I fashioned a splint and Laura helped me wrap up Josh's arm so that it was immobilized. He was comfortable enough after that to go to sleep, and slept until morning.

Late that night Kunonga, the Lands Officer, arrived in a pickup truck. I went out to speak to him briefly, then he spent some time talking to the war veterans and the other invaders. After a while they crowded onto his pickup and sped off into the night, leaving a mess of mango skins and pips behind them.

In the morning, another pickup arrived. It was the police. They'd persuaded Kunonga to remove the invaders the previous night and now they'd come to see evidence of the mango theft.

I think it was the first time in six years that invaders who had been put in place by a Minister had been removed. It was an amazing answer to prayer.

We took Joshua to the doctor and he put his arm in plaster.

CHAPTER 15

Our advocate, Jeremy Gauntlett, wanted to come to visit us at Mount Carmel before the Supreme Court case, so that he'd know what he was fighting for.

He and Adrian de Bourbon, our other advocate, arrived like pack horses with their cases loaded with sugar and other basic commodities that we were unable to procure in any of the shops at the time because they were empty. I showed Jeremy around. He saw the well-managed orchards and the crops and the cattle, but he also saw the burned-out shell of the safari lodge and the land devoid of the game that had so recently roamed across it. He saw the squatters' huts, and the poverty and destruction that the squatters had brought with them. The evening was dusty and warm and dry, and the scents in the air were strong. I could tell that he was moved by what he was seeing. He went very quiet.

When we got to Harare on 15 May 2006 for the Supreme Court hearing (challenging the constitutional validity of Amendment 17), we discovered that Justice Sandura was not on the bench. All the judges were party faithful appointees.

It was the first time I'd heard Jeremy in action and as soon as he started to speak, I knew why he'd come so highly recommended. His mastery of language and the clarity of his argument made me think of a great composer conducting an orchestra in an inspired piece of music. He spoke with authority and fluency and left no room for doubt regarding the rights and wrongs of our case. On the fundamental rule of law issue, he submitted that our right of appeal to any court had been wrongfully extinguished and Zimbabwe had been left with a unique constitution unlike that of any other in the world. He went on to argue the discrimination issue.

It was an historic day. As far as I know, it was the first case of racial discrimination against whites in Africa to be argued in an African court. The judges had few questions to ask.

Adrian was brief and to the point in his argument regarding compensation. It was a very simple issue. Acquisition of anything cannot be said to be complete if the people acquiring it do not pay.

The government side had little to say in their turn. What could they say? The judges even berated them for their weak argument. But Mike and I went back to the farm knowing that life was going to continue to be tough. We knew we weren't going to win: the Chief Justice had taken a farm, as had almost all the other Supreme Court and High Court judges, so how could they possibly rule in our favour? Right at the beginning of the land invasions, Adrian had argued that judges who had received farms should recuse themselves. Even though he was chairman of the Bar, he was verbally attacked and threatened by the Chief Justice for having done so. Later there was a physical attack on one member of his family and Adrian left the country.

However, we did know that while our case was *sub judice* and we were waiting for a judgment, we couldn't be legally removed from the farm. We also knew that if the judgment was against us, it would be a sign that the judiciary had nailed their colours to the mast. They would no longer be able to retain any international credibility as independent, non-partisan judges. I expected a long wait for their judgment. When decisions are hard to make, people generally prevaricate.

Before we said goodbye to Jeremy and Adrian, we discussed a new international court that I'd been told about, called the SADC Tribunal. It turned out that, after fifteen years of preparation, the Southern African Development Community's new Tribunal was due to open its doors for business in Windhoek, Namibia, the very week after our hearing in the Zimbabwe Supreme Court. We started preparing to take an appeal to SADC.

In September 2007, Mike was summonsed to appear in the local magistrates' court, charged with contravening the Gazetted

Land (Consequential Provisions) Act, which was passed into law in December 2006. Like many other farmers all over the country, he faced serious charges for the crimes of living in his own house and continuing to farm his own land. All the Chegutu farmers were due to appear in court on 1 October. It was a hot day and the Chegutu magistrates' court looked tired, cramped, and chaotic. All the farmers – large and small, young and old – had to squeeze into the tiny dock together. Mike was cramped in at the back, trying to avoid falling through the floor, as there was a broken floorboard. Eventually Dave Drury asked if one farmer could stand in the dock on behalf of all the rest, which was agreed.

Mike and all the other farmers were remanded out of custody, but they were all given trial dates and still faced serious criminal charges.

Five days later we lodged an urgent application at the SADC Tribunal to try to get relief from prosecution. Delays and postponements dogged us from the start. Our SADC Tribunal hearing was due to begin on 20 November 2007, but the Zimbabwe government apparently didn't receive notice because they claimed their fax machine was broken. It was postponed to 4 December and then was finally heard on 11 December.

Mike and I were driving to the airport to go to Windhoek, Namibia, where the SADC Tribunal sat, when we were stopped at a police roadblock. It was 5:30 in the morning.

The policemen signalled for Mike to pull off the road.

"You overtook on a solid white line," one of them said. "Where are you going?"

"We are going to Windhoek in Namibia," Mike replied.

"Why are you going there?"

"We are going to take the president to court in the SADC Tribunal," Mike said simply.

There was a slight pause. "You may proceed," the policeman said, waving us on in obvious approval.

Mike and I arrived in Namibia the day before the hearing. I was incredibly struck by seeing all the fence lines intact as we drove past the farms on the way to Windhoek. None of the grass was burned, and although everything was very dry, it was heartening to see a landscape that looked well managed and cared for. There were no potholes in the roads. In the city, everything was clean and looked well maintained.

We'd arranged to meet up with Andy Thompson from Explore Films in the UK, who had emailed me after reading an article about our taking on President Mugabe at the SADC Tribunal. Andy wanted to make a film about the case. I knew that publicity was the very soul of justice and that it was crucial that people knew about the case and the injustices that were causing so much suffering in Zimbabwe. Andy gave me a crash course in documentary film-making and a small camera to smuggle back into Zimbabwe. By this time it was extremely dangerous to allow film crews onto the farm.

When we arrived at the Tribunal, we discovered that it had been gutted by fire shortly before our hearing. I hoped that this was not a message for justice in the future of southern Africa. Our hearing was transferred to the Namibian Supreme Court.

It was an historic day. Ours was the first human rights hearing in the world's second permanent international tribunal for human rights violations. The SADC Tribunal is the African counterpart to the European Court of Human Rights at Strasbourg. The judges came from Mozambique, Botswana, Angola, Malawi, and Mauritius. Robert Mugabe, in his capacity as President of the Republic of Zimbabwe, was cited as the respondent. The judges filed in and we stood up, bowed, and then sat down again. Jeremy argued the immediate, pressing danger of incarceration that we were being threatened with and asked that we be legally protected until the main hearing.

Advocate Prince Machaya argued in response that we hadn't exhausted domestic remedies because we were awaiting a judgment from the Supreme Court of Zimbabwe. He explained that such judgments sometimes took up to two years to be handed down. I saw a couple of the SADC judges shake their heads in disbelief at this. He was asked if the Zimbabwe government would adhere to any judgments that the SADC Tribunal might make. Advocate Machaya said that it would.

Two days later the order came out, granting us interim relief. It said that the Zimbabwe government should "… take no steps – or permit no steps to be taken, directly or indirectly, whether by its agents or by orders, to evict from or interfere with the peaceful residence on and beneficial use of the farm occupied by the farmers, their employees, and the families of their employees".

We flew back to Zimbabwe feeling hopeful.

***

Soon after we got back, Mike heard shots on the farm. He rushed off, and followed fresh tyre tracks to a vehicle in the bush not far from his house in the game area. While he was waiting for the poachers to return, he was rushed from behind and thrown to the ground. The poachers gave him a pummelling, which broke some of his ribs. They took off his shoes and tied his hands and feet together with his shoelaces, trussing him up like a goat. Then they lifted him up and dumped him unceremoniously in the back of their vehicle before bumping around on rough tracks and taking him off to the next door farm that one of them had taken a plot on.

When Angela told us that Mike was missing we searched the bush, but there was no sign of him. When it got dark I decided to go to the police.

I couldn't see Mike's vehicle at Chegutu police station and I was just about to leave when I decided to go into the charge office and see if he'd been there earlier. Mike emerged from behind the door like a ghost. He had blood over his face and shirt and he was dirty and dishevelled. After he had been carried around in the poachers' vehicle, he was unceremoniously chucked onto the concrete floor of the police station. There he'd had to sit, tied up, on the floor behind the charge office desk.

I was so pleased to see him that I gave him a big hug, not knowing that his ribs were broken. He'd borne the whole beating and abduction incredibly stoically. I took him home and we managed to recover his vehicle from the bush.

Despite Jonah Zindoga and the other squatters clearly possessing a weapon that they'd used to kill animals on Mount Carmel, and despite their having beaten a 73-year-old man, they all got away without being charged. They told the police that they'd been looking for missing cattle and had fired shots when they got lost. Not a very convincing story.

The poaching continued. We found one of the young giraffe that had pulled away from a wire snare but still had the wire around its head. It seemed all right, so we monitored it and watched it grow without any apparent problems. After perhaps two years it disappeared. I found its carcass on a foot patrol. Its skull had grown around the wire until eventually the wire was underneath its cranium. I brought the skull back home. To me it was a picture of the land reform programme in Zimbabwe – the slow and traumatic death of so much.

By the beginning of 2008, with the safari lodge a blackened shell of a ruin, there wasn't an animal left on Mount Carmel. After that, whenever Mike saw a wild animal, his eyes would fill with tears. Even right up until his death, three years later, if he saw one on television, he would turn the set off. It was too painful for him to be reminded of the destruction of his lifetime's endeavour to reintroduce and protect the animals he loved in the country he loved.

***

Shortly after the SADC Tribunal's interim relief order of 13 December 2007 granting us protection from eviction, Peter Chamada and some of his thugs drove into our garden in a Toyota Prado in the middle of the night. He made a fire on the lawn not far from our bedroom. Early in the morning I managed to get out and drove to Mike's house to get Andy's camera from his safe. It was just after dawn when I returned home, with the sun rising behind me. I walked toward Chamada with the camera in full view on my shoulder. We had the same conversation that had happened a thousand times before on a thousand farms, but this one was recorded and was later included in the 2009 documentary film *Mugabe and the White African*.

"Good morning. How are you, Mr Chamada?" I enquired.

"How are you?" he replied.

"What are you doing here?" I asked.

"I'm here for my land," he said.

"Your land?"

"Yes, that you've taken. It was given to me four years ago by the government."

"No, that's not correct. We've been to the SADC Tribunal, as you know."

"Who is SADC? I am SADC," Chamada asserted.

"SADC has given us full relief," I informed him, "until the main case."

"I am SADC," he repeated, "and SADC has the same feelings that I have."

"SADC has said that you can't interfere until after the main case is heard," I told him.

"Is that why you refuse to get out of this farm? Tell me."

"This is my home," I said, with feeling.

"It is your home? Well, you're in the wrong home. Who did you pay? The African or another white fellow?"

"We paid transfer duties to the Zimbabwe government. We bought it on a willing-seller, willing-buyer basis. We didn't steal it."

"Now that's unfortunate, because we realized without land we have nothing," Chamada continued.

I put him right: "You have got land. I've been to your house in Harare."

"So you've been raiding my home also!"

"No, I've just driven past it."

"What were you coming for?"

"I was coming to see where you live," I said simply.

"And do what?"

"Well, if you want to steal my house, maybe you can give me your house?" I said with a smile.

"The land belongs to the black peasants. It belongs to the black poor majority," he insisted.

"And Ministers are the black poor majority?" I asked with irony. "Every time you come, you come in a brand new car. This is a brand new Toyota Prado worth about 50,000 US dollars. Last time it was a brand new white twin cab. Before that it was a Jeep Cherokee."

"How about you?" he butted in, pointing at our utility pickup. I should've panned the camera round to our ancient Ford Laser, which was over twenty years old, and the beaten-up Mazda pickup, which was twelve years old.

"This has nothing to do with our land!" Chamada insisted.

"If you've got all this money, why can't you buy somewhere?" I asked.

"The land belongs to the black peasants," he continued. "Look at you! You are so greedy!"

"I'm so greedy?" I was incredulous.

"You're so greedy!"

"You come to steal my house and my farm and yet you say I'm greedy? I paid for everything, Mr Chamada."

"You paid for it? Where? I can't buy land in the UK," he said, untruthfully. "Everything my father has in London and America is frozen. You've taken it. My father isn't even allowed to go to your country. But you're still here."

"But you can own land in the UK, Mr Chamada. It's only government ministers who are subject to targeted sanctions because of what they've done to this country."

"No, my friend. You take all the land from us, you starve us, you bring sanctions and you want to cripple us so that you can take us over. This country will never be a colony again," he said forcefully. "I will sleep here until you are out. I mean it. I want you out. We are so tired of you guys. You come here. You grab every nice thing away from us – everything nice."

"Mr Chamada, we only own about 2 per cent of the land in Zimbabwe," I said, rather overestimating the amount of land that white people were still living on. "Can't a white person be a Zimbabwean any more?"

"Not any more."

"Why not?"

"Our president told you, crystal clear. He indicated to you that we don't want anything to do with you people. We have nothing to do with you!'

'So a white person can't own a house?" I asked.

"No. We're not happy with you!"

"We can't own any land? Can't do any farming?" I persisted.

"We're not happy with you white fellows, because we've realized your attitude. It's cantankerous. We want to deal with friendlier people – men from China, men from India. Not you. We don't want you any more – get it?"

"But we're Zimbabweans," I said, desperately.

"We don't want you in particular. Just go!"

"Just because we're white, hey?" I asked, sadly.

"I'm not talking to you any more. I am happy and I am telling you the land belongs to us. End of story."

We ignored him after that. He positioned himself on the lawn with his fire, not looking very happy at all. One of his men carved "F*** you Ben" into a tree in the garden. They left after a few hours, but we knew they'd be back.

Sure enough, just over a month later on Sunday 21 January 2008, Chamada was back again, drinking beer and demanding to know why we still hadn't moved out. I told him again that we had relief from SADC. He just laughed at us, then drove off.

The following day our Supreme Court judgment was handed down in Harare. "The application is dismissed," said Justice Mlaba simply. The judgment itself was sixty-one pages long, but we couldn't get a copy immediately afterwards because it wasn't finished. The judges had nailed their colours to the mast: the judiciary and the executive were one and the same. It was the final confirmation that there was no longer any independent justice in Zimbabwe. The Supreme Court clearly believed that they couldn't alter or overturn any decisions made by the president. When the rule of law is overturned, it becomes rule by law.

The *rule of law* refers to a state of constitutionalism where the law (not parliament) is supreme and where all government power is subject to the law. It is the antithesis of authoritarianism, and it provides that individuals' rights may only be interfered with to the extent authorised by law.

Rule by law means the opposite. It refers to a police state in which government invokes the law (indeed creates law) to "justify" excessive use of government force. Detention without trial laws are common examples of these. When a country is under rule by law dictatorship is complete.

About two weeks later, Chamada drove back into our garden and demanded that we leave. He kept shouting and sounding the car horn, keeping the children awake until the early hours. We informed the police but they were unclear about how to deal with our SADC Tribunal relief. An election was coming up, which made things more complicated. If the police didn't uphold the Tribunal ruling, we made it clear they would eventually become accountable. Chamada and his men headed off.

Meanwhile, the local magistrates handed down a judgment stopping Mike's trial until the High Court appeal had taken place. It was a huge relief. I asked for a written copy of the judgment to show to the police and to the invaders when they came to the farm, but there was nobody to type it up. "I'll do it," I offered. "The magistrate can sign and stamp it when he has read it and agrees that I've typed it up correctly."

I felt it was important that I didn't strike up any conversation with the magistrate while I was typing. When he'd signed and stamped the typed judgment and given it back to me, I paused at the door on my way out and said, "God bless you."

171

"This law goes against our conscience," he replied. I knew that apart from a small minority, most people felt the same.

***

On 25 March 2008, four days before the combined Presidential and Parliamentary election, we went back to Windhoek for the final hearing of the main action in the SADC Tribunal case. Seventy-seven more commercial farmers were applying to join themselves to our case, hoping to get the same relief as we had been granted. Prince Machaya, again acting for the Zimbabwe government, said that he didn't object to the Campbell relief continuing, but it couldn't be extended to the other farmers.

The argument went on and on. I remember the Botswana judge asking the crucial question, which went to the heart of the matter: "Are Zimbabwe rights different from the SADC Treaty rights?"

The Zimbabwe government, who asked for more time to look at the other seventy-seven applications, employed delaying tactics. The Tribunal allowed them more time, but granted interim relief to the other farmers who were still on their farms at the time of their applications.

The Campbell case demonstrates the differences between the rule of law and rule by law very well, and this is indeed why Jeremy Gauntlett and Jeffrey Jowell refer frequently to this dichotomy in this context. The land reform programme is a classic example of rule by law. The Government of Zimbabwe invoked the law (its self-serving constitutional amendment) to authorise government excesses. But the SADC Tribunal applied the rule of law, whereby infringements by states with individuals' rights (e.g. expropriation) is only lawful within the constraints of the law (i.e. expropriation in the public interest, for a legitimate reason, and against reasonable compensation). Because of the Government of Zimbabwe's failure to comply with the latter, its conduct was held to be unlawful despite it being facially "authorised" by Zimbabwean law.

CHAPTER 16

It was shortly after this second visit to Windhoek, while Zimbabwe and the world were waiting for the 2008 election results to be announced, that the violence started in earnest.

One night, while Laura and I were away, a vehicle arrived outside Mike and Angela's house. Mike went out to investigate. It was Gift Konjani, a brave MDC campaigner who knew us well. I'd even preached at his church in Chegutu.

Gift could hardly speak because there was so much blood around his mouth. He had other wounded men with him. Mike invited them all in and started to patch them up while Angela made them some food. One of them had a hole in his head that Mike said seemed to go right through to his brain. Another had most of his ear hanging off. Gift had blood pouring from a wound by his nose.

"What happened?" Mike asked, turning the camera on to record as they sat around the yellowwood table in the dining room.

"I received a report that one of our members had been killed, so I went to console the family," Gift explained. "I met a group of militia, and they attacked us. Some of them had stones, which they started to throw at us. It was in full view of the police. Then the police took their rifles and started shooting at us."

Their clothes were soaked in blood. Blood dripped down onto Gift's already saturated shirt as he spoke.

"So what's the plan?" Mike asked.

"We need to go to Harare for some medical treatment."

Mike organized some fuel for them and they headed off into the darkness.

"Thank you so much, Mike. God bless," Gift said.

The pictures that Mike took of Joshua Bakacheza, one of Gift's men, were perhaps the last taken of him alive. He was abducted, tortured, and shot. Gift eventually found his decomposing remains dumped in the bush two weeks after his murder.

Shortly after that there was a large *pungwe* on Chikanka, the resettlement farm less than ten kilometres away from Mount Carmel, where we'd hoped to create a proper resettlement model. A number of the men there were singled out for having been polling agents for the MDC opposition party. In front of a crowd of over 300 people, one man had a heavy rock hurled down onto his leg, smashing the bone into fragments. Afterwards Bruce managed to help to get the man some medical treatment. Nobody was left in any doubt as to what would happen to him or her if they did not support Mugabe.

There were *pungwes* all the time. Our farm workers were forced to attend one at Giant Mine where a Mount Carmel tractor and trailer were commandeered by Major Tauya, who was supervising the *pungwes* in the district. The driver was detailed to collect firewood at night with no lights, causing an accident on the main road involving a bus-load of school children. Fortunately nobody was killed, but one of the farm workers had to have his leg amputated. The *pungwe* went on regardless. Our workers told us that one teenage boy was very severely beaten with sticks for apparently sympathizing with the MDC. He collapsed, toppling forward, with his fist raised to the sky trying to shout ZANU–PF slogans and died in agony some months later.

Gilbert Moyo and his gang were moving around Chegutu district, systematically evicting any remaining white farmers. On 6 May they arrived at the home of our good friends, Bruce and Netty Rogers of Chigwell Extension farm. They were also protected by the SADC Tribunal order.

Netty was out when they arrived. Bruce called her, saying that three thugs had turned up, threatening to kill him if he wasn't gone in two minutes. "They say a mob is coming and if we're still here when they arrive, they'll kill us," he told Netty. "They say they are hungry like lions."

Netty went straight to Chegutu Police Station and saw Assistant Inspector Bepura, who wasn't interested. Bepura is thin and sly. Whenever anything happened on a farm, he would act like a snake, coiling himself around any police officer that wanted to help, then squeezing the man tight until he was unable to do anything. Netty managed to make an official report though, and reminded the police of the SADC protection.

Back on the farm, she and Bruce discussed what to do. They had nowhere else to go and everything they owned was on the farm. They were told that Chief Inspector Gunyani of the Chegutu police had said that a white Datsun pickup army truck was driving into the area to clear the illegal invaders off the land. So Bruce and Netty decided to stay.

A little before dark a white Datsun pickup did arrive, with about fifteen people on it. Bruce and Netty looked at each other. The army had arrived. But they were clearly feeling belligerent. They smashed the lock on the gate, drove into the garden and, within minutes, were smashing all the downstairs windows and the front door.

Bruce and Netty went upstairs with the dogs. Bruce crouched against a wall, keeping an eye on the stairs, his shotgun in his hands, while Netty squatted beside him, hanging onto the phone.

Suddenly, Bruce screamed, "Move! Get out of the way!" Netty responded to the urgency in his voice and sprang back. A split second later, a shot exploded toward them. Pellets whizzed past their heads from a shotgun fired no more than six metres away.

After the shot, things went quiet for a bit. Bruce and Netty phoned the police and some other farmers, who went to the police station on their behalf to try to get help. Eventually Bruce got through to Assistant Inspector Bepura and told him that his door had been broken down and he and Netty were being shot at from inside the house.

"Call back in thirty or forty minutes, as I'm in Kadoma," Bepura said casually. This was clearly a lie: one of the farmers trying to get police to react saw him at the police station at Chegutu at about the same time. When Bruce called back, he didn't answer.

Several shots were fired at the farm workers' houses and Bruce and Netty heard shouting and threats and orders being given. Then the gang came back with the farm workers and their wives and children, who were made to sing *chimurenga* songs and chant the usual hate slogans. It was dark by now, and the noise was overwhelming and continuous. Netty spoke to her friend Kerry Etheredge on the phone: "If we don't get out alive, please tell our children we love them."

One of Bruce's oldest workers, a tractor driver, was forced upstairs and told to take Bruce's shotgun. Bruce refused to relinquish it, believing that help would come eventually. He told the tractor driver that he could stay upstairs with him if he wanted to. The thugs shouted up to the old man, "If you don't come back down, we'll kill your son."

They sent more workers up, using them as a human shield. Bruce and Netty struggled to identify them in the darkness. As each one came up the stairs in the gloom, they let them past to crouch behind them in the dining area. Then Netty glimpsed a man in a white T-shirt creeping up behind a woman farm worker who had a little baby on her back.

"Shall I spray?" she asked Bruce urgently, clutching her mace spray.

There was so much noise that she didn't hear his reply. She knew she didn't have time to ask again. She stood up and pushed the spray button, aiming it directly at the man's face.

There was pandemonium as everyone scrambled for the door, with people pushing and shoving to get out. Everyone upstairs started coughing, their eyes watering. Babies were screaming and women were crying.

The thugs shouted more threats and then broke down the back door. They had already lit fires outside on the lawn and now they threw burning logs into the house, which began to fill with smoke.

Bruce and Netty realized that they would be burned alive if they stayed much longer. They knew they would be locked up if they tried to shoot their way out. They decided to take their chances with the thugs.

"If we come down now, will you let us and our dogs leave in peace?" Bruce shouted down the stairs.

"Yes!" a man replied.

"What's your leader's name?" Bruce asked.

"Moyo!" the voice shouted back.

Bruce and Netty walked slowly down the stairs, with the phone on and their two dogs beside them. It was dark, noisy, confusing, hot, smelly, and very frightening. The logs were still burning on the floor in the centre of the lounge.

Three or four thugs jumped on Bruce. The dogs fled out into the night in terror. It was the last they would ever see of their little Jack Russell. Bruce tried to unload his shotgun in case it was used against him. He couldn't do it, in all the chaos, so he pulled the trigger, emptying several shots into the ground. Then he was hit on the head and fell down unconscious. Netty tried to reach him but she was grabbed around the throat. She was terrified and started screaming.

"Stop screaming or I will f****** kill you right now," yelled one of the thugs into her ear. She was getting more and more desperate as the throttling grip on her throat tightened.

She looked down and saw an arm, which she grabbed. She brought it to her mouth and bit the wrist as hard as she could. After that, someone hit her hard in the head and she lapsed in and out of consciousness. She and Bruce were both kicked and viciously beaten with iron bars and tyre irons. As the blows continued to rain down, Netty wondered how long they'd take to die.

After what seemed like an eternity, she was told to get onto the vehicle, which was about ten metres away. Bruce had disappeared and Netty was worried that he'd been taken away and killed. She was too badly injured to move, so the thugs dragged her by the legs over to the vehicle, then pulled her upright by her hair. To her immense relief she discovered that Bruce was lying tied up on the floor of the vehicle.

The thugs searched Netty, running their hands down her body and inside her clothes, making her feel sickeningly violated. They found her safe key and her car keys and stole one vehicle on the spot, roaring off in it at high speed.

"Then they screamed at us," she told me later. "Their mouths were only millimetres from our faces and their spit flew onto our skin. Their hatred was so great you could almost feel it, and the air was thick with evil. They shouted, 'We are professionals from the Zimbabwe National Army! You are going to die!' They went on and on, but we didn't say anything. Only when they yelled, 'You are British and you have no place in Zimbabwe,' did Bruce finally speak. He had just been groaning but now he said calmly, 'No. My grandfather, my father, myself and my children were all born in Zimbabwe. I am a Zimbabwean.'"

As she and Bruce lay there, Netty heard her captors discussing how they were going to kill them. Should they kill them both immediately, or take one or both of them away and kill them elsewhere, or kill one now and the other later? How should the killing be done? What should they do with the bodies?

"We were both surprisingly calm," Netty told me. "It was as though we'd become resigned to our fate. I remember asking God to give me the courage to die with dignity."

The thugs burned Bruce's feet and ankles with their cigarettes, but he still didn't cry out. He just shifted his feet when the pain became unbearable. He even managed to get one of his hands free and was busy trying to untie his feet when they discovered what he'd done.

Meanwhile the whole farming community was desperately trying to get the Chegutu police to intervene, but it was clear that they were under orders to let the thugs have their way. Bruce's aunt, Sheila, was beside herself with worry. She went to Kadoma Police Station in tears and explained the situation to the sergeant in the charge office. Somehow her tears and prayers got though to him. Amazingly, he took her to see the leader of the "Black Boots". She realized that this man could save Bruce and Netty. Desperate to persuade him to do something, Sheila went up to him and hugged him. "I'm not letting you go until you send your men out," she told him.

It was an act that undoubtedly saved Bruce and Netty's lives. Already they were in a terrible way. They both had multiple fractures and extensive deep tissue bruising, as well as grazing over much of their bodies. Bruce had two broken vertebrae in his back and a broken nose. Both he and Netty had fractured cheek bones. Netty also had a fractured orbital socket, two fractured ribs and a perforated ear drum.

The man who had been trapped in Sheila's bear hug gave orders for the Black Boots to go out to the farm. When they arrived, the place went eerily quiet, Netty said. She heard voices and then one of the thugs yanked her out of the vehicle by her shirt. "This is it. This really is the end," she thought. Silhouetted against the headlights she could make out more armed men, but when she reached them they told her that they were policemen from Kadoma. They asked her what had happened and she gave them an outline of the attack and told them that Bruce was still tied up in the back of the truck.

They told her to go and get something warm from the house, but she refused, as she knew if she went back inside she'd be grabbed and beaten again. So they went with her as she walked unsteadily in. It was quiet now. Flickering light from the fires that had been lit inside the house showed that the place had already been ransacked and looted. Most of Bruce's clothes and shoes had gone and the gun safe was standing open. Five weapons and all the ammunition were missing. Later, while they were in hospital, absolutely everything they had was taken, down to the last teaspoon.

The police didn't ask Moyo or his thugs a single question. Netty and Bruce were taken to Chegutu Police Station, where they tried to make a report. They weren't allowed to. No one in authority would come to see them. Assistant Inspector Bepura was apparently drunk. After waiting for a while in utter frustration, they were taken to hospital, where they had scans and X-rays into the early hours. By the time they were allowed out, their medical records had all disappeared. Back at the police station at Chegutu it was the same story. Despite a full report being handed in, this too had disappeared. There was no trace of the assault, or the attack on their farm or the destruction and looting of their house and workshops. Later, the Chegutu district administrator, Michael Mariga, took the place for himself.

The press got hold of pictures of Netty and Bruce and they were shown all over the world. Things quietened down in the district a little after that but nobody was arrested.

The same day, the Deputy Attorney General, Advocate Prince Machaya, wrote to the SADC Tribunal to request a postponement to the hearing that was due to take place on 28 May. The Tribunal refused, so we went ahead and booked our flights.

***

When we got to Windhoek, we discovered that one of the government lawyers had got together a group of people who had offer letters on various farms. They were trying to claim that their rights would be prejudiced if the Tribunal ruled in our favour. Papers had been submitted the previous day requesting that they should be joined to the proceedings on the government side.

The Tribunal took a fifteen-minute recess and came back to rule that the new papers were not properly submitted and they did not have a material application.

Advocate Prince Machaya then made an oral application to postpone the case. He claimed that the Zimbabwe government had not had the resources or the manpower to complete their papers. One of the reasons he put forward was that they couldn't find all the legal authorities on the internet. Another was that they were busy running an election. He also said that they would have had time to prepare if they hadn't had to travel all the way to Windhoek.

Mike said disgustedly to me, "They have enough resources when it comes to beating up the opposition!" I'd spoken to Laura that morning and she'd told me that a massive campaign of violence had been stepped up against the workers on the farms around us. Many of them had had their limbs broken. And there was certainly no lack of resources or manpower in the size of the government legal team in Windhoek, some of whom had rolled up to court in top-of-the-range black Mercedes.

On our behalf, Jeremy pressed the issue of urgency, pointing out that even farmers who were under the protection of the court were being forcibly evicted. "There is continuing turmoil," he said. "This is about the lives and livelihoods of a lot of people. If the State doesn't have the resources, what about us? They have a university and a law school to help them. We could have assisted them with material. We could have, but we were not asked."

Despite widespread international media coverage over the previous weeks, Machaya claimed that he was not aware of the evictions! He said that the issue of the Tribunal proceedings was meant to be discussed in cabinet the previous day but he hadn't been informed as to the outcome. He stated that the Minister of Justice concurred that there was an obligation on Zimbabwe to comply with orders of the Tribunal.

I was dismayed when the Tribunal judges went along with the government's application for more time to prepare their case. The main hearing was delayed again by almost two months to mid-July 2008. The Judge President said the postponement was "in the interests of justice". The Tribunal was clearly bending over backwards to give the government every opportunity to defend itself.

Mike and I went straight back into mayhem. Our farm workers were forced to attend a ZANU–PF *pungwe* on the next-door farm. All night long we heard the drums and the slogans and the chanting, fiercely denouncing the whites and the British. Everyone was told that they would be shot if they voted the wrong way. They were warned that the next week they would have to attend all-night *pungwes* every single night. We prayed for our workers and none of them was beaten that night.

Workers on other nearby farms didn't escape the violence. Just over the river, two men were beaten with barbed wire for supporting the MDC opposition party. A couple of farms away, farm workers had had their arms and legs broken. Others had had their houses burned down. I spoke to one man who had been to visit his 87-year-old mother close to the Nyamapanda border. "I was stopped at the river," he told me. "Nobody was allowed past the roadblock. I was held there for two days without food or water. Each of us was taken off and interrogated. Four men didn't answer the questions correctly, so they were asked, 'Do you want short sleeve or long sleeve?' The first one said, 'I want short sleeve.' They cut off his whole right arm. The other ones said they wanted long sleeves, so their right hands were cut off so that they couldn't vote." The man winced and closed his eyes. Then he said quietly, "I saw the hands wriggling on the ground!"

Posters sprang up everywhere with pictures of Mugabe and slogans such as "Get Behind the Fist!" and "100% empowerment".

Then we got word of a massive *pungwe* that was due to take place on Mount Carmel. It was called the "Mount Carmel programme", which sounded ominous. That afternoon Mugabe himself arrived unexpectedly in Chegutu. Everyone was told to go and hear him speak. The Mount Carmel *pungwe* was due to start immediately afterwards. Mike and Angela got off the farm, knowing that it was unsafe to stay.

The *pungwe* started just after dark. Everyone who'd been to the rally had to come. I heard tractors and other vehicles going along the road and turning into the pack shed next to Mike and Angela's house. People had been bussed in from miles around. Major Tauya was leading the event. Everyone was checked for cell phones and told that they would be killed if information leaked out about what was being said. They were also told that if they voted for the opposition, it would mean war. The drumming and slogan chanting went on hour after hour, all through the night.

I couldn't sleep, not knowing what was going to happen. As the dawn chorus started, the chanting stopped and a terrible noise broke out, like a massive swarm of bees on the rampage. In the half-light, I went outside. The ground was covered in frost. All the people who were suspected of having sympathy with the MDC opposition party, or who had been the party's polling agents, had been singled out and had cold water poured all over them. I saw Ifoss, the child of one of our farm workers. He had a strained look on his face for one so young. He'd obviously not been able to sleep either. He knew what was happening. "They are beating them now," he said.

Laura's brother Bruce had tried to get the police to come out and stop the *pungwe*, but it was clear that they were under orders not to. I tried to drive off the farm but there was a roadblock at the end of the track manned by some militia. Soon after that the electricity and both the cell phone networks went down. We were totally cut off. We felt very uneasy.

Our other neighbour drove along the main road past the farm on his way to Chegutu and was attacked. Major Tauya's youth placed burning logs on his bonnet and tried to tear him and his girlfriend out of his vehicle. He managed to get away and drove to the police station but still they wouldn't react.

Bruce eventually decided to try to come out himself. He came alone. Nobody would have volunteered to come with him and he didn't expect anyone to. Miraculously, just before he arrived, the roadblock was removed and everyone evaporated. The *veld* was left with no memory of the night's terror except for the marks of over fifty fires by the pack shed.

The next night Netty Rogers called from the Etheredges' farm, where they were staying after their own house was trashed. Gilbert Moyo was causing trouble again, arriving on farms with gangs of men and ordering people out, looting property and intimidating farm workers. I went to try to persuade the Chegutu police to do something, then spent much of an uneasy night at the Etheredges' before Moyo was ordered back to his base camp by the army that was running the election campaign. A couple of nights later they came back and started looting. It was clear that new authority had been obtained and Edna Madzongwe, the President of the Senate, was the beneficiary. The Etheredges had to get out in a hurry at four o'clock in the morning.

We couldn't go onto the farm because there were roadblocks of rocks and felled trees in the way. We parked on the road, as near as we could, and I started filming, but the thugs began stoning us, so I retreated.

Peter Etheredge went over to the other side of the river and filmed Senator Madzongwe's men looting his house. Even then, the police wouldn't budge.

I went back to the police station.

"You must deal with these crimes," I told the officer-in-charge, Chief Inspector Gunyani.

"We do not have transport," Inspector Manyota informed me.

"But Inspector, you can use my transport," I offered.

"We are not allowed to use your transport," he replied.

"So when will you have transport?" I asked.

"Very soon…"

184

We waited for hours in the police car park. When the police vehicle eventually came back, it was immediately used for another task. Meanwhile Chief Inspector Gunyani was in and out of Chegutu all the time on the four-wheel police motorbike.

"What about the motorbike?" I asked. "Can't you send men out on that?"

"Ah no! We cannot fit."

"But it's not far," I said. "What about going in relays?"

"We do not have the manpower."

"But Inspector, you don't need much manpower. All you need is two weapons. How about the policemen at the roadblock? It would only take them half an hour to walk to the farm."

"No. We are busy. Come back later."

It was incredibly frustrating. Several of us spent the best part of a week going back and forth to the police and waiting there for hours at a time while the Etheredges' tractors and other vehicles were being driven off the farm, full of loot, and pneumatic drills were used to go through the walls of the reinforced concrete safes. Meanwhile the Etheredges' farm workers were having a very hard time, being intimidated, threatened, and attacked by the thugs. At the station the police had put up a big banner proclaiming "Zero toleration for pre- and post-election violence in Zimbabwe"

Most of Laura's linen workers from Mount Carmel were made to go to one of the nearby farms, which had been taken by the invaders. Everyone was locked in, inside the security fence. They were made to chant slogans all night. During the first night they weren't allowed to sit down even once. One of the relatives of one of our workers had been a polling agent for the MDC. He was very severely beaten and tied up with barbed wire and put into one of the sheds, close to death. The thugs burned down his mother's house and made her dig a grave for him. Then they paraded a mock coffin made out of cardboard in front of everyone.

I drove back to Chegutu Police Station and spoke to Assistant Inspector Sasa, as all the other officers were out. She is a very large lady, too big to fit into a uniform, so she wears bulbous dresses. I explained the whole desperate situation and pleaded with her to help.

"This man will die if you do nothing," I told her. She sat there like a bullfrog, unmoved and completely opposed to helping in any way whatsoever. I felt washed out, exhausted, impotent, and utterly frustrated. The callousness of the police in the face of so much suffering made me think that they had no feelings at all.

Something inside me suddenly snapped. I couldn't bear it any longer.

I shook my fist at the ceiling and screamed at the top of my voice, "*Pamberi* ZANU–PF! *Pamberi* Robert Mugabe!" Tears rolled down my cheeks. I was surprised at the violence in my voice as it echoed emptily around the police station. I felt somehow estranged from it, as though it wasn't my own.

"I will report you for denigrating the president," said Inspector Sasa calmly.

I got up from my chair with such force that its legs scraped across the concrete floor. She could do what she liked. She could come and arrest me and throw me in the darkest cell she could find. I didn't care. I strode out of the dingy room, past the peeling paint and all the policemen sitting in the charge office, and drove away, in fury and despair.

I tried to pull myself together and think of something to do. I decided to go to Harare to try to persuade some of the observers who were based there to come out to the farms to observe what was going on. I cried when I spoke to them about all the violence. I knew that the injured man would be dead if something didn't happen quickly. And there were hundreds more in the same position across the country.

On my way back to the farm I saw a group of eight vehicles parked at Gadzema, the broken-down mining hamlet six kilometres from our house. All of them were black, with black-tinted windows so that you couldn't see inside. They had no number plates and there was something horribly sinister about them. There was layer of fine red dust over their black paint work and I knew that they must be one of the CIO mobile death squads that had been moving around the communal lands assisting with the intimidation campaign.

Our pastor managed to persuade a group from the Pan African Parliament Election Observer Mission to go out to the farm where Laura's linen workers were trapped. However, when the observers got to the fence the militia wouldn't let them in, despite being shown evidence of their status and being told that President Mugabe had invited them to the country. There was nothing they could do. They were forced to turn back, and the violence continued.

Eventually some policemen from Selous arrived and the injured relative of one of our workers was able to get some medical help. He lived.

In the meantime I managed to contact another group of Pan-African Parliamentarians. They agreed to meet me at Chegutu Police Station. They went straight into Inspector Manyota's office. I followed them, but the inspector promptly told me to get out. I turned around and walked sadly back to my car.

Two minutes later Inspector Manyota ran out. He was a changed man.

"Have you got transport?" he asked.

"Yes, of course."

"I am sending you with the policemen!" he said.

We set off in convoy. On the way there I got a call from Laura. My heart sank as soon as I heard her voice. I knew there was something wrong.

"There's a group of youths, all armed with sticks, surrounding the house," she said. "They want me to come out. It's about the T-shirt."

"I'm coming with the observers, as fast as I can," I reassured her.

I knew the T-shirt would cause a problem. Laura had seen a ZANU–PF T-shirt on our washing line and in a fit of uncontrollable rage, brought on by everything that ZANU–PF were doing to us and our workers, had thrown it in the boiler, telling the linen workers that she didn't want to see such things on her washing line again.

When we got to the Etheredges' place, we saw a heap of mangled furniture beside the main road, covered in winter dust. The observers wanted to take pictures. Laura called again. I could hear the fear in her voice. Our dog, Ginger, had just been beaten with a stick, she said. I was desperate to get over to her.

"Why don't you come to my farm for some tea and we can discuss the whole situation?" I suggested to the observers.

They weren't in any hurry. "Is it safe?" they asked.

I didn't lie to them. I just told them, as reassuringly as possible, that my wife and children were there. I didn't want them to be frightened off. I prayed. Then I said, "My wife has made you a cake. It's only just down the road here."

"All right, we'll follow you," they agreed.

Just after we drove away, the Etheredges were attacked, in full view of the police, who stood by and watched. Apparently they'd "forgotten" to bring the magazines for their rifles. The Etheredges had to make a run for it. They managed to escape with only a few welts on their backs from being hit with sticks.

I drove as fast as I could over to Mount Carmel where Laura and the children were waiting. All was quiet.

"What happened?" I asked Laura.

"They were youngsters whom I didn't recognize," she explained. "They stood at the open gate, shouting, but it was as if they were too afraid to come past it. About two minutes before you arrived they headed off, running like a pack of dogs toward Mum and Dad's. They'll probably come back later."

Laura went inside and came out again with the tea and cake. We sat on the veranda with the observers, enjoying the afternoon sun and the view of the green garden and the beautiful brown African *veld* all around us, as though everything was normal. That was the thing – people who just visited only saw the surface. They didn't see the darkness below. It was as though a shroud covered everything. The surface was calm, but underneath the whole country was trembling and crying in terrible anguish.

After each new atrocity, after each terrifying *pungwe*, I'd see our workers come back in the morning, tight-lipped and silent, going through their days mechanically, with terror written all over their faces. There was no more laughter among the women, just a black, all-consuming fear that made us all heavy with dread at the thought of what might happen next.

We were becoming numb in the face of so much suffering. What could we do? How could we help any of these people? How could we help ourselves? The law, the law enforcement agencies, our judges, our neighbours, our own abilities, the human rights agencies, the international community, and the church – everything that we believed should protect us seemed to have evaporated. All that was left was God.

The Presidential run-off election was scheduled for Friday 27 June, three months after the disputed March election. We could hear the drums at the polling station next door. Everyone knew how to vote – they'd been coached at the *pungwes*. They were lined up in order, in groups of ten, each group with a leader. Each person in each group could be traced back to the number on their ballot paper. They were all told, "If you vote for the opposition, your head will be chopped off." They knew it was true. By the end of the day not a single person had dared vote for Morgan Tsvangirai. Violence had won again.

CHAPTER 17

Two days after the election, at around the time that Mugabe was being sworn back into power as President, his twenty-eighth year in office, the radio sprang to life. Laura and the children and I had had Sunday lunch at home with Mike and Angela, who'd just left.

"Ben! Ben! Ben! This is Bruce."

"Reading you," I replied, leaning over to push in the red button.

"I've just heard that Frank Trott has had his ribs broken and a gun put to his head by Gilbert Moyo, over on Twyford farm. Some of the workers over there heard the gang say they were coming over to 'Campbell's'. They're heavily armed. Over."

"OK, copy that. I'll go and warn Mike and Angela now, over." I knew that their radio was on the blink, so I tried their cell phone, but couldn't get through.

We knew that the looting and violence was being organized against us. A small group of nuns had come to the farm a few days earlier, under the guise of buying seed potatoes, to warn us. They had overheard a conversation that indicated that the Minister of State for Policy Implementation, Webster Shamu, was behind it. We took the information seriously and had previously written to the Commissioner of Police asking for protection.

As I drove around the corner to Mike and Angela's house, I was greeted by two gun men pointing guns straight at my head. A group of thugs had arrived. One of the men holding a gun was wearing a bright shirt with Robert Mugabe's face emblazoned on it. It was Gilbert Moyo.

I ducked down to avoid the bullets and jammed on the brakes, then thrust my truck into reverse. I managed to back around the bend, then, shoving the gear lever forward into first, wheeled around back out the way I came in. I was gaining speed when a large rock smashed through the side window, hitting me on the right-hand side of my head. It was a piece of granite and it broke in half on impact. I went down, dazed, and smashed into a tree, stalling the car.

My head was pouring with blood and I was covered in broken glass. I reached for the keys to restart the truck, but someone grabbed them away from me. Several men leaned into the truck and dragged me out. I couldn't do anything. They were viciously strong, determined, and well trained in violence. They didn't say anything or ask me anything. I was surprised by the strength of their violent attack. I felt like a rag doll in their hands.

My shoes and jersey were ripped off and my shirt was torn open. I was sad about the jersey. It was very warm and had been a gift from my grandmother. Immediately, without any questions, the blows rained down; heavy, vicious blows from the thugs' rifle butts. I tried to protect my head as best I could with my hands. Something sharp was thrust into my right arm near the elbow. Someone kept hitting my back very hard.

After being beaten for some time, I was tied up with a strong green nylon rope they took from my car. I was already very sore all over and my right eye was so swollen that I couldn't see out of it. I was dragged along the driveway, through the dust, until I could make out two shapes lying under the bauhinia trees outside the garage. Mike and Angela.

Mike's head was discoloured and misshapen from being beaten with rifle butts. Blood was soaking into the dust where he lay, coagulating into dark, crusty patches. He was groaning and barely conscious. Angela's head was visibly bruised and she had red marks on her face where she'd been beaten with sticks. Her left arm was badly broken.

None of us could do anything. We just lay there, helpless in the dust, lapsing in and out of consciousness, at the mercy of Mugabe's thugs. I heard lots of shooting and I could see them carrying loot out of Mike and Angela's house and piling it into their vehicles.

I knew that one of the vehicles that Moyo was using had belonged to Kobus Joubert. The DISPOL (police officer commanding the district) had been out to his farm, about ten kilometres away, while Moyo was looting and killing some of his animals. Although she had stopped him from looting further, she had allowed him to take Kobus's vehicle. More recently Kobus, who was still on his farm, was shot dead in his bed one night.

I learned later what had happened to Mike and Angela. After having Sunday lunch with us, they'd gone to find a calf that had been separated from its mother. They'd managed to catch it and had got it on the back of the Land Cruiser. Mike wasn't happy with the look of its mother's teats, so Angela was just driving off with some milk in a bottle to feed the calf when Moyo and his gang had torn up the driveway in a lightning attack.

Jonah Zindoga, the squatter from the neighbouring farm who had been poaching our game and had beaten up Mike six months earlier, breaking several of his ribs, had been bicycling up and down the road. He was obviously keeping a look-out. His brother, Simberashe, was one of the leaders of Moyo's gang.

The gang arrived just as Mike was trying to call Bruce on his cell. When he heard the vehicles, Mike came out to see who it was. He was attacked immediately. They grabbed him and started beating him brutally with sticks and rifle butts.

Angela, who was in the Land Cruiser, saw what was happening and leaped out, running straight toward the thugs, shouting, "Stop!" They had about fourteen guns between them at that stage but Angela charged them single-handedly, with no weapon herself.

They grabbed her violently, breaking her left arm in several places and beating her with sticks. They tore big chunks of her hair out and beat the bare patches on her scalp. One of the thugs urinated on her head. Then they tied her to Mike with a thick blue nylon rope, which they took from the workshop.

Just after I'd left the house, Kelly, one of Mike and Angela's dogs, had arrived, panting and in distress. Kelly had never come to our house of her own accord before and Laura immediately realized that she'd come to ask for help. So she called Bruce. Bruce arrived on the main road while we were all lying tied up and injured on the driveway. He realized that something was dramatically wrong when he saw my vehicle skewed across the driveway with all its wheels shot out.

Bruce didn't know what to do – he was all by himself. He parked on the driveway and came into the garden on foot to try to assess whether or not we were still alive. He kept the phone line to Laura open. "Shall I shoot into the air?" he asked her.

"Yes!" she said. He fired some shots into the garden and this panicked the thugs, who fired volleys of shots back. I believe they thought that he had several people with him. Bruce retreated to his car to try to make some phone calls and get the police to do something.

The gang finished taking all the weapons and valuables from Mike's safe, then picked up Mike and me and dumped us on the floor of Mike's station wagon. Angela was put on the back seat, flanked by two men with rifles sticking out of the windows. They drove out, straight past Bruce's vehicle, as though they didn't see it. Bruce was lying concealed in the grass a few metres away. They eventually saw him and started running towards him. He fired some shots in the air and with that all hell broke loose. He got into his car while they fired several volleys of shots at him but he managed to drive past Mike and Angela's house. He looped round back to our house where Laura and the children were. Grace, who was soon to become Bruce's fiancée, had arrived there too with Megan, Bruce's daughter. Bruce advised them not to go onto the main road where the shooting was still going on. They must get out through the northern boundary.

Meanwhile Mike, Angela, and I were taken to the Bronkhorsts' farm just down the road. All I could see from where I was lying were telegraph poles and the tops of trees. I desperately tried to see where they were taking us but it was impossible to really know.

It was painful bumping along the rough roads. My head was banging on the floor and I couldn't do anything about it because I was tied up. Mike and I were like two bags of maize bouncing around as the truck careered along at high speed. I didn't know it then, but I had a twelve-centimetre skull fracture as well as broken ribs. Mike's injuries were worse, though, and all I could hear from him was constant groaning.

Bruce had come back out onto the main road to try to tail us. Our captors started chasing him, travelling at speeds up to 150 kilometres an hour, Bruce said later. The thugs had more than twenty guns between them, and they kept firing them out of the windows as they screamed along, peppering Bruce's vehicle with bullet holes. They even shot at passing traffic.

At one point they set off down the old strip road near Stockdale farm. Bruce stopped to try to make some phone calls. He was on the phone to Bruce Rogers, who was telling him to watch out for an ambush, when a bullet whistled through his open side window, missing his head by inches. A second bullet was deflected off the perspex. The gang had stopped around the corner and had come back on foot with their rifles. Bruce drove off.

A number of people from the community went to the police station to try to get help, informing them that we'd been beaten and abducted and that Mike and Angela's house had been looted. Even though the election was now over, the police didn't respond. We even drove past a police vehicle, which was crawling along the road in the opposite direction. The guns were bristling out of the windows of our vehicle but the police did nothing. It's a quiet stretch of road with no more than five or ten cars an hour. It was obvious that the police were monitoring and directing the whole show.

Laura and the children heard the shooting and after Bruce told them to get out of our house, she loaded the dogs and a few possessions into the Ford Laser while Grace drove her car with the children in it. The Laser, at over twenty years old, is low to the ground. It was never designed for dirt tracks in the bush, but it was evident from all the shooting that Laura had to go out through the bush on the northern boundary rather than risk being shot at on the main road.

Megan started crying.

"You mustn't cry, you must pray," Grace told her. The children prayed and Megs stopped crying.

When they got to the northern fence, neither Grace nor Laura had wire cutters. It's a tall game fence that Bruce had put up to try to protect the wildlife before it was all poached away. Laura said a prayer, and out of the bush walked a man with a dog. "The man had a lovely face," she told me later, "and the dog looked healthy and well fed." This was very unusual in a land where even the people are hungry. Laura had never seen the man before, and has never seen him or his dog since.

Laura briefly explained the situation to him. Without a word he pulled some wire cutters out of his back pocket and walked over to the fence. He cut through it and opened it out. As she and Grace drove through he told them which tracks to take. They got to the police station without further incident.

At the police station she explained the situation. "My brother is being shot at. My parents and husband have been badly beaten and they've been abducted." One of the policewomen started laughing at her. Laura made to go around the counter and give the women a slap but she was restrained by some of the other people in the community who were there on our behalf.

Mike, Angela and I were still trussed up in the back of the car. Hours went past and it got dark. We eventually ended up deep in the bush at a large militia camp located near the Pickstone Mine on the road to the Ngezi Dam. The thugs hauled us out of the vehicle, dumped us on the ground, and poured buckets of cold water over us. This was the standard treatment meted out at the *pungwes* to anyone who hadn't shown enough support for the ruling ZANU–PF party. Often people were forcibly baptized in the names of the spirit mediums of the First *Chimurenga* and were made to roll in the dust while they were beaten with sticks.

The gang sang anti-white *chimurenga* songs and waved their guns over us. They kept talking about killing us. Then I was picked up by my belt and the bare soles of my feet were violently beaten. Each blow convulsed my whole body as I swung there. In the light from the camp fires I could see my tormentor raise his *sjambok* high over his head with both arms before bringing it down on the soles of my feet, again and again.

Angela was allowed to sit by one of the fires. It was a frosty night and we were shivering, having had cold water poured over us. Fortunately Mike was still wearing the woollen sports jacket he'd put on for church that morning.

The thugs were passing round a joint of *dagga* and they offered some to Angela to have a drag. She refused. They then wanted to take the rings off her fingers, but her fingers had swollen and the rings wouldn't come off. Someone said, "Chop off her fingers." Another man went off to get a *panga*. "You don't need to chop them off, just use soap," Angela told them. They pulled all her rings off and took them away.

Next they ordered Angela to sing a *chimurenga* song. She refused but they insisted, so she started singing the first thing that came into her head, "If you go down to the woods today, you're in for a big surprise!" The "Teddy Bears' Picnic". One man grabbed a stick from the fire and thrust the burning end down her throat. Fortunately another man restrained him so the burns were less severe than they might have been.

Mike had been rolled onto his back so he was staring up at a sea of threatening faces, with darkness all around. At one point he regained consciousness. "Give me back my watch," he shouted defiantly. Laura had saved up and given him the watch when she was a teenager. It had been on his wrist ever since. Then he lapsed into unconsciousness again.

I was left tied up face down in the dirt. I plucked away at the knots for a while and eventually managed to untie myself. There was no moon and it was a very dark night. I thought I could probably get away without being shot if I made my break quickly and disappeared into the bush. Then I thought about Mike and Angela. When the thugs realized that I'd escaped, they would almost certainly shoot them. I decided against making a run for it. A little later they discovered that I'd untied myself and so they tied me up again, but this time much tighter. Soon I couldn't feel my hands at all. The nerves got damaged in my left hand and I get a strange tingling sensation there to this day.

By then a huge number of people were praying for us. Miraculously, fear did not enter my head at all. I wasn't afraid of death in the slightest. I knew that I was probably going to die, but I made my peace with God. I said to him, "If I'm going to die and go to be with you today, I am ready. But if you've still got work for me to do here, I'm ready for that too." I was given a total peace about whatever was to happen.

At one point Angela felt abandoned by God when she thought that Mike and I were probably going to die. She felt prompted to "look upwards". As she did so, and saw the stars burning down from high above, a sense of God's presence flooded through her. She had an assurance that God was in control and that somehow things were going to be OK.

Months later, Giftmore, a messenger at the CFU with whom I'd maintained contact, told me that when he heard of our abduction, the image of Shadrach, Meshach, and Abednego in the fiery furnace had immediately come into his mind. Because of this, he said he knew God would protect us.

The thugs really laid into me again, beating my feet savagely with the *sjambok*. With every blow that landed I cried out, "Jesus!" "Jesus!" "Jesus!" Over and over again.

It was then that the miracle happened. It's one of the most significant things that has ever happened to me. The hardest words Jesus ever said were, "Love your enemies." I knew it was right, but I'd found it impossible to love the people who were doing these things to us and our friends and workers.

When they left off their beating, and as I was lying in the dust again, it was almost as though those words of Jesus from the Sermon on the Mount hit me physically. "Love your enemies," and "bless those who curse you." Suddenly I felt a love for the people who were doing these things to us. No hatred or anger or bitterness came near my heart. This wasn't natural – it had to be supernatural.

I saw a leg right in front of my face and I knew what I had to do. I managed to reach out and touch it and said, "May the Lord Jesus bless you." I saw another and I reached out again, saying, "May the Lord Jesus bless you," and another, and another.

It was an incredible experience. In my physical captivity I felt totally free. I had a real compassion for those youngsters. Most of them at the camp were young teenagers, taken away from their parents and their schools, and indoctrinated into violence at the ZANU–PF re-education camps. I knew that they were lost souls, needing love and the forgiveness that only Jesus can bring when people repent.

At the same time that this miracle was happening, Laura, who didn't know whether any of us was still alive or not, read a Bible passage from 2 Chronicles 20, about what the Israelites did when they faced a vast, destructive army. God told them, "Do not be afraid or discouraged… stand firm." The story goes on to say that the Israelites began to praise God, despite the enormous calamity that appeared to be about to unfold. When they started to worship God, the army that was invading Israel turned on itself and destroyed itself. Laura began to praise God. She was confident that he was in control.

The thugs wanted us to withdraw from the SADC Tribunal proceedings. They put a gun to Angela's head and made her sign a document pledging that we wouldn't continue with SADC. They also made her sign a piece of paper giving them the car for three months. Mike was still unconscious most of the time. I could see now that one of the fingers of his right hand was grotesquely swollen and sticking out at a horrible angle.

We were loaded back into the vehicle and bumped along a dirt track for another thirty kilometres or so. I thought we were probably being taken to a quiet place to be shot. Mike and I were covered by a blanket and Angela had been blindfolded. I still had a tremendous sense of peace in my heart. I wasn't afraid of what the gang could do to me.

At about midnight we were untied and dumped in the dirt by the roadside. As the thugs left, one man said, "We're sorry for what we've done." Mike and Angela couldn't walk. I knew we had to get help urgently. I saw a light from a house not far away and stumbled toward it. I climbed through a hedge and knocked on the door. When the occupants came out and saw me, they were clearly afraid, but they let me use their phone. The concussion subsided and my head was suddenly clear. I could remember telephone numbers again. I reached Laura on the first call. I asked the residents to explain to her where we were so that she could come and fetch us. It turned out that we'd been left between two churches in Kadoma.

CHAPTER 18

The whole community had been trying everything they could to get the police to react. No one from the Chegutu, Kadoma, or Selous Police Stations would move a muscle to go to Moyo's base camp near Pickstone Mine. After hours of trying, Dirk Visagie and Dana Nel decided to go there themselves. Everyone knew that was where we would be taken. Just before Dirk and Dana reached the dead zone close to the camp, where there was no cell phone signal, Laura managed to get through to them with the news that we'd been found. They turned around and came back to Chegutu.

When I think of it now, I want to cry. Those two men, and Bruce, should get medals for their courage. They went unarmed to try to persuade those violent thugs to release us. They were willing to go to a notorious base camp where everyone knew that people were regularly being tortured. They knew that there was a strong probability that terrible things might happen to them there too – and yet they went. There is no virtue that is more admirable than the courage to go into a life-threatening situation to help people who are in mortal danger.

When Laura, Bruce, and my sister-in-law Cath and her husband Alex arrived at the place where we'd been dumped, Laura didn't recognize her dad. Mike was barely alive and was being supported between two people, his head hanging down. He had broken bones all over his body and his face was grotesquely misshapen and black from the bruising. Laura said that we smelt terrible – of blood and sweat and urine – and she wanted to vomit. She and Bruce put us into the car with the heater turned on full blast, because we were all very cold.

On the way to the hospital we were stopped by the police at a roadblock only a few hundred metres from where we'd been dumped. Moyo, in his stolen vehicle with his stolen guns, had gone though the same roadblock a little earlier without hindrance, despite the police knowing full well what was going on. The police wanted to know why Bruce had beaten-up people in his car. He explained that he needed to get us to the hospital quickly. They wanted to delay him further and started to be difficult. Bruce floored the accelerator and drove on through.

At Chegutu hospital half the community was waiting for us. It was such a heart-warming sight that it's stuck in my mind more than anything else. We were given warm, dry clothes. Heidi Visagie took pictures of us for record and legal purposes. I was shocked when I saw the photographs a few weeks later. I had no idea that we looked so terrible. Although there were no drips in the hospital, one was found by Maureen Taylor in the community before Mike's veins collapsed completely. Another hour and he would have died. Once we'd all been stabilized, we were taken by ambulance to the Avenues Clinic in Harare. But one of the nursing sisters, who was obviously CIO, wanted us to be taken elsewhere so that everything could be hushed up and we could quietly disappear. We decided that the Avenues was not a good place to remain, so the ambulance took us to Dandaro Clinic instead.

It was a desperate place, crammed with the victims of Mugabe's violence. There was no money and breakfast was sometimes just *mealie-meal* porridge, with no salt or milk or sugar. Laura visited some of the other patients and tried to encourage and help them. One man she got to know had had his arms tied behind his back with barbed wire. The ZANU–PF thugs had then smashed a rock down on his hands so that all his fingers and other bones were crushed into fragments. His legs had been smashed too. Two months after the attack he could still do nothing with his hands, nor could he walk. In all that time he hadn't had a single visitor, because his family didn't know where he was. He didn't know if they were still alive. Even so, the people in hospital were the lucky ones. Most of the victims in the rural areas were unable to get any proper medical help.

For me, the next few weeks were a bit of a blur. I couldn't eat anything for nearly the whole of the first week because of the pressure on my brain as a result of my head injuries. Whenever I tried to eat, I vomited. I got thin very quickly. Once the internal bleeding stopped, Mr Auchterlonie came to operate on me. He was about eighty years old but still had a steady hand and a very sharp mind. He cut a two-inch-diameter hole in my skull and released the pressure.

When I woke up, the first question I apparently asked Laura was, "What's the exchange rate now?" It was a constant concern, as the currency was in freefall, devaluing by hundreds of per cent in a day. The hundred trillion dollar note was shortly to come out – the largest denomination note in history. Within a few weeks it would be valueless again though. The next thing I wanted to know was whether I'd be well enough to attend the SADC Tribunal hearing, which was due to take place in eleven days' time. Mr Auchterlonie said there would be no way, but by God's grace I healed quickly and was discharged from hospital just in time.

The first thing I did was go down to the farm to see our workers. They were so excited to see me alive and on the mend. I felt the tears welling up because I was so moved by their reactions.

Mike was still flat on his back most of the time and was too badly injured to be released from hospital, let alone make the journey to Windhoek for the Tribunal. He made a statement from his hospital bed, lying there in pain and struggling to get the words out.

"It seems that if you go against Mugabe, then they pull out all the stops and try to get you, but I'm afraid that's not going to work too well because we are still going to go against Mugabe," he said. "The fact that they came out and hammered us has made us more determined to carry on with the case. The fact that they asked Angela to sign a piece of paper which said we wouldn't continue just shows that the thorn is quite deep in the flesh. We will continue at all costs.

I should be dead by now if they had their way," he continued, "but we don't always let them have their way."

I was still in a wheelchair when I went to Windhoek. Dad came over from England and met up with me at the airport. It was an emotional reunion. He and Mum have been so incredibly supportive in so many ways.

On the morning of 15 July 2008, before we went to court, we prayed together. I read from Proverbs 29, which says, "Fear of man will prove to be a snare, but whoever trusts in the Lord is kept safe. Many seek an audience with a ruler but it is from the Lord that man gets justice."

I prayed for the five judges who had flown in to hear our case. I prayed that they would fear God and not men. I prayed that they would understand that it is God's law, and his ways, that are so badly needed in Zimbabwe. I prayed that they would have clear vision, clear minds and strong hearts. And I asked God to confound the ways of wicked men who wanted to pervert justice, and who wanted the stealing and killing and destruction to continue.

Before the case got underway, there was another ploy to delay it still further. Gerald Mlotshwa, a young ZANU–PF lawyer, tabled an application to join 346 other people to our case, claiming that they might be adversely affected by the outcome.

Apparently the Judge President asked Mr Mlotshwa if he could read, saying that the order sheet was set and he couldn't spring a new application just before a hearing started. Due process must be followed. Mlotshwa swore and left the chambers.

When we were all in court, ready to start, the Judge President said he wanted to get into the main case straight away. For a moment Jeremy Gauntlett, our advocate, was lost for words, but within a few seconds he'd rearranged his thoughts and his papers and had launched the argument of the main case. He stuck to the fundamental principles of law, starting by saying that Article 1V of the SADC Treaty guaranteed human rights, democracy, and the rule of law in the SADC signatory countries. He submitted that it was open to the state to distribute land, but the distribution needed to be done according to the rule of law. The Supreme Court of Zimbabwe had tried to maintain that domestic law was more important than international law, but once a country is signed up to an international treaty, that country is thereafter subject to international law. He called the Zimbabwe government's argument that the treaty was just a guideline for economic integration "a cynical, morally bankrupt argument", adding that, "If one thing is to be learned, it is that you cannot have development without the rule of law."

Jeremy then launched into his first major attack on Amendment 17 to the constitution, which denied us access to the courts. He called this law the "most crass measure" he'd ever come across in thirty-two years of legal experience, then went on to attack Justice Mlaba's judgment in the Zimbabwe Supreme Court, which had held that parliament could do as it wished.

Finally, Jeremy introduced the discrimination issue, pointing out that the taking of land only affected white farmers. There was never any question of farmers who were incompetent, or farmers who were bad employers, being removed from their land. The only characteristic shared by the dispossessed farmers was that they were white. He also addressed the fact that there was discrimination in the giving out of the land in that the recipients of the reallocated land were politically appointed.

To close, Adrian de Bourbon argued the compensation issue. It was very simple: in all international and human rights law, compensation was a necessary ingredient to taking of property.

Advocate Prince Machaya, the Deputy Attorney General, argued on behalf of the Zimbabwe government. He said that the SADC Treaty merely outlined the framework and the context of human rights and wasn't legally binding. He stated that Amendment 17 had been brought in because the Land Acquisition Act was impractical. Zimbabwe was a sovereign power in which property rights could be infringed in the public interest in order to redress colonial imbalances. If that was what parliament intended, it had the sovereign right to go ahead and legislate accordingly. He denied any "ethnic cleansing" of white farmers but was unable to give any reasons to show why that wasn't what was happening. He didn't try to deny that the land had been given to the ZANU–PF *chefs*.

Jeremy fired back, noting that Article 6 (1) of the SADC Treaty stated that the principles and objectives of the treaty were binding provisions, and commenting that we weren't in court for a public debate on politics.

We came back on the second day for the urgent application regarding the Zimbabwe government's refusal to protect us and our workers. There was a noticeable tension in the courtroom.

Jeremy started, "There are four questions…."

He was interrupted by Advocate Machaya, who said, "The allegations should be before the main case… why is it necessary to hear the case?"

The Judge President responded, "We are masters of our own proceedings. This case is listed. I can't see a problem… this case must proceed this day and this moment."

"May I proceed?" Jeremy asked.

"I would like to ask indulgence for a postponement of one hour to talk to the government of Zimbabwe," Machaya persisted.

Jeremy jumped in, "The application was put in thirty days ago. Full notice was received. My learned friend had every opportunity to object. It was the understanding yesterday that it would be heard at 9:30 a.m. today."

"What difference will one hour make?" commented the Judge President. "The listing was a long time ago. The respondent's delaying process is now normal behaviour in this court." He adjourned the proceedings until 10:30 a.m.

When the government team came back in, the atmosphere was very tense.

"I have received instructions that the government of Zimbabwe takes this application very seriously," Machaya said. "There have been developments in Zimbabwe and we want to file additional evidence. I will not make submissions until I have got evidence. I want to be excused from the proceedings."

We were staring disaster in the face. Jeremy responded, "The application was properly enrolled. It complied with the rules. The thirty-day notice was given. Article 32 (5) of the protocol says that any failure of a state to comply must be reported to the summit for its decision. We no longer have the human or financial resources to carry on from hearing to hearing. The Tribunal's task is to build a house of justice. Zimbabwe means 'house of stone'."

The Judge President was adamant. "This case has been properly filed. The court will deal with the facts before it. There is no reason to postpone." He had a quiet voice and a Portuguese accent but he was very clear. "We are building a house of justice in this region," he added.

Unbeknown to Jeremy or the Judge President this fitted in with the Bible passage that Dad had read out to us early that morning from Psalm 127: "Unless the Lord builds the house, its builders labour in vain."

While the Judge President was still speaking, the Zimbabwe government representatives were standing up and putting away their papers. They filed out to the front and then, before the eyes of the whole court, marched across the centre of this "house of justice" and out and away. Advocate Machaya was the last to leave. I was sitting in my wheelchair at the end of a row. I reached into my pocket and pulled out a little booklet of Bible readings entitled *Daily Strength*. I gave it to him as he passed, knowing that if he continued to go along with justice the Mugabe way, at some stage he would need it.

It was extraordinary behaviour by the government's legal team. I've never heard of another case in any international court anywhere in the world where the respondents have staged a walk-out.

Undaunted, Jeremy pressed on: "My clients have done nothing more wicked than coming to you. I have never before come across a case where the litigants have had violations committed against them on account of their going to court. The internal law of Zimbabwe appears to permit it to ride roughshod over international legal obligations." He cited some of the many instances of the police refusing to attend life-threatening situations because they were "political" and mentioned the eviction orders sanctioned by magistrates despite Tribunal protection. He spoke eloquently about the lawless evictions by thugs of farmer after farmer, despite Tribunal protection. He drew attention to official army involvement in the evictions and the incriminating silence of the Zimbabwe government. He mentioned Deputy Attorney General Johannes Tomana's letter saying that, "Provisional orders cannot suspend prosecutions."

Finally Jeremy described our torture and the "sinister perversion of justice to try to suppress litigation". His colleague, Elize Angula, one of our wonderful Namibian lawyers, held up the pictures of Mike, Angela, and me that Heidi had taken after we'd been attacked. Until that day I hadn't seen what we'd looked like after our beatings and it was a shock to see what a state we were all in. The judges shrank back visibly when they saw the distressing images.

After Jeremy had finished, all we could do was go home and wait for the judgment. In the plane on the way back, Dave Drury found himself sitting next to Mlotshwa. Mlotshwa complained to the South African Airways stewardess, "How could you put me next to my sworn enemy?"

It was dark in Harare Airport when we landed, and I was straggling behind the others, out of my wheelchair. Three men came up and flanked me, wanting to take me down to the deserted lower car park for questioning. I called out to Dave Drury, who came to my rescue. Mlotshwa tried to threaten him, but, raising his voice for everyone to hear, Dave said, "Don't you try to intimidate me, Gerald!"

We got into the car and sped away home.

CHAPTER 19

There was huge international pressure following the attacks on us and following the contempt of the government for the SADC Tribunal. It resulted in some moves toward justice.

Thanks to some private investigators and the tracking system in Mike's car, Gilbert Moyo was found crouching in a cupboard holding a gun, not unlike the discovery of Saddam Hussein in 2003. Moyo and various members of his gang were arrested for a while, although none of them have ever been brought to trial. Some of the weapons stolen from different farmers across the region were recovered, as well as some of the loot: stoves, fridges, furniture, tractors, and other vehicles.

We went back to our houses and started trying to pick up the pieces of our lives. Journalists from around the world wanted to come and see us. Those of us still on our farms had become a very rare breed indeed, and we were even rarer because we were prepared to countenance committing the crime of speaking to journalists.

Richard Mills was an Irish award-winning war photographer and he had been moving around the district taking pictures of broken farmers and farm workers, recording the absolute carnage that had been created over the previous months. After lunch with us, he played rugby with the children in our garden. As he was undercover, he then headed up to Harare to a safe house. In the morning he was found hanging dead in his room.

Whether it was foul play or suicide I don't know. While he was on the farm with us there was no way he seemed suicidal, but perhaps the culmination of seeing so many utterly hopeless situations had produced a similar hopelessness in him too.

We eventually got a date of 28 November for the Tribunal judgment.

A great many people wanted to come with us to Windhoek to hear it. So much hinged on the outcome. If we lost, we knew that there would be no future for any of us. If we won, and had people with a strong moral voice behind us, there was the promise of a new era in the history of southern Africa.

We organized a bus but the government refused to grant a temporary export permit. So everyone had to pile into cars or get on the plane. It was now five months since the attack on Mike, Angela, and me, and Mike was still very weak.

Driving into Windhoek, I noticed a rivulet that was just beginning to flow down a dry river bed. I'd never seen that before. There was no dramatic wall of water, just a rounded front of liquid sliding down over the sand and quenching the parched ground. It appeared symbolic.

On the night before judgment day I couldn't sleep. At three o'clock in the morning I realized that Peter Etheredge, in the bed next to mine at the Klein Windhoek guesthouse where we were staying, was awake too, so we got up and had some tea. It was raining hard outside – beautiful strong African rain that just poured and poured. There was a dry river bed right beside the guest house, which only flowed every few years. Peter went out in the rain and came back exclaiming, "Come and look at this!" I went out and saw that the river had started to flow in a great, rushing torrent, running right across the road. Windhoek had a quarter of its annual rainfall in the hours before the judgment was handed down. Elize Angula said it was a sign from God.

Dave Drury had left his shoes outside on the open veranda and they were brimming with water when he came to put them on. He told me that he had said a little prayer for his feet before slipping them in and squelching off to hear the judgment.

I was pleased that the judgment was to be handed down in the SADC Tribunal building itself. When we had first gone to the

Tribunal, nearly a year before, it was a burned out ruin. Now it was ready for business again.

We got there early and took our seats at the front on the left-hand side. Chris Jarrett, who had had to borrow some trousers the previous time because, as he put it, Mugabe had stolen his trousers along with everything else, had accidentally left his borrowed trousers behind in Zimbabwe. He rushed off to buy a new pair but he's a very large man and the biggest size he could find wouldn't pull above his knees. Fortunately the judges were a bit late arriving so Chris had more time to scour the town. He walked into court with the bottoms of his new trousers rolled up so they wouldn't get wet in the puddles, beaming all over his face. He was very pleased to be there and was confident that Mugabe's land grab programme would be smashed to smithereens.

Justice Mondlane started to read the judgment. I felt sick. It was nerves. We had a tremendous responsibility. If the judgment went against us, we'd all be out in the cold. It would be the end. The last few whites would be thrown out and Zimbabwe would descend further into hunger and economic ruin. After the judge had been reading for about an hour, all I wanted to do was go to the back of the court and vomit. I concentrated on not being sick.

It was a very detailed judgment, citing all sorts of international treaties and human rights law. Gradually it became apparent that it was all coming together. Toward the end, each point we won felt like a physical blow of the hammer on the desk and my head started reeling.

The first point, the sovereignty issue, was the most significant. The Tribunal held that Mugabe could no longer misrule Zimbabwe as he willed. The democratic process could not extinguish fundamental rights, even if the people had apparently elected the Members of Parliament who had brought in the unjust laws. Dictatorship was out. Tyranny had to flee. There were standards of governance and human rights that must be adhered to.

My nausea finally vanished when we won the racial discrimination argument. For half a century white people in Africa had been forced out just because their skin was the wrong colour. They hadn't tried to fight it. No one would have listened to them if they had. They had simply left, often with nothing but a suitcase. In Zimbabwe, only a fraction of 1 per cent of the population was now white. In many other African countries, there were almost no white people any more. At last, we'd been given some hope. As white people we had been given the legal right to remain in our homes, in our little places under the sun. An international African court had decreed it. White people could be African too. We could no longer be discriminated against just because of the colour of our skin.

When the judges filed out, I didn't know what to say. I shook Mike's hand. A wave of emotion swept through the courtroom. Before I knew what was happening, Deon Theron, who had been appointed vice president of the Commercial Farmers' Union, was in my arms and we were both sobbing. Then I was in Elize Angula's arms and there were tears streaming down her black cheeks.

"I am so happy," she said. "You have won on all counts! This is an important day for Africa. There is hope for justice in Africa. I am so happy!"

"You don't have to give up law now," I said, for this is what she'd threatened to do if we had lost. She'd said that if the judgment went against us, there could be no future for human rights or the rule of law in southern Africa.

Even some of the press, hardened to so much on the African continent, had tears in their eyes, as did many of the diplomatic corps. The British Ambassador's eyes were wet. It was a significant moment. Something huge had just happened.

Mike's hearing was much impaired as a result of the beating and he hadn't heard a word, so he was rather bemused to see everyone crying. He wasn't sure exactly what we'd won and what we'd lost. In the end the only thing that we didn't get was costs, and that was a split judgment.

Josephat Tshuma, President of the Law Society of Zimbabwe, summed it up well during the press briefing we held afterwards. He said, "Governments come and go but justice doesn't go. The Tribunal has given us hope. There is an alternative to chaos."

The Zimbabwe government had conceded defeat before the judgment was even read. They knew that they couldn't win. Mutasa had already accused the judges of taking bribes and he was reported as saying that the government would disregard the judgment and would accelerate the land reform programme instead. He dismissed the call to protect farmers.

When we got back home, we met with the legal fraternity and the farming leadership from all the different factions. Suddenly there was a new sense of oneness of purpose and policy. The judgment had set things out for us all in clear, unequivocal terms.

It didn't last long. At his birthday rally on 28 February 2009, President Mugabe was back on the warpath. "Land distribution will continue," he said. "It will not stop. The few remaining white farmers should vacate their farms, as they have no place there. Our land issues are not subject to the SADC Tribunal." He described the ruling as "nonsense" and "of no consequence".

Within a short time the violence was back in full swing.

Angela was outside one evening when she looked up and saw an amazing sight. It was a cloud in the shape of a hand and it was very clear. The fingers were all there. The joints were there. The palm was cupped directly over her head. Angela felt certain that it was God's hand over us, protecting us – a prophetic vision in the light of what was about to be unleashed.

Peter Chamada tried to get an eviction order against us from the magistrates' court. When this failed, I believe Minister Shamuyarira fired him; he was replaced with a man called "Landmine". Landmine was a different character altogether. He had the strutting arrogance of a bantam cock and a peculiarly frightening voice. It was obvious from the start that he was high up in the CIO and had full authority to be as violent as he liked.

We first met him one April morning in 2009 at the beginning of the main Mount Carmel mango harvesting season. He roared up in Mr Shamuyarira's maroon Prado and marched straight in through Mike's kitchen door with a gang of thugs. Bruce was there, busy packing mangoes for a thirty-ton refrigerated lorry that was due to arrive from South Africa that afternoon. Landmine demanded that he get out immediately.

"Who are you?" Bruce asked.

"I am Landmine Shamuyarira," came the reply.

The farm workers had recognized the Prado and immediately realized what was going on. They all came straight to the house and demanded that Landmine should leave. It was a totally spontaneous action: they'd all seen enough of farm invasions and they knew from what they had seen on all the looted farms in the area that they'd have no future if Shamuyarira took over.

Landmine and his gang were outnumbered. He beat a tactical retreat and drove off spitting threats, leaving about ten thugs behind. I went to police to try to get a reaction but it was like talking to a brick wall.

The farm workers' blood was up. There was an exchange of words and while Bruce was in the office, the remaining thugs had been loaded onto a couple of vehicles and driven off the property. The workers took them to a proper resettlement area to the north-west where the government had bought farms in the 1980s. They left the thugs there and came back. I was extremely impressed with the workers' expression of loyalty, but there was a knot of unease in my stomach. I knew that when the workers started to help us, the state machinery would come down very hard on us all.

That afternoon the police came out in Senator Muduvuri's lorry, about twelve of them in riot gear and armed with automatic assault rifles. Laura was out in the car with the children when she saw the lorry turning down the dirt road near Gadzema. She knew that they must be on their way to Mount Carmel, so

213

she dropped in on Bruce and warned him before coming back to our house.

The lorry stopped at our gate. Chief Inspector Zengeni was hostile. "We are looking for the people who were instigating violence this morning," he told Laura. She knew he was referring to the farm workers, not the invaders.

Laura responded, "Why are you sending out all these policemen to arrest innocent people? When my husband and parents were abducted and beaten up, the police didn't send one vehicle!"

"Do not provoke me! I will arrest you!" Zengeni threatened, unbuttoning his pistol from its holster.

"I've been waiting for you to arrest me. Go ahead!" Laura said.

Some of the policemen started laughing, and then they piled back into the senator's lorry and drove off at high speed to the beer hall on Hakulandaba's farm next door.

Then Laura and the children heard shots being fired. There was chaos in the beer hall as people scrambled and fled. The police used tear gas and poured all the beer onto the ground. Eight people were arbitrarily arrested and beaten with rifle butts before being taken off in the senator's lorry to Chegutu Police Station. There they were beaten with armoured cables before being thrown into the cells. Some of them were key Mount Carmel farm workers who had been busy in the pack shed, packing the mangoes for the export order at the time when the invaders were driven off. They hadn't even known what was going on, let alone been involved.

That evening Landmine returned, this time with Senator Muduvuri's lorry and a large group of thugs from the senator's bar in Kadoma. They were quick and savagely ruthless. First they disarmed the Mount Carmel crop guards and took their weapons and ammunition. Then they captured some of the workers, clearly targeting the older men – the ones with the most influence. They threw one man, Sinos, into the fire that they'd lit on the lawn outside Mike and Angela's house. He managed to roll out but they picked him up by the feet and dropped him several times on his head onto the hard concrete workshop floor. Then they beat him with sticks and irrigation pipe risers, and urinated on him. They loaded him and some other workers into Shamuyarira's Prado and took them, virtually unconscious, to the police station.

Grace was at the station when Landmine arrived. She saw Sinos being carried in and dumped onto the floor. Then the policeman on duty grabbed his head and smashed it against the charge office wall. Grace heard the sound of his head hitting the concrete. Other injured workers were carried in and thrown down.

It was clear that Sinos was badly injured, he was motionless and couldn't speak. Grace eventually managed to persuade the police to allow him and the other workers to get medical treatment and they were taken to hospital. Sinos had a fractured skull. After he'd been treated, Grace was able to take him away to a safe house to recuperate.

Meanwhile, back on Mount Carmel, Landmine broke open the lock on Mike and Angela's kitchen door, gaining access to the house. The situation was very precarious. There was no way that Mike would survive another beating. There was just one locked internal door between Landmine and Mike and it wouldn't take more than a minute for the invaders to break it down. Mike sat on a chair holding a pistol. His hands were so weak that I doubt he would've been able to pull the trigger. He couldn't even load the gun. The thugs started threatening to come through.

"I will shoot if you break down the door," said Mike, in a voice that had become small since his beating. The invaders left the kitchen, but it was anyone's guess as to where they'd come in next.

I crept in, unarmed, through the darkness, to be with Mike and Angela. Laura's sister, Cath, long since evicted from her ranch, had come down from Harare to stay with them and she let me in without the thugs knowing.

It was a very uneasy night. Outside, drums and shouting and threats went on constantly. I didn't sleep at all: my mouth was dry and I couldn't eat. We just made endless cups of tea and tried to keep each other calm, while keeping an ear out for where the invaders might break in next.

I managed to get out at dawn and drove up to Harare to see Dave Drury. We wrote a letter to the Commissioner General of Police in the hope that he might order his subordinates to act.

While I was away, Mike and Angela were given an ultimatum by Landmine.

"You will be out in two hours!"

There were a number of intimidating incidents that day and by the time I got back, Mike and Angela had had enough. They were getting out. They knew from the previous night that the situation was life-threatening. If the authorities had allowed the thugs to beat our workers to within an inch of their lives, what would they be allowed to do to us? It was clear that there were orders from the top that we were to be taught another lesson. I think a policy decision had been taken to make an example of us.

Mike and Angela packed what they could into their vehicle. Some of the farm workers had been hiding in Angela's garden since the thugs and then the police had come looking for them. Mike and Angela hid them underneath some carpets and took them and their children to safety. They drove out into the darkness and that was it. They left all their belongings and their whole history behind them. They were never been able to go back.

Landmine put up barricades on the road but I managed to get through with a few very brave friends to sleep in Mike and Angela's house. In the morning everyone had to go to work. We decided that the best thing to do was to lock things up as best we could and try to bring some pressure to bear to get the invaders arrested. We drove out through the roadblocks, past the fire on the lawn and past Shamuyarira's Prado and that was the end. We never managed to sleep there again.

Dave Drury came down the next day to try to get the farm workers out of jail. Grace and I saw Landmine arrive at the police station with some of his thugs. They went inside, then one of them came out, got some money out of the car and took it back into the police station. It was brazen. I went in.

Assistant Inspector Sasa was there.

"What is Landmine's real name?" I asked her.

"This is a police matter," she replied.

"Yes, but I need to know the name of the man who is committing these crimes against us."

"Go and see Chief Inspector Zengeni."

So I went to Zengeni and asked for Landmine's name. "You are provoking me," he said, and refused to tell me. It was obvious that Landmine was high up in the CIO. Eventually we found out that Landmine's real name is Lovemore Madangonda.

After a wait of several hours, Dave was allowed to see the workers. They showed him the marks on their bodies where the police had beaten them.

"What did the police use to beat you with?" Dave asked.

One of them pointed to a cupboard in the interrogation room. "It is from there," he said.

Dave reached in to where the man was pointing and pulled out a piece of armoured electrical cable about a metre long. Its size corresponded exactly to the welts that each of them had on their backs and buttocks. Dave marched out of the room to show us and called Grace to go with him to show Chief Inspector Manika. The chief inspector was embarrassed but dismissive. Torture is so common that it has become normal.

In court Dave asked the magistrate to order an independent medical examination of all the workers. But the magistrate compromised and ordered that only a government medical officer should examine them. It never happened. Instead they were all sent to a maximum-security prison nearly a hundred kilometres away. There was a cholera epidemic on, and prison was not a good a place to be. There was also no food there, so Bruce and Grace drove down every day to bring food and visit the workers and make sure they were being looked after. In Chikurubi Maximum Security Prison, life expectancy isn't long: 720 of the 1,300 inmates had died in the previous twelve months. After a couple of weeks, once their torture welts had gone, Dave managed to get an order from the High Court in Zimbabwe ordering that the workers be released.

In the meantime I asked Dave to initiate proceedings in the High Court. Amazingly, a number of our evicted friends risked their lives by coming to stay at our house, which became a sort of commune for refugees. Although it was at times terrifying living out there during those months, being among friends who had a strong faith in God gave us tremendous strength.

The invaders acted quickly, clearly trying to intimidate us to move. Early one morning, a very sinister looking black panel van with no windows, similar to one of the vehicles used in our abduction, arrived at our open gate. I walked toward it with my heart pounding. A number of our linen workers were on their way to work, and the black van turned around and went away. Through the windscreen, our workers saw a number of unknown men crowded into the back. It was a warning, calculated to terrify us.

CHAPTER 20

During early April 2009, a UK-based ITV television news crew came out. They wanted to try to get to Mike and Angela's house to see what was happening there. I told them we'd have to go on foot, in the dark, as the invaders had put a large roadblock of felled trees in the way. Cath dropped us off close by and we started to walk.

I was nervous. I knew I couldn't afford to get beaten over the head again. We walked along the gravel road as the bush was too thick to get through. We got past the roadblock and were just going over the gate into Angela's garden when we heard movement. We were being ambushed. Stones started to fly as we took to our heels. Fortunately Martin Geissler, ITV's Africa Correspondent, who was with me, was a marathon runner and very fit. I led the way. Martin was hit on the leg by a rock and went down but I saw him scramble up again. In the darkness we had to concentrate on every foot fall. We were going at full sprint, adrenalin pumping and every muscle straining.

When we got to the barrier of trees across the road, I took it in two bounds. My marathon-running friend, spurred on by the flying rocks, tried to take it in one steeple-chase hurdle but his toe caught a branch, which sent him sprawling again. I saw him roll down onto the gravel. Our pursuers were close behind us. I had to make a split second decision: should I stand and face them and try to help Martin, or carry on running to get him help? My decision was influenced by the fact that last time I had been captured by invaders, only about a hundred metres from where I now was, I had had a grim time of it. To my shame I decided to keep running, leaving Martin to whatever rescue bid we could effect with the vehicles.

I became aware of one pursuer right on my heels. He was fast and incredibly persistent, but I was just managing to gain on him. I had shouted for the vehicles and I saw Cath's headlights coming toward me. She slowed down and I yanked the door open and leaped into the front seat while the car was still moving, locking the door behind me.

"Drive!" I commanded.

But she didn't floor the accelerator. In that moment my pursuer caught up with us. In one gymnast's leap he vaulted over the side of the pickup. To my great annoyance he was now on the back.

"Cath, what are you doing?" I shouted angrily. I was about to grab the man and throw him off the truck when I realized that it was Martin, the athletic ITV journalist! We'd both managed to outrun the thugs.

We got back to the house still breathing very hard, patched up Martin's grazes, and filed a news report. It was the fastest few hundred metres I'd ever run. With the relief of having got away, we all had a good laugh.

Eventually some police did come out to take a look at Mike and Angela's place. We found that Landmine and his thugs had broken into the house and looted a few things. Outside the pack shed there was a queue of people buying mangoes from Landmine and we found that the pack shed itself had been broken into. Over fifty tons of export mangoes that Bruce had harvested lay rotting in wooden bins on the floor. I managed to film it, but the police still refused to do anything to apprehend those responsible.

We also managed to contact Giles Mutsekwa, the Joint Minister of Home Affairs (MDC-T), and pleaded with him to come out to the farm and see things at first hand. In the end a large delegation came out on 17 April, the first official visit by a group of high-ranking officials in all the nine years of the farm invasions. We had both Ministers of Home Affairs, the Deputy Prime Minister, the Minister of Lands and Land Resettlement, the Minister in the Prime Minister's office and all sorts of dignitaries.

I led the convoy of vehicles with Laura and the children. They were excited to meet the Deputy Prime Minister, Arthur Mutambara. As we approached the locked gate that Landmine had put across Mike and Angela's open driveway, a man with a gun came up threateningly. When he saw the rest of the convoy he backed down.

We'd told the farm workers what was going to happen and they all arrived. The workshop area was full of people and journalists. The Deputy Prime Minister addressed everyone and then said he wanted a closed meeting. I suggested that we go to the pack shed. All the tons of export fruit were still lying rotting on the floor.

Everyone was given the chance to have their say. We explained the desperation of our situation, and that of the farm workers.

At the end of discussion the Deputy Prime Minister said, "We have agreement. You will be working again this afternoon!"

"Can we have that in writing?" I asked.

"No," he replied, and my heart sank. "We are the government and we are giving you that assurance."

"Can you explain that to the police?" I asked, desperately.

"Yes," he agreed. "Both the Ministers of Home Affairs can do that."

Before he left, Laura saw Lands Minister Herbert Murerwa talking to one of the thugs. He was smiling and she saw him give the thumbs up sign.

At two o'clock, when Bruce went over to get the work going, the thugs were there with guns. They chased away all the workers and Bruce and the BBC film crew he was with had to leave in a hurry.

Shortly after this Landmine roared in through our open gate at dusk one evening, drunk.

"Let me in, I want to talk!"

"Can you hear me?" I replied.

"Yes," he said.

"Then let's talk through the door," I said. Ruth, Anna's godmother, who had been evicted from her own farm, was upstairs trying to film, so I was able to see later that Landmine was waving a pistol around. It was fortunate I didn't go outside – anything could have happened.

"You must be out!" he said. "I will continue my tactics until you are out! I am coming back!" With that he got back into his car and sped away.

One night we heard the sound of tractors and *chimurenga* songs and saw lights coming toward us. I knew trouble was on its way and I was very afraid, but I tried not to show it. The invaders came to the house and started issuing threats. Our night watchman was chased away and they burned his overalls. The flames went up into the thatch of the workshop but fortunately it didn't catch fire. One of the thugs burned some sacks and held them up close to the thatch. There was lots of shouting. Then they started ploughing, using the Mount Carmel tractors. Our whole driveway was ploughed up and the lawn and some of the flower beds were turned into a mass of furrows. It was impossible to drive the 500 metres to the main road because of the ruts.

On another occasion, some Spanish journalists were visiting us and while they were here, the thugs shut off the generator and then went over to Laura's linen workers. We could hear them shouting and threatening to kill everyone who continued working for the white man. Then we saw little gaggles of people filing away, trying to leave as quickly as they could. The thugs clearly meant to terrify us all that day. Many of them were armed with rifles and they took up positions around the garden and pointed the guns at the windows of the house. We drew all the curtains and hid in various rooms. No shots were fired but it was very intimidating. One of the Spanish journalists was sweating so profusely that rivulets were running down his face. He told me that he'd faced dangerous situations in Iraq and Afghanistan but had never been as scared as he was in our house on a farm in Zimbabwe.

Eventually the thugs were warned off through diplomatic pressure, and our Spanish visitors were able to leave. We were alone again in the uneasy quiet of the beautiful African *veld*, not knowing how the peace would be broken next.

After that, all the linen workers were terrified. None of them dared come to back to work. Those who lived in houses only 50 metres away abandoned them and went to live with relatives elsewhere, only creeping back at odd hours of the night to check how things were. It was eerie living there under that leaden atmosphere of fear. I became very silent. I felt I always had to be on the alert. I became very intolerant of idle chatter and found loud noises extremely distressing.

The worst part was the way that the invaders' tactics were forever changing. We never knew what they'd do next. Each time they arrived, our mouths would go dry and no amount of tea would take the dryness away. My stomach would go into knots, I had no appetite and couldn't eat. We jokingly called it the Mugabe diet – it was far more effective than any of the thousands of other diets that people pay to go on. We laughed about setting up our house as a health spa for weight watchers.

Throughout this time the invaders were busy reaping the maize and the mangoes and selling them off. We couldn't stop them. From the house we could see the maize sheller spewing out its plume of chaff as the thugs reaped the crops that they'd never sown. Hour after hour and day after day and week after week it went on, gradually getting closer to us. I could never get used to it. We saw pickup trucks and lorries in the orchard reaping the mangoes. When they'd finished with the mangoes and the maize, they started on the sunflowers and the oranges.

We won the case in the High Court to stop the invasion and evict the thugs. Time after time I went to the Deputy Sheriff and the police but they always had an excuse for not implementing the eviction. "We have no manpower." "We have no transport." "This is only a provisional order – you need to get a final one…" I knew they were trying to wear us down until we gave up. I wrote to the Prime Minister. I tried to publicize everything that was unjust and wrong, but it just carried on and on.

In the evening Ruth would often play the piano and we'd sing rousing hymns. It gave us courage. Some of the songs made tears roll down my cheeks, but I wasn't embarrassed. It was good to be moved from deep within. Sheer courage alone couldn't sustain us over the months and years of intimidation that we'd suffered. Only God could keep us going. Words and stories from the Bible jumped to life in our hearts and we found incredible comfort in them.

The thugs continued to intimidate all the farm workers in the various villages, who were told to get out of their homes. The electricity was closed off and they were prevented from getting water from the borehole. They all had to walk to the river or the neighbouring farm with buckets. One night the invaders came to Peter Asani's house. Peter was Mike's old foreman and had worked on the farm almost since Mike bought it. He had now reached retirement age. They broke down his door at midnight, when everyone was asleep, hit Peter's wife with a rifle butt, and pulled Peter outside.

"You are Peter!" one of them shouted.

"Yes," he agreed. With that, the thugs dragged him to their lair in Mike and Angela's garage where he was beaten for an hour and a half with sticks on the soles of his feet. His bones were broken and he couldn't walk. They then put him in their car and took him to the police station, where he was locked up.

But he was the wrong Peter. The thugs had been after someone else. Grace and Bruce eventually managed to get Peter to the hospital where he was cared for. It was months before he could walk again.

One day I was driving off the farm from our house when I saw a vehicle loaded with people coming down the dirt road at great speed. I immediately thought it was the invaders and was gripped by a sick feeling in the pit of my stomach. Then I saw it was James

Etheredge in the driving seat. He pulled over beside me and I saw a group of farm workers in the back. James was visibly shaken. There was lots of fresh blood, wet and very red, smeared all over the white paintwork in the tray, and bullet holes through the side of the vehicle. Several people were wounded. I told James to come back to the house quickly so that we could try to help.

The police had fired the bullets when James and his brother Peter had driven onto their farm to check on their orchards. They were about to reap their 6,000-ton crop of oranges when the President of the Senate, Edna Madzongwe, took over again. Their scantily refurnished house was looted again. The third homestead on the farm was broken into by the police. Peter was immediately arrested and put in jail for apparently stealing his own fruit. James managed to get around the corner and away before more bullets could hit them. The workers lay in the back of the vehicle and kept their heads down. The police had definitely been firing at the people, not just at the tyres of the vehicle.

One man had a very ugly wound. A bullet had starting spinning after going through the metalwork of the vehicle and entered his leg, creating a real mess. The exit hole was so big that I could've put my whole fist into it. His bones had been smashed to pieces. I tried to do what emergency first aid I could to stem the bleeding, but knew it was important that the man got to Harare quickly. We covered them over with blankets so that the police wouldn't stop them on the road, and they left.

The Etheredges abandoned further attempts to reap their crops. It was too dangerous to try any more. Every day we would see the Etheredges' stolen tractors carting stolen oranges to Chegutu for sale. One man who apparently tried to steal some oranges from them was assaulted so badly by the senator's men that he died the next day.

All over the district the last few farms were cleared in similar ways. The human rights abuses got worse and worse and there are thousands of stories of crimes against humanity, just from our district alone. No one would do anything to stop the terror.

One afternoon Chief Inspector Manika and Assistant Inspector Bepura dropped in. Manika told me that he wasn't going to be around that night as he had to get instructions regarding the civil case we had initiated against him and the Commissioner of Police. He said he was going on to see Shamuyarira's men. "They are unpredictable," he said. "We can't guarantee your safety. I advise you to get your children out." There were some old tyres in the back of his vehicle. He said he was going to see Landmine before going to Harare.

I knew there was no point in remonstrating with him. He knew that all he had to do was to follow court orders or arrest the invaders for theft and break-in and assault – and all the numerous other crimes they had committed and then we would be safe. He never did.

That night the gang arrived outside our house, with much noise and shouting. They set up plough discs in various places around the house and started beating them with metal bars, making an incredible din. One of them had brought along a ship's bell that had been stolen from Mike and Angela's house, which he rang interminably. They lit tyres and dragged them around on the lawn, the flames leaping up into the night sky.

I went into the office and tried to make some telephone calls, sitting there in the darkness with my leg shaking uncontrollably from fear.

One group started to break in though the dining room door and another group through the main front door. They had burning tyres with them, which they wanted to pull through the house. The flames were close to the long curtains in the dining room.

Laura came running through to me and said quietly and incredibly calmly, "They are in the house."

Then they pulled a burning tyre in through the front door. As they dragged it forwards, the breeze fanned the flames and fire leaped up into the thatch.

Laura slipped upstairs to the children. Some of the thugs had already been up there and taunted them. Josh said afterwards,

"I just ignored them and didn't look at them." Laura prayed with the children and read the Bible to them while the nightmare continued.

Landmine appeared to be the only one with a firearm, and he kept in the shadows in the background. The rest of them picked up whatever they could find to use as weapons – croquet mallets, hockey sticks… It would've been funny if it wasn't so serious. "Out!" they shouted. "Get out!" "This is our land!" "Go back to America!" "The white man must go!" All the usual threats that we'd become so used to.

They ripped the phone away from the aerial and took it. After that we were on our own.

The gang split into various groups and were trying to hustle us out of the house. Eventually they agreed that we could have fifteen minutes to collect the things we needed. I stood near the burning tyre in the court yard.

"What is the one thing we have in common?" I asked them. I knew this was the right sermon for the situation, the same sermon that I had given to the thugs a few years previously. Now that they were in the house and the threat was real, I felt unbelievably calm and not afraid at all. I could even see the comic side of things as they stood there with their raised croquet mallets and other sporting paraphernalia. In all the hubbub, a number of them started listening.

It took me a long time to get to the bit about death. "You can kill me tonight," I told them, "but that's not going to help you. Each one of you is going to have to face the one certainty of life one day, sometime in the future. You've got a choice. Either you do things God's way or you don't. It's your choice, but if you don't do things God's way, what will happen to you when you face death?"

I kept asking them questions and getting them to think about judgment day and the love of God who sent his only Son to die for us all so that we might have forgiveness and life.

There was a big countdown toward the end of the fifteen minutes. We hadn't packed as much as a toothbrush. They began

227

to hassle us and physically push us out of the door. I knew that once we were out of the house and into the darkness of the *veld* beyond, things would get worse. We'd be in their territory then, and anything could happen. As they inched me toward the door, I kept trying to talk to them and hold their attention.

Then I saw the strangest thing. A policeman, wearing his hat and in full uniform, walked through the front door. The effect was immediate. A sudden hush descended on the night. It was as though the headmaster had unexpectedly walked into a room of naughty schoolchildren. In the silence, without a word being spoken, the thugs filed out of the front door, one by one, in an orderly line. They left singing *chimurenga* songs into the night.

Bruce and Grace were behind the policeman's arrival. Without Manika and Bepura at the station, the other policemen had been persuaded to come out on the back of Bruce's vehicle. Bruce had driven with his foot flat on the accelerator. If they'd arrived five minutes later, it could have been a different story.

Although no one was arrested, at least the thugs were told to leave us alone. We later discovered that a few things had been stolen, but there wasn't much missing. I put in the usual request for a police guard. "The thugs will come back as soon as you leave!" I said. I was assured that they wouldn't. I didn't tell them that I suspected their officer-in-charge had given the thugs the tyres to burn because I didn't think it would help.

Fifteen minutes after the police had left, there was the sound of *chimurenga* songs coming toward us again. The thugs drove back in through the gate and came around the house. My heart sank. I wondered if they had new orders. I frantically made a call to Bruce to bring police back.

The invaders, in their frenzied state, bashed the metal plough disks again, shattering our fragile equilibrium once more. They made threats: "We will burn your house! We will eat your children!" And then they were gone again.

We lived on through that night and the next. For a time things were quiet. The sighing grasses that swayed and waved in front of the house were like the golden waters of the Zambezi River. It was a happy colour, the colour of a salmon river with the sun sparkling on its clear water and golden sandbanks underneath. Anyone who came to see us on the farm who didn't know what was going on would have imagined that everything was fine and working normally. The birds carried on singing. The sun still shone. After a few weeks, some of the linen workers filtered back and carried on their chatter in the factory. But we knew that if we strayed, the crocodiles were waiting. The drone of the tractors stealing our crops was a warning to us that the peace was an uneasy one.

At night we were kept awake by the sound of their parties. Often we'd see them coming back from Gadzema on one of the tractors loaded up with beer. We heard that they'd been demanding sex for mangoes.

It was hard to think of the thugs living in Mike and Angela's house just two kilometres away, sleeping in their bed, eating their food, milking their cows – even eating a couple of them – stealing their things and destroying their history and everything they'd worked for. As time wore on and they stripped more and more away, we gave up trying to make police reports unless there was something life-threatening happening. I would periodically write to senior politicians in the Government of National Unity, but was never graced with a reply. A few of my open letters were published in the press, but nothing ever led to the re-establishment of the rule of law. It was disheartening.

CHAPTER 21

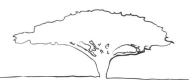

Way back, on 5 November 1984, during a time of prayer at our church in Chegutu, Anne Cranswick spoke the following prophetic words: "My people, listen to what I say. The state of this country will become worse and still worse. Corruption will be as you have never seen it before. Law and order, education, medical facilities, agriculture, transport, and finance will break down, be chaotic. People will be in a state of despondency. My tribe will be scattered…"

Less than a decade and a half later, the prophecy was coming true. It was indeed chaos, and through the chaos our hearts wept and wept as lives and the beauty all around us were destroyed. People we loved were taken, or had to leave, and chaos continued to reign on the farms we loved. We wept until we were dry and there was nothing left inside to weep out any more.

I saw men and women who used to have a twinkle in their eye and a vision and purpose for each day become broken and brittle like dry wood. They had nothing left to live for. It was a time of sitting and waiting and withdrawing into a life of meaningless depression. Some turned to drink to numb the pain.

Earlier a gang had come in and cut down all the mukwa trees on the farm with chainsaws. Mukwa is a beautiful hardwood, much sought after for furniture making. The trees lay dead with their branches extended, like slain giants. So it was in Zimbabwe. People lay felled, like the mukwa trees drying out in the sun. Eventually the smaller branches become so brittle they could be broken with just a tiny bit of pressure. In the same way men and women were broken too, or burned up because they'd become too dry to resist the flames.

We were driving back to the farm after church one Sunday when we saw a fire. It looked like it was close to the house. Mike and

Angela had come down from Harare to have Sunday lunch with us and I could see Angela standing near the gate with a hose, red in the face from the heat and looking very stressed. There was a strong wind and the fire was galloping in from the south. I drove straight into the garden and ran to help. A number of people had come from the main Mount Carmel worker village and from next door. We tried to burn back from the firebreaks but the wind was too strong and the fire jumped over the breaks. We ripped branches from the trees and tried to smother the flames, beating furiously. I only had one knapsack sprayer as the thugs had taken all the rest. It was impossible. Sparks were flying through the tinder dry grass, igniting new fires even before the main fire reached them. I hadn't realized how difficult it was to put a grass fire out without the proper equipment. Normally firefighting was relatively simple.

The crackling of the flames was deafening and the heat was intense. My face and arms were soon scorched red. Before we knew it, the flames had enveloped one of the workers' houses and spread through the roof. The wind blew them into an inferno and within seconds the whole roof was alight. Sparks flew onto nearby roofs. The houses were all burning too quickly to save anything from inside them. I shouted, "Let's save the factory! You can live in the factory," but there was so much noise and emotion that nobody responded. They were wailing and crying. They had lost everything.

I ran over to the factory to try to do what I could, pouring water and extinguishing the fire as it came near. I was keeping it at bay, when I saw that a fireball of thatch had blown from one of the workers' houses over the trees onto the roof of our own house. The flames licked up to the ridge in seconds, where they leaped and spread, fanned by the wind.

I ran into our bedroom, grabbed the safe with all the documents in it and threw it on the lawn. I ran in a second time and got the camera and Swiss army knife from my bedside table, then charged across to the computers in the office, frantically tearing out the leads. I ran out with them and that was it. A little round

231

table and three chairs were rescued from the kitchen. Mum, who was staying with us at the time, got a small bag from her room, and we managed to get the cars out as Laura had had the presence of mind to grab the car keys. The rest we could only watch burn. We could do nothing more.

We took shelter at a distance and watched. It was so quick. I took pictures as the house burned, and from the first picture at 1:20 p.m. it took just three minutes for it to turn into a raging inferno. The noise of the fire was tremendous. Everything was exploding in the intense heat. The glass in the windows melted and beams came crashing down, bringing ceilings and walls with them.

We saw one of the stolen tractors with the 2,000-litre spray tank on the back being driven around by the thugs. They were laughing at us. They drove along the line of the fire and put it out as they drove, stopping it from getting into our crops because they hadn't finished reaping them.

A baby genet ran out from the bush onto the haven of green lawn close to our gate and died there. The cattle herders pushed the cattle to water through the black scorched wasteland all around us. They plodded along slowly in single file, a pathetic picture of poverty in the desolate landscape where there was nothing for them to eat.

Topsy, our little Scottie, was missing. We later found her incinerated remains in the spare room, underneath where the bed had once been. She wouldn't have suffered for long. We also found the remains of Jackson, one of the cats. Brownie, another cat, died in the *veld* close to the cattle grid on the driveway but we didn't find the remains of her sister. Laura had seen her shoot out of our bedroom window when the fire first took hold. Maybe she died later.

People from the church came out with some tea and we cried and somehow found it within us to laugh. I remembered some words from the book of Job: "What the Lord has given, the Lord has taken away. Blessed be the name of the Lord" (Job 1:21). I said them out loud. Laura and I discussed rebuilding. We agreed that we wouldn't thatch next time.

It was hard that night to tear ourselves away from the house. It was still smouldering in places. We only left when it was nearly dark. All we had left were the clothes we stood up in. We spent the night with Mike and Angela in Harare but I didn't sleep for a second. Whenever I closed my eyes, all I could see were flames burning orange and bright before me, so I quickly opened them again.

We discussed what we should do. There was no doubt that we must rebuild, but we agreed I should go to South Africa the next day as planned for the first screening of the documentary film *Mugabe and the White African*. I sat through the film and watched the whole of the trauma of the previous year pass before me. In the back of my mind I could still see the flames, crackling, illuminating, consuming. The tears came again. I didn't try to stop them.

After buying some clothes and toothbrushes and other necessities for herself and the children, Laura drove back to Chegutu. She was told to go to a house that another family had moved out of the previous day. As she arrived, a generator roared into life and the sudden light revealed virtually the whole community waiting for her. They'd all come to help and showed her around excitedly.

"Now come in here and have a look at this!" one of them would say as Laura walked from room to room. There was a fully stocked fridge in the kitchen, with a stove and pots and pans and cutlery and plates and cups and glasses and washing-up liquid and cloths and everything that was necessary for a kitchen to function. There was food in the pantry and in the freezer. There were beds and bedding, and clothes on coat hangers in the cupboards. There were even uniforms so that our children could go to school the next day. There were toiletries and flannels and towels and a first-aid kit in the bathroom, and chairs and flowers and plants in the sitting room. Curtains had been put up and pictures hung on the walls. It was incredible: a house that had been completely emptied the day before was now fully furnished and ready to be lived in.

I spoke to Laura on the phone that night from South Africa to find out where she and the children would be sleeping. "You won't believe what the community has done for us," she told me. "It's the most amazing outpouring of love."

The next day Laura phoned again and I immediately knew that something was wrong.

"They've burned Mum and Dad's house too," she said simply.

There was nobody on the farm who could attempt to salvage Mike and Angela's treasured possessions. It was devastating to know that everything had gone: the furniture made by Angela's father and Mike's grandfather from beautiful African hardwoods; the pictures and photographs of all the old relations; the old cutlery and crockery sets; the silver; the letters and diaries. Even the photograph of Angela when she was a little girl, which her father had carried through the German POW camps during the war, and which had survived prisoner-of-war camps and death marches, was gone. Grandpa had kept it until he died, when he was ninety. All the family history was gone. It was the place where Laura had grown up and our children had grown up. Now it was all gone.

"The bastards!" I replied, with feeling. I hadn't used that word of anybody in years.

Later we were told that the invaders were looting inside Mike and Angela's house and had set the fire to cover their tracks. We even got an affidavit from one of the thugs detailing what had happened. However, they had dumped a few broken bits of furniture on the driveway, and Laura was allowed to go and take them away. She wasn't allowed near the burned ruin of the house or the outhouses, where we understood the thugs were storing some of the furniture to cart away later.

A few days after the fire my Mum took the children back to the ash heap that was once our home and told them about castles and ruins and happy times in history. They recalled pleasant memories of living at the house. Josh said to Mum, "Now, when I see a ruin, I'll think of all the good times that people must have had at the place before it became a ruin." In our bedroom there was still a pile of ash from the books and magazines that had sat on the bedside table that Laura's grandfather had made for her. A few pages hadn't been completely burned. They were from Laura's Bible. Right on top were the words of Psalm 37, often known as Zimbabwe's Psalm. Laura had underlined them and the underlining was still visible: "The salvation of the righteous comes from the Lord; he is their stronghold in times of trouble. The Lord helps them and delivers them; he delivers them from the wicked and saves them, because they take refuge in him."

One day some time later, when we went back again, the cat that Laura had seen leap out of the bedroom window during the fire suddenly appeared. She had somehow survived – a tiny glimmer of hope in a world that had died. Sometime after that Laura found a few photographs that had been stuffed into a drawer of a piece of furniture that the thugs hadn't wanted from Mike and Angela's house. One of them was dog-eared and partly obliterated. It had "STALAG VII A" stamped on the back. It was the picture of Angela as a little girl.

We made sure we went back as much as we could to the ruin of our home, although it was very painful to see the devastation. After a time, though, with watering, the garden was resuscitated and we managed to rebuild a couple of the workers' houses, out of pole and dagga. The linen workers worked hard to clear the rubble and sift through the debris to find the odd metal object that hadn't burned.

We rented a tractor and started carting sand into place to try to rebuild the factory and some of the house, but the thugs stepped in and started threatening the workers, forcing them out of their newly built homes. After a while we gave up trying to rebuild. There was no point in reconstructing our house just for someone else to move into when it was finished. The key thing was to work toward creating a new environment in which everyone could live and build and thrive without fear and intimidation. Eventually the few buildings that we had managed to save, along with the newly built workers houses, were burned down anyway. The garden died, the transformer was stolen, the armoured cable to the borehole was dug up, the fence was rolled up and taken away, and all that now remains are memories of things past and the foundations of the buildings.

As we look to the north and see so many decades of tyranny in so many countries of independent Africa, things seem hopeless. But there is still hope.

When there was no food in Zimbabwe and we had to drive six hours to do our grocery shopping over the border in Botswana, I had seen how proper leadership had created development and wealth in that desert state. It all stemmed from servant leadership, based on Christian principles and not on the fear of the spirits.

Now our film was being shown in Gaborone, at the 10th Annual Human Rights Festival, organised by Ditshwanelo, the Botswana Centre for Human Rights. Early in the morning of the showing, I decided to climb a hill. There were a lot of cars parked at the bottom. Everyone who knows Africa will know that African people, who are mostly very poor, are unlikely to waste valuable energy climbing hills merely for the sake of enjoyment. As I went up and chatted to the other climbers, most of whom were black, I realized that in Botswana hill climbing was a regular pastime. That seemed incredible to me, and strangely it gave me great hope.

At independence in 1966, Botswana, a land-locked country with 70 per cent of its surface covered by the Kalahari Desert, was one of the poorest countries in Africa, with a GDP per capita of about US$70. Led by founding president Sir Seretse Khama KBE, Botswana broke the pattern of most other post-independence African states and forged ahead into the ranks of middle-income status to become the fastest growing economy in the world.

Khama was committed to upholding the rule of law, property rights and maintaining sound fiscal policy. The constitution prohibits the nationalization of private property. Botswana was developed through the wealth it created, with significant investment in roads, hospitals, schools, and other infrastructure. Khama kept the government small and did not allow corruption. For the past fifteen years, Transparency International has ranked Botswana as the least corrupt country in Africa. For the first eleven years after independence, Botswana didn't even have an army. The Botswana Defence Force was formed in 1977.

Although diamonds were discovered in 1967, the first mine only began production in 1972, by which time the country had already made remarkable progress. Currently mining (predominantly diamonds) is the mainstay of the economy, followed by tourism, industry, commerce, and agriculture.

In most incidences, diamond discoveries in post-independence Africa have led to much suffering as different groups wrestle for control and fund private armies to retain them. In Botswana, diamond revenues have been used wisely to fund economic development. From being third poorest in mainland Africa, Botswana is now the second richest in terms of per capita income. It has achieved an average annual growth rate of about 9 per cent with a GDP (purchasing power parity) per capita of about US$14,800. The World Economic Forum rates Botswana as one of the two most competitive nations in Africa.

While I was in Botswana, I was taken to parliament to meet MPs, ministers, and permanent secretaries. Those few days are etched in my mind as days of great hope. Here was a non-racial African society with a government that was forging forward. Its foundation dates back to the Scottish missionary Robert Moffat's mission in the nineteenth century, when a young man – later to become Khama the Third – became a committed Christian and revolutionized the way things were done in his society. The Khama family continued that Christian tradition and are leading the way forward for the rest of Africa.

In Zimbabwe there are also some sparks of hope. I see Foundations for Farming, set up by the person whom I believe to be Zimbabwe's most successful farmer, Brian Oldreive – who is the most humble man I know – as a bright light for the future. He and those with him live by faith, teaching the poorest of the poor godly farming principles based on conservation agriculture right through the continent, laying the foundations for the future.

237

***

I have snuck back to our farm a few times. The first time I was with the Al Jazeera television crew. A bare-chested policeman clutching an automatic weapon, who was living with the thugs, came tearing around the shell of Mike and Angela's house and promptly arrested us all. We were taken off to the police station at gunpoint. They released us after only a few hours, probably because the news crew was from Al Jazeera.

I have managed to return a number of times since then without getting arrested. Now not a single borehole is operational and the pump at the river also hasn't worked since the invaders took over. I haven't been able to get to the orchards but I understand that none of the 40,000 trees have been irrigated or sprayed or fertilized, despite Minister Shamuyarira having taken over all the equipment and materials needed to carry on farming operations. As a result, many of the citrus orchards are dead or dying. My tree nursery, which had about 8,000 fruit trees in it, is dead. My small macadamia nut orchard is also dead. No crops were planted last season.

Despite several attempts, we were unable to rescue Ginger the horse. He used to stand over the table on a Saturday morning when we had a family breakfast at Mike and Angela's house. He is also dead.

We have been back to the SADC Tribunal and the Zimbabwe government has been judged to be in contempt three times. After the Tribunal's third contempt ruling on 16 July 2010, the case was referred to the SADC Summit which was due to be held in Namibia in August 2010. We registered one of the costs judgments in South Africa and attached a house belonging to the Zimbabwe government in order to pay the lawyers' costs. At the SADC Summit in Namibia (16–18 August 2010), the SADC Heads of State failed to confront President Mugabe over Zimbabwe's refusal to honour the SADC Tribunal's rulings on the land grab programme. At the end of the summit, a communiqué was issued which read: "The summit decided that a review of the role and terms of reference of the SADC Tribunal should be undertaken and concluded within six months."

238

The deputy executive secretary, Joao Samuel Caholo told journalists that the Tribunal would not be able to conclude any old cases or take on new ones before the end of the review. The outcome will be critical for human rights in the region. After the announcement of the review, Jeremy Gauntlett wrote: "What is happening now is a defining moment. Either the members of SADC will accept that through their Treaty commitments they have bound themselves under international law to accept and defend the overlapping trilogy of internationally recognised human rights, democratic institutions and the rule of law, and subject themselves to the scrutiny of a regional Tribunal in that regard, or they will show that they are going back on that. In that event, words only will be left: words of complicity between political leaders shrugging off the constraints of law."

Whatever the outcome, we will ask the Tribunal to adjudicate a value on the Zimbabwe government's contempt when it reopens.

Back in Chegutu, Assistant Inspector Bepura is still at the police station, ensuring that court orders are not followed. Presumably, when the violence starts again in earnest, he and Sasa and the others will ensure that the perpetrators will once again escape arrest. Chief Inspector Gunyani retired to his plot of land soon after we served civil papers on him regarding our assault. Ironically, after we served civil papers on him, Chief Inspector Manika was sent to join the United Nations' peacekeeping mission in Kosovo and, despite complaints, is believed to have completed the assignment.

It has been difficult for us to adjust. Although Laura restarted the linen business in Chegutu town, it's not really working. I need to get a job that pays but I can't find one.

The children are doing well at school and have developed a secure faith in God through this time of testing. Anna, at the age of four, was asked by a tall black journalist, "Are you afraid of black people after everything that has happened?"

"Only the ones with blood-shot eyes," she told him.

Back in Harare, Mike and Angela, without a home of their own, came to live with us. Mike gradually got weaker. It was difficult for him to walk, talk, and eat because of his head injuries. The doctors did what they could but damaged brain cells continued to die and fluids accumulated in the spaces. Sometimes his breathing became very laboured.

I couldn't help remembering the drought year when Laura and I lived in Zambia. The game became weak with hunger and many animals died. Etched in my memory is the picture of a great kudu bull. His skin was stretched tightly over his bones but his head was still magnificent, with the great horns spiralling up and back as he ran through the skeletal trees. Then, as he grew increasingly weak, there was a wobble to each stride until, after less than a hundred metres, he went down. With an effort, his majestic head came up again and his limbs scrabbled on the hot, baked earth as he attempted to raise himself. At last he could try no more and his great head went down for the last time. It was an almost unbearably tragic sight. Mike reminded me of that bull while he was still running; he often went down, but always he struggled up again undaunted, and kept going.

During early April, Bruce was forced to endure a *jambanja* outside his house on Carskey farm. For five days and nights, drums were beaten continuously and a ZANU–PF mob chanted anti-white songs and slogans right the way through from dawn to dusk and then to dawn, over and over again without a break. Finally we all agreed that he had no option but to leave. Members of the thinly-spread Chegutu farming community came out to help – they are all experienced at packing now, having done it so many times before over the past decade – and his remaining goods were loaded onto the waiting trucks. His workers were also forced to leave their houses, swelling the ranks of the homeless and destitute.

As a result, Mike co-instituted an application in a further important matter which would take fifteen Heads of State in southern Africa to court for effectively suspending the SADC Tribunal, another landmark case. No individual in legal history has ever done this, but Mike believed that the only mechanism for achieving justice was through the Tribunal.

Ten days later, on Wednesday 6 April, Mike was too weak to walk. He could hardly talk and he couldn't eat. He knew his time had come and that morning said, "I am going to die today." The Bible reading for the day was from Psalm 55 verse 6: "Oh, that I had the wings of a dove! I would fly away and be at rest."

Family and friends poured into our house and he recognized every one of them and called them by name. He was asked, "Have you made you peace with God?"

"Yes," he replied.

"And have you forgiven the people that hurt you and your family?"

There was a shadow of pain and then Mike replied again, "Yes." It was the biggest thing he had ever done.

Mike died shortly afterwards. Thousands of tributes poured in from all over the world. This white African was no longer part of the troubled land of Zimbabwe. We laid Mike to rest on De Rus farm, which belongs to the Cremer family. As the Last Post sounded, and we shovelled the red soil of Africa down onto his coffin, I looked up and saw tears in the eyes of hundreds of African mourners, both black and white, who had come to pay their respects to a great man.

On the faces of so many of those still alive there is a tired, washed-out, fearful look. The resurgence of ZANU-PF violence aimed at forcing people to vote for Mugabe in the next election is of escalating concern.

However, I still believe that with strong, godly leadership the fortunes of the country can be turned around. Until that day, though, people will continue to suffer and fear will engulf the land like a malevolent cloud. Only when the miracle occurs and hope is rekindled by people whose hearts are brave enough to face the oppressor and throw off the yoke of oppression will transformation take place.

AppeNDix 1 – GLOSSARY

Agritex Department of Agricultural, Technical and Extension Services

Black Boots the Support Unit, or riot police, known as the "Black Boots" due to their footwear

boss boy the right-hand man of the boss/owner

CFU Commercial Farmers' Union

chef a term that was picked up by Mugabe's men in Mozambique during the war in the 1970s, it refers to senior party officials

chimurenga revolutionary war

CIO the Central Intelligence Organization or secret police

dagga cannabis

Gukurahundi "the early rain which washes away the chaff before the spring rains". The term refers to the massacres carried out by President Mugabe's North Korean-trained 5th Brigade between 1983 (only three years after independence) and 1987 in the predominantly Ndebele regions of Zimbabwe. About 20,000 people in Matabeleland and the Midlands died or disappeared. In September 2010, the *Gukurahundi* massacres were classified as a genocide by the internationally recognized group Genocide Watch

JAG Justice for Agriculture

Jambanja a state-sponsored, violent confrontation initiated to force farmers and farm workers off the commercial farms

kraal a traditional African village of huts, typically enclosed by a fence

lowveld land in the lower areas of the country

mabhunu a racist term for a white farmer

mbanje cannabis

MDC Movement for Democratic Change party

mealie-meal ground maize flour

mopani an African hardwood tree

mudzimu ancestral spirit

Nyami Nyami water spirit or river god of the Zambezi River

n'yanga witch doctor spirit medium

nyati buffalo

Operation Murambatsvina "clean out the filth" – where 2.4 million people were affected as homes and businesses were bulldozed in 2005

pamberi the word used at all the rallies and *pungwes*, meaning "forward" in Shona

panga a half-metre long knife

pungwe all-night indoctrination meeting designed to instil fear through denunciations, public beatings, and killings

recuse the disqualification of a judge (or prosecutor or juror) by reason of prejudice or conflict of interest

rule of law is to rule and accept the supremacy of law itself, usually in the form of a justiciable Bill of Rights in a relatively rigid constitution. The ruler is the law itself and no one is above the law

rule by law is to use law as an instrument of oppression where there is no respect for human rights and there is usually no constitution and a justiciable Bill of Rights. The ruler is the executive (usually a dictatorship) who uses oppressive law to rule

SADC Southern African Development Community (comprises fifteen member-states, including Zimbabwe)

sjambok heavy leather whip traditionally made from hippo hide

skull bashing intimidation

svikiro personal spirit medium

terr terrorist

veld southern African term for open grassland or bush

vlei wet low-lying open areas with black soils that work like a sponge

ZANLA Zimbabwe African National Liberation Army, the military wing of the Zimbabwe African National Union (ZANU) which fought in the Rhodesian bush war

ZANU Zimbabwe African National Union, the political party led by Robert Mugabe

ZANU–PF Zimbabwe African National Union–Patriotic Front

ZAPU Zimbabwe African People's Union was a political party formed in 1961. With the signing of the Unity Accord in 1987, ZAPU was absorbed into ZANU–PF, effectively achieving a one-party state

ZIPRA Zimbabwe People's Revolutionary Army was the military wing of the Zimbabwe African People's Union (ZAPU) which fought in the Rhodesian bush war

ZIJIRI Zimbabwe Joint Resettlement Initiative

ZUM Zimbabwe Unity Movement, which was formed to contest elections in 1990, ten years after independence and soon quashed

APPENDIX 2 - TIMELINE

1889 ····o British South Africa Company (BSAC) gains a mandate to colonise what becomes Southern Rhodesia

1890 ····o Pioneer column arrives from the south at site of future capital, Salisbury (renamed Harare after Independence)

1896–1897 ····o First *Chimurenga* (revolutionary struggle) against colonial rule by BSAC

1960 ····o NDP (National Democratic Party) founded by Joshua Nkomo; joined by Robert Mugabe who was elected Information and Publicity Secretary in 1961

1961 ····o ZAPU formed with Joshua Nkomo as President and Mugabe as Information and Publicity Secretary following banning of NDP in 1961

1962 ····o ZAPU banned by Rhodesian government

1963 ····o (8 Aug) Split within ZAPU led to formation of ZANU by Rev Ndabaningi Sithole (led party until 1976), Herbert Chitepo, Edgar Tekere, Leopold Takawira, Mugabe, and others. Joshua Nkomo continued to lead ZAPU.

1964 ····o Mugabe imprisoned from August 1964 until November 1974

1965 ····o (11 Nov) Rhodesian Unilateral Declaration of Independence (UDI) from Britain, by Prime Minister Ian Smith

1966 ····o Madzimbamuto v. Lardner Burke case (landmark human rights-based challenge regarding the rule of law in Rhodesia and Emergency Powers detention)

····o (28 April) Rhodesian Bush War or Second *Chimurenga* begins: Armageddon Group (ZANLA) attempts to blow up power lines near Sinoia (Chinhoyi)

····o (17 May) attack on Nevada farm, Hartley (Chegutu) district

1972 ····o Upsurge of insurgency activity leads to escalation of Bush War

····o (22 Dec) Attack on Altena farm, Centenary, by ZANLA

1974 ····o (Nov) Mugabe and other leading nationalists released from detention

····o Mike and Angela Campbell purchase Mount Carmel farm

1976 ····o Patriotic Front (PF) formed as a political and military alliance between ZANU and ZAPU

1978 ·····o (9 Jan) Attack on Rainbow's End farm, Chegutu district
·····o Ian Smith yields to international pressure for a negotiated settlement

1979 ·····o British-brokered all-party talks at Lancaster House in London lead to a peace agreement and new constitution

1980 ·····o Elections: Patriotic Front alliance partners split into their respective factions and compete separately as ZANU–PF (led by Mugabe) and PF–ZAPU (led by Joshua Nkomo). Election won by ZANU–PF
·····o (18 Apr) Zimbabwe Independence – ZANU–PF comes to power, Mugabe becomes Prime Minister

1982 ·····o Thornhill Air Force court case following sabotage attack

1983– ·····o *Gukurahundi* massacres in Matabeleland and Midlands
1988 provinces carried out by Mugabe's North Korean-trained 5th Brigade

1986 ·····o (14 June) Mugabe's Rufaro Stadium speech – refers to "the language of the gun"

1987 ·····o (22 Dec) Mugabe becomes Executive President; signing of Unity Accord between ZANU–PF and PF–ZAPU (led by Joshua Nkomo) under the name ZANU–PF

1990 ·····o (23 Mar) Presidential and Parliamentary elections; attempt to create *a de jure* one-party state fails; government begins amending constitution

1992 ·····o Land Acquisition Act enables compulsory purchase of land

1994 ·····o Ben Freeth marries Laura Campbell

1997 ·····o Freeths start to build own home at Mount Carmel
·····o (Nov) Mount Carmel farm listed for acquisition

1998 ·····o Mount Carmel farm delisted
·····o (Sept) Land donors' conference

1999 ·····o Establishment of Movement for Democratic Change (MDC)

2000 ·····o (Feb) Referendum on new constitution defeated; within three days, invasion of commercial farms (referred to as the Third *Chimurenga*) begins on Saffron Walden farm near Norton
·····o (18 Mar) High Court rules that farm invasions are illegal
·····o (15 Apr) Murder of David Stevens on his farm at Macheke
·····o (18 Apr) Murder of Martin Olds on his farm at Nyamandhlovu
·····o (24/25 June) Parliamentary elections
·····o Invasions on Mount Carmel farm

2001 ·····o (Aug) Mount Carmel farm invaders resettle on Carskey farm

·····o (Aug) Colin Cloete becomes President of CFU

2002 ·····o (9 Jan) Heidi Campbell dies with unborn twins due to malaria introduced by invaders on Carskey farm

·····o (9–11 Mar) Presidential election won by Mugabe, condemned as seriously flawed

·····o (17 Mar) Murder of Terry Ford on his farm at Norton

·····o (May) New legislation regarding Section 8 Acquisition Orders

·····o (June) 2,900 commercial farmers ordered to leave their land within 45 days

·····o (Aug) CFU Congress

·····o (Sept) Ben Freeth suspended from CFU

2003 ·····o Zimbabwe leaves Commonwealth

2004 ·····o (27 May) Supreme Court hearing of Quinnell case (Banket farmer test case)

·····o (Sept) Offer letter for "acquisition" of Mount Carmel farm given to Minister Nathan Shamuyarira

2005 ·····o (31 Mar) Parliamentary elections – marred by political violence and intimidation

·····o (19 May) Operation Murambatsvina begins; 700,000 poor people rendered homeless

·····o (14 Sept) Amendment 17 to Zimbabwe Constitution nationalizes all listed land

2006 ·····o (15 May) Campbell case hearing in the Supreme Court (Dec) Gazetted Land (Consequential Provision)s Act becomes law – farmers who fail to comply and vacate their farms risk two-year jail terms

2007 ·····o (11 Mar) Brutal police attack on peaceful prayer gathering of political opponents and civil society leaders

·····o (Oct) Prosecution of Mike Campbell and others for committing crime of farming

·····o (11 Oct) Campbell files a case with SADC Tribunal challenging acquisition of Mount Carmel

·····o (11 Dec) First hearing of Campbell case at SADC Tribunal

·····o (13 Dec) SADC Tribunal rules in favour of Campbell; grants interim measure prohibiting the government from taking any steps to evict him from his farm or to interfere with his use of the land

2008 ·····o (Jan) Supreme Court dismisses Campbell's application

·····o (25 Mar) Second hearing at SADC Tribunal – postponed to allow 77 other commercial farmers to join Campbell case as interveners

2008 ····o (29 Mar) Parliamentary and Presidential elections. Results not announced for six weeks

····o (6 May) Attack on Bruce and Netty Rogers on their Chegutu farm

····o (28 May) Third hearing at SADC Tribunal – government delaying tactics result in postponement to July

····o (27 June) Presidential run-off election, preceded by unprecedented government-sponsored violence; MDC leader Morgan Tsvangirai forced to withdraw

····o (29 June) Mike and Angela Campbell and Ben Freeth abducted and beaten

····o (16–17 July) Case of the 77 farmers, including Mike Campbell, plus first contempt application heard by the SADC Tribunal.

····o (15 Sept) Power-sharing agreement (GPA) signed in Harare

····o (28 Nov) SADC Tribunal judgment in favour of Campbell and interveners

2009 ····o (11 Feb) Inclusive government leaders sworn in

····o (28 Feb) Mugabe says SADC Tribunal judgment is "nonsense" and of "no consequence"

····o (4 Apr) Invasion of Mount Carmel by "Landmine" (Lovemore Madangonda). Farm workers beaten and imprisoned; all farm work stopped indefinitely

····o (5 Apr) Mike and Angela Campbell evicted

····o (17 Apr) Visit to Mount Carmel by Deputy Prime Minister and other ministers

····o (May) High Court orders evicting "Landmine" disregarded. All household effects and farm equipment stolen

····o (5 June) Zimbabwe government held to be in contempt by SADC Tribunal for the second time

····o (30 Aug and 2 Sept) Freeth and Campbell homesteads destroyed by fire

2010 ····o (June) New wave of attacks on commercial farmers

····o (July) Zimbabwe government held to be in contempt by SADC Tribunal for the third time

····o (Aug) SADC Summit leaders put SADC Tribunal on a six month review

····o (Sept) *Gukurahundi* massacres declared a genocide by Genocide Watch

2011 ····o (19 Jan) Amid escalating ZANU–PF violence, Finance Minister Tendai Biti warns Zimbabwe could face a bloodbath at the next elections

····o (2 Mar) Prime Minister Tsvangirai calls on SADC, the AU, and the international community to monitor the situation and for a binding roadmap as a precondition for the next election

Appendix 3

BEN FREETH'S OPEN LETTER TO MUGABE IN 2005

Dear Mr Mugabe,

It has been said that the battle for land is the greatest single cause of strife and warfare between human beings. I am sure you can testify to the truth of this. You will know that your parliament has now passed the bill that aims to drive the last white men off the land as well. We sit on the eve of the senate ratifying this and you, Your Excellency, signing it. Before you do so I wish to give you some food to reflect upon.

I have listened to many history lessons on how terrible the white man is and how terrible colonialism was. Repeat something often enough and it becomes accepted; and all subsequent actions against the white man, whatever they may be (even if he or his family had nothing to do with colonialism) appear to become justified.

You will know though that the history of colonialism in Zimbabwe started more than a thousand years ago – first with the Bantu tribes, of which you are a part, moving from the north forcing the San people out; then with Shaka Zulu forcing Mzilikazi out to the west of the Drakensberg mountains; then with the British (who had come, like your people, from the north) forcing the Boers out of the Cape; then with the Ndebele destroying Boer trek parties coming from the south; then with the Boers retaliating and the Ndebele being forced out of the Transvaal to the north; then with the Ndebele forcing the Shonas to the north; then with the Rudd and Lippert concessions and the various other agreements with the Shona chiefs where written legal history was made for the first time…

The history of colonialism is not quite the simple history that it is often made out to be. There has been much blood shed by all parties concerned.

With the arrival of the colonial white man, and the favourable conditions that this brought for the population, the black population doubled in the first thirty years; and carried on doubling thereafter. The white people were also increasing in number. It was at that time that the Land Apportionment Act of 1930 came into being. It was made, as you know, on the strength of the Carter Commission, which reported that territorial segregation was what the black people wanted for purposes of security of tenure. The Land Apportionment Act set aside thirty acres for every black man, woman, and child. White men were then barred from buying land in those areas. Contrary to the repetitious propaganda, every serious farmer knows that land in these now communal areas can be made to produce every bit as well as other land in Zimbabwe.

In the 1940s ownership with title was given to the most skilled black farmers in small-scale commercial farming areas. By the 1960s black farmers were able to buy land in white areas. Since that time quite a number have done so, including many high-profile people within your party.

It is regrettable that no serious move was made then by Smith, or later by you, to give the land to the people in the rest of the communal areas through the provision of title.

But the repeating of history does not change the principle that if a man buys a piece of land and develops and uses it productively, he should be able to continue to utilize that piece of land; unless it is compensated for in accordance with international norms [some of which you have signed up to]. Over 70 per cent of those that have been chased off their land by your government bought their land under your government since 1980. Your government had right of first refusal on all land transfers. Your government issued certificates to say that they did not want those specific pieces of land that were being sold. Your government accepted transfer duties from those that were purchasing the farms and taxes from those who were selling them. And now your government has taken those farms and not paid for them.

Zimbabwe whites reduced land holdings by over a third between 1980 and 2000 [from over 30 per cent to 18 per cent of Zimbabwe's land total]. This was all on a willing seller willing buyer basis. Unfortunately the land that your government bought from the whites then [that we as the tax payers paid for through our taxes in conjunction with the British] was never given by the state to the rural poor people. Much went to your party hierarchy. The rest was never actually given to the rural poor because, I presume, your party did not want to lose control over it.

The rural poor who were allowed to go onto the land were never given ownership of the land. They could not develop and invest in land that was not theirs. The rural poor got poorer; and still, especially because of the last six years, they are getting poorer today. Conditions are so poor for population growth that the population is actually shrinking and the economy is the laughing stock of the world.

We are now in the position where the state, through the party, has taken all of the land by vesting it in you, Mr President. Nobody owns any of the land apart from you [there are a few exceptions, like the reserve bank governor, who, realizing the importance of title, bought his farms while your government was still saying that it did not want them through certificates of no present interest]. All land is now yours, Mr President. If you do not like someone, you can remove them.

The last 400 of us whites are liable to be chased off the land any day from now because of your apparent hatred for us, and because there are many in your cabinet and your party that covet what has been developed by us. There is folly in this situation and there is evil motivation behind it. If we want the people to eat and prosper, it is time that a holistic legal system of individual ownership be put in place and respected.

This black Africanism movement that you revel in, and, with it, the hatred of the white man, is bringing poverty to your people [who also include the white man]. Almost all are getting poorer through this Spirit. What all right-thinking people should be saying is that the 18 per cent owned by white farmers should be recognized as such: they bought it and developed it; and unless they are compensated for it, the state [through the party] has stolen it. Many white men won't come back, but at least pay them what they are due so that the land can be properly freed up for people that wish to produce on it. The ones that want to stay – leave them be.

On the 82 per cent of Zimbabwean land that the white farmers do not/did not own, as well as much of the rest that the whites will not come back to, the rural poor need to be given ownership. Only then will they have security of tenure so that they can buy and sell and lease it out and invest and protect it as individual owners will generally want to do.

It is giving the individual ownership that counts. The ones with a propensity to work and develop can then do so. Not all people are farmers – in most developed countries it is less than 2 per cent of the population that are in agriculture – and because of the economies of scale, they have large food surpluses. Why are you wishing to perpetuate an inefficient peasant feudal system based on subsistence agriculture where food becomes short and the towns begin to die?

In Zimbabwe do the young really want to break their backs like Cain, hoeing the land as peasants? Do they not want to be professionals, tradesmen, and businessmen? Should land be just given to people who want something for nothing? Should land be just handed out to people who have not got a realistic chance of keeping that land productive with the people employed and fed? Should land be dished out at all if there is no proper ownership system in place?

The system of vesting all the land in yourself as the president and in removing the white man from the land has happened in country after country to the north… it is a tried and tested formula that ensures people control for a while, but abject poverty for generations. Africa is the poorest continent on earth and getting poorer; and yet God has given us more arable land than any other continent; and most of that land is in the tropical belt where we can out-produce every other area with the right investment and skills.

Why don't we turn the tables back on their feet? Why don't we call all this nonsense off and say we have failed God and we have failed the people? With God's help we have a chance to allow the healing of our land; to become an example of how things should be done and to make Zimbabwe great. But, Mr President, I believe that you know that God will not help those that continue in the ways of wickedness. A house built on the foundations of hatred will crumble and fall.

I do not know whether you will sign the law that will put us in jail if we stay in our homes and commit the criminal offence of farming. I pray to God you do not…

Yours sincerely,

Ben Freeth, Chegutu.

APPENDIX 4 - UPDATES

Ben Freeth MBE

On 13 October 2010, Her Majesty Queen Elizabeth II presented Ben Freeth with an MBE (Member of the British Empire) "For his services to the farming community in Zimbabwe."

Ben attended the investiture at Buckingham Palace with Laura and their three children, Joshua, Stephen, and Anna. Ben was part of a group of almost a hundred people from across the world who had been recognized on the Diplomatic Service and Overseas List – published during June on the date of the Queen's official birthday.

The British honours system is one of the oldest in the world and recognizes merit, gallantry, and service.

Independent review of SADC Tribunal

A report of 14 February 2011, issued by a Geneva-based company conducting an independent review of the SADC Tribunal over the previous six months, found that SADC law should be supreme over domestic laws, and that all decisions made by the court should be binding and enforceable within all member states. The review was conducted by WTI Advisors Ltd, an affiliate of the World Trade Institute. Its key findings were:

- The SADC Tribunal has the legal authority to deal with individual human rights petitions.
- SADC Community law should be supreme to domestic laws and constitutions.
- Decisions of the SADC Tribunal should be binding and enforceable within the territories of all SADC member states.
- The SADC Tribunal was legally established in terms of the SADC Tribunal Protocol.
- The SADC states waived the requirement to ratify the SADC Tribunal Protocol which became a part of the SADC Treaty by agreement and is binding on all SADC member states.
- Zimbabwe may not turn around to say the Tribunal was not legally constituted when they participated in all the proceedings of the SADC Tribunal and nominated a judge for appointment.
- A member state may not rely on its national laws (including norms of constitutional status) as a defence against a violation of an international obligation.

MAPS

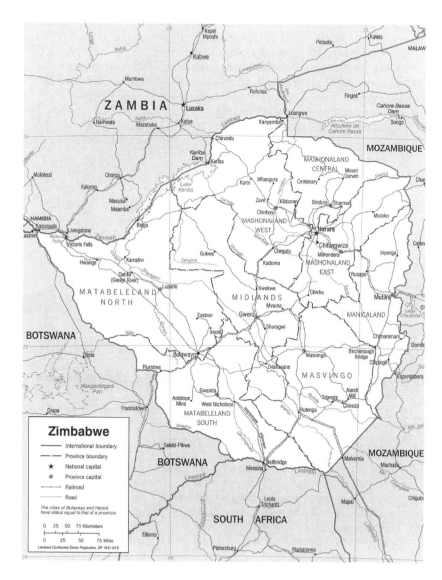

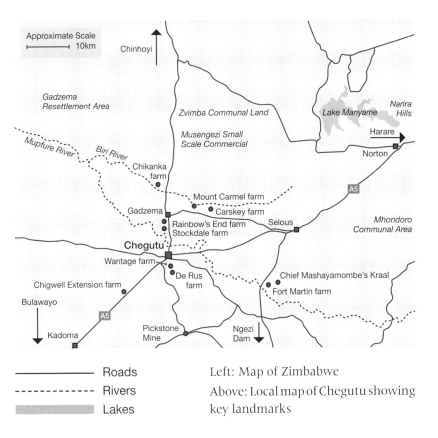

——————— Roads	Left: Map of Zimbabwe
- - - - - - - - Rivers	Above: Local map of Chegutu showing
▓▓▓▓▓▓ Lakes	key landmarks

Map left © 123rf; map above © Lion Hudson Plc 2011

The documentary film about the Campbell's and the Freeth's
struggle against Mugabe is available to buy on DVD